# Blind Vision

James Pittar

Copyright © 2019 (James Pittar)
All rights reserved worldwide.

No part of the book may be copied or changed in any format, sold, or used in a way other than what is outlined in this book, under any circumstances, without the prior written permission of the publisher.

Publisher: Inspiring Publishers,
P.O. Box 159, Calwell, ACT Australia 2905
Email: publishaspg@gmail.com
http://www.inspiringpublishers.com

A catalogue record for this book is available from the National Library of Australia

National Library of Australia The Prepublication Data Service

Author: James Pittar
Title: Blind Vision
Genre: Non-fiction
ISBN: 978-1-925908-12-1

Front Cover Photo - Anne Henshaw
Back Cover Photo - Murray Fraser

# Foreword

The loss of any one of the five senses at any time through our life is devastating, unfortunate and challenging. Above all, one may say, the loss of sight forces an individual to have a greater dependency on the rest of the community for the rest of their life. This does not mean that a person loses their independence! With an aware community and courage every day, a blind person is an active member.

Every day, every hour a blind person has additional challenges, a sighted person takes for granted. "Where did I leave my keys for the house?" Truly close your eyes and from somewhere in your home try to find them, oops you knocked them off the table, bend down and pick them up. Mind your head on the edge of the table, if you bump your head and it bleeds, you may not know or determine the severity. Oops, bugger, now you are in the middle of the room and not sure which way you have turned. Where are you?! These circumstances are a daily challenge for a person with any degree of blindness or sight impairment, we can list many, send a text without sight, how much toothpaste did you just place on your toothbrush? To alleviate these challenges a blind person endeavours to establish a routine for their everyday actions, so to venture out of their normal routine requires valour every minute of every day.

Living without sight requires you to trust in other members of your community, asking for their assistance and taking assistance offered or maybe not, by a member of the community, this takes spirit and patience. James has proved he has this in "truck loads"! He has a big heart and determination and a never say "I can't do it" attitude to life. James has ventured out of the normal routine of daily life to travel the world and achieve remarkable feats on the way. On the world stage, he has inspired, impressed and humbled the world's greatest athletes as well as people like us! He will provoke you to go out and try something new no matter how small.

To see how much trust, respect, patience and determination James Pittar possesses will change the way you view life and the challenges you might feel you face and be overwhelmed.

It is all for these reasons that we continue to respect and be amazed by our friend James Pittar, and it's a privilege to call him our friend. For us, it has been an honour, as well as fun, to be his coach in swimming and to be his personal fitness trainer. We have both laughed, cheered until we had no voice, cried, reminisced, debated, planned and fallen asleep with exhaustion over the many years with James and its been a pleasure and a privilege to be part of his journey.

This book will inspire you to live life to the fullest and maybe, just maybe, try something you never thought you could do.

Matt Logan Personal Trainer and friend since 2003,

Narelle Simpson Swim Coach and friend since 1993.

# Acknowledgements

Oscar Trimboli, who encouraged me to pursue this dream in February 2015 and willingly gave his time and his encouragement to help me finish the task. Stephanie Ayres, my Editor, who took my unformed memoir and massaged it into a polished biography, her knowledge and patience were invaluable.

Narelle Simpson, my coach, for never questioning my ability to complete challenges, keeping my training on track and supporting me throughout my career. Matt Logan, my trainer, for keeping my mind and body fit to meet both my sporting and personal goals; and for his friendship.

My family, particularly Jenny and Annica, for their love and support. And many thanks to the friends and fellow swimmers who contributed their knowledge and memories to add depth and colour to my story.

**Dedication**

I would like to dedicate Blind Vision to:

Joan Constance Bell (1904-1991) ( Granny)
Heather Joanna Pittar (1935-2015) ( Mum)
Des Renford (1927-1999)

*"You can never cross the ocean unless you have the courage to lose sight of the shore."*

— Christopher Columbus

# Contents

1. Getting prepared .................................................................. 1
2. Crossing the channel .......................................................... 21
3. My early life ........................................................................ 37
4. High school ........................................................................ 51
5. Racing in the pool .............................................................. 65
6. Representing Australia ....................................................... 81
7. Rowing ............................................................................... 91
8. Manhattan Island ............................................................. 107
9. Martha's Vineyard ............................................................ 121
10. Gibraltar ........................................................................... 141
11. Monaco to Alcatraz .......................................................... 153
12. Cook Strait ....................................................................... 167
13. Getting married ................................................................ 187
14. Turkey and Thailand ........................................................ 201
15. Catalina Channel ............................................................. 215
16. Islands and piers ............................................................. 229
17. Molokai Channel .............................................................. 243
18. Bering Strait .................................................................... 259
19. Freedom Swim ................................................................ 285
    Epilogue .......................................................................... 293

# Chapter 1
# Getting prepared

*When the night has come*
*And the land is dark*
*And the moon is the only light we'll see*
*No I won't be afraid*
*Oh I won't be afraid*
*Just as long as you stand, stand by me*

— 'Stand by Me', Benny King

These were the words running through my head as I took my first steps across the moonlit sand of Strouanne beach. My legs felt like jelly and my face was stinging like hell, but I'd never felt better. I was the first blind person ever to swim the English Channel. It was an achievement more than seven years in the making.

It all started one stormy December evening in 1990. It had been pouring with rain all month and tonight was no different. I was swimming at North Sydney Pool, where the Spine Care Foundation was running a swim-a-thon. The swim went well, but it was what happened afterwards that would shape the next seven and a half years.

I'd never met Des Renford, but I knew exactly who he was. How could I not. With a success rate of about 12 percent, even a single crossing of the English Channel is an incredible feat. But that wasn't enough for Des. He crossed the English Channel nineteen times from nineteen attempts. To say his record is impressive is an understatement. And that night, I got to meet him. We only chatted for a few minutes, but by the end of our conversation I already knew that's what I wanted to do: to swim the English Channel. Of course, I said nothing to anybody – I wasn't interested in the criticisms I knew would follow. I could almost hear it now. 'A blind person swimming the English Channel? Don't be ridiculous!' And so I kept my dream to myself. Hidden in the back of my mind, away from friends, family, and anyone else that might want to taint it with their doubts and disapproval.

I'd been competing in swimming pool events for a few months now, but this was the first time I really considered turning my attention to longer distances. And I didn't waste any time. Only a few months later, I entered my first competitive open-water ocean swim: 2.5 kilometres from Palm Beach to Whale Beach. It was a far cry from the 34 kilometres I'd face if I ever did make it to the English Channel, but it was a start! I would swim with my brother Tony. Tony's good like that – he's always been willing to help me out with my swims, and even when he can't make it he always calls to see how I am going.

It was a beautiful, sunny day without much swirl and we felt good about my chances – of finishing, that is, not of winning. I'm a slow swimmer at the best of times, let alone when I'm sandwiched between nine hundred other competitors. The starting gun fired, and the first two or three hundred metres felt almost too easy. Sure enough, no sooner had the thought entered my mind than I felt a sudden kick in the ribs, closely followed by another blow to the throat. But undeterred, I powered onwards. Together, Tony and I swam around the rocks into Whale Beach. I had successfully completed my first ever ocean swim.

The following May Tony turned twenty-four and marked the occasion with a massive bash at his place. One of his friends took it upon himself to document the night, and was cavorting around the group with a video camera and a microphone asking what everyone would be doing in the next five years. He was getting a lot of blank faces and drunken slurs in amongst a bunch of pretty standard responses – completing exams, getting a job, going out, getting married. But with a successful open-water swim now behind me, when my turn came to answer I felt ready to face the music. 'I'm going to swim the English Channel', I announced. Heads turned and voices whispered. 'He's had too much to drink', they laughed. 'No way that's going to happen!' The fact that I saw the ridicule coming didn't make it hurt any less. However, I do believe it strengthened my resolve. I didn't swim the channel within five years – but I did do it in seven.

Over the following year I entered a few more short open-water courses, but if I wanted to reach my goal I knew I'd need to step up my game sooner or later. So in late 1992, I decided to have a crack at a 6-kilometre event for the first time. The setting was Narrabeen Lakes, home to some of the most polluted water in Australia at five times the national average. Not that it was going to stop me from swimming!

A mate from work had agreed to swim it with me, though he may not have been so quick to volunteer if he'd realised quite how circuitous the course was. When the race began, instead of living the dream I felt as if I was living a nightmare. By now I was an old hand at the standard up-and-back courses, but Narrabeen Lakes' shoe-shaped course was something else! At one point, the course even doubled back on itself. But as the distance between me and the rest of the pack widened, at least I knew I wasn't getting in anyone's way. Well, not at first.

Swimming blind with a man who'd never swum with me before, I probably shouldn't have been surprised when I veered off course. Suddenly I was swimming across the tide of competitors – among them Australian marathon swimmer Shelley Taylor-Smith – as they powered back towards the finish line. I wanted to sink into the deepest recesses of the lake as they all stopped for me one by one. So did I finish the course? Yes... eventually. But no matter how long it took, nothing could get in the way of my pride at having completed a 6-kilometre event. My mate said he felt like he'd swum more than 6 kilometres, and I've no doubt that we did!

As we walked back to the car, Shelley Taylor-Smith's coach intercepted. 'You're the reason Shelley lost,' he spat. As if I needed someone to point it out to me. Maybe the 100 metres I'd cost her was the difference between a win and a loss, but right then I didn't care. I'd completed a 6-kilometre event with a mate, and that was all that mattered. Shelley would go on to win an incredible fifty-one FINA open-water swimming events, two World Championships and five Manhattan Marathons in her career. Surely whether or not she won today at Narrabeen Lakes was neither here nor there. But as I would come to learn, for Shelley it was always about winning no matter what the cost.

In early 1993, I did the 8-kilometre Bridge to Bridge on the Nepean River. The swim itself went well, but more importantly, afterwards I got another opportunity to sit down and chat with Des Renford. But this time was different. His son, Michael 'Murph' Renford, was there with him. At the time I didn't pay it much mind; I was just thrilled to be able to sit down with Des again, and I listened eagerly as he dispensed pointers about swimming the English Channel. Little did I know that over two decades later Murph Renford would still be one of my best friends. With boundless enthusiasm and generosity, he's a force to be reckoned with – just like his dad.

Sitting down with the Renfords reinforced my desire to swim the Channel, but unfortunately my meeting with them came at around the same time that I had a few disappointing swimming pool competitions. I ended up so disenchanted with it all that for a few years there I shifted my attention to rowing. But that's not to say I'd given up on my dream of swimming the Channel. It was always in the back of my mind, and I never let my skills slip. I just wasn't making any real progress – until the autumn of 1997.

I was swimming at Manly Pool, the usual, when my coach, Narelle Simpson, suddenly said, 'What do you want to do now in your swimming career?' Narelle had been my coach for four years now, and she brought a real empathy that I'd never experienced with any other coach. That's what drew me to her – she wasn't all about technique and logistics. She was about understanding people and helping them reach their goals, whatever they may be. So her question kind of took me by surprise. She already knew what I wanted.

'I want to swim the English Channel.'

'Well, what are you waiting for?' she challenged. 'Go out and do it.'

For a minute I was taken aback. I don't know what I was expecting, but her response lit a fire in me. It was then that I realised that had been her aim all along – to remind me of what I wanted. To remind me that it wasn't just going to happen by itself. I had to make it happen.

I went straight home to my parents and announced, 'I'm going to swim the English Channel.'

My mother was thrilled, absolutely thrilled. Just as she has been for every marathon swim I've ever attempted. Some have worked, some haven't, but it's never mattered to her. She just loved that I got out there and did it, and she never placed any bounds on what I could do. One day she said, 'James, we've got a swim for you. Madagascar to the mainland of Africa.'

'How far is that?'

'Oh, around 9,400 miles. Should be easy.'

She always knew how to make me laugh.

Dad, on the other hand, was far from impressed. 'So how many people have swum the English Channel?' he asked cynically.

'Well, based on past attempts, you've got a 12 percent chance of completing it.'

'How many have done it on the first attempt?'

I took a deep breath. 'You know the Sydney Football Stadium?' He nodded slowly. 'And you know how hard it is to stay dry at the stadium when it rains?' He nodded again, waiting for the punch line. 'Well, you've got more chance of staying dry at the Sydney Football Stadium when it rains than you do of swimming the English Channel on the first attempt.'

The statistics were hardly encouraging. But we knew what we were up against. It was never going to be easy, but the challenge had been set, and I fully intended to rise to meet it. 'So we'll do it in 1999?' I asked Narelle the next weekend, intending it as a rhetorical question. But Narelle had other ideas. '1999? You wish. Try July '98.' That was less than fourteen months away. But Narelle brushed it off like it was nothing. 'No worries mate. Twelve months of training. You'll be right!' And so the training began.

That, and putting together a team we knew we could rely on. People who think of the English Channel as an individual achievement have obviously never been there. Without your team out there with you, you don't stand a chance. Of course, that goes double when you can't see! It's about the way your team goes with you, how you get fed, how you listen to the whistles, how you take instructions. And above all, the way they manage to keep you going when you're ready to give up. Choosing the right team could easily be the difference between success and failure.

Narelle spearheaded the whole operation because she worked at Manly Pool and knew a lot of great swimmers and kayakers. She immediately approached Brooke Withers, a Learn-to-swim coach and masseuse, and Bill 'Sticks' Tricker, a lifeguard so named for his rangy legs. Narelle had introduced me to them both back in 1995, not long after we'd met. They're both exceptionally kind people, and great at what they do, so I was stoked when they agreed to be part of the team. But I could never have predicted just how important they would turn out to be in my career. They would be my staunchest supporters over the next two decades, the stalwarts of my team and the people I turned to through thick and thin.

In fact, once Sticks became part of my team, I wondered how I ever survived without him. He's one of the most caring people I've ever known. He's always ready with good advice, delivered in the most respectful way. He's scoured the newspapers for years to send every last article about me to my family. And he takes any and every opportunity to promote me and my swimming career. Outside of my family, he is my greatest supporter. Every Saturday morning he was out on the water first thing to blow the whistles for me, and when training was over, he refused to leave until he saw me off safely in a taxi. He never let me down, and he never would.

Ian Byrne was another magnificent source of support. Narelle introduced me to Ian because he had swum the English Channel in 1995. He was a fountain of information for me and my parents, and finally managed to make Dad see that this wasn't an unrealistic goal for me – something I never thought possible! Ian was always there to spur me on at my training sessions at Manly Pool with an infectious enthusiasm that never waned even for a second. Sometimes he'd dispense advice; other times he'd simply stand quietly and be there for me. But no matter what the conditions, I could rely on his support. That and his unwavering sense of fun.

I still vividly remember the time I was swimming at Manly Dam and I heard his warbled voice through the water. I lifted my head out of the water and his words suddenly became clear. 'Watch out for the brown snakes!' he yelled. I stayed where I was – this was typical Ian Byrne humour – but we both burst out in nervous laughter the next week when a picture was published in the *Manly Daily* of a brown snake found in the Manly Dam!

Every weekday now I was training at home in my parents' pool. I would tie a tethered wrap around my waist, anchor it on a fence post, and swim in the one spot for two or three hours. I did it all through winter, in the middle of the night, in raging storms – the worse the conditions, the better the preparation. At least that's what I told myself! As far as I knew it had never been done before, but I was determined to work with what I had – and what I had was a pretty darn small backyard swimming pool.

I believe this was one of the great things that got me across the English Channel. Yes, it prepared me physically, but more importantly, I learned what it was like to do a very boring activity for a very long time. I prepared my brain for a long, relentless, and often mind-numbingly boring swim. To me, swimming the English Channel is not about how good a swimmer you are (though it certainly helps!). It's about how well you can steel yourself mentally against both the cold and the length of the swim. And nothing could have prepared me better than those tethered swims in my own backyard.

For me, that's what it was all about: the training. I believe the key to success is just to do as much training as you can, as many kilometres as you can. It's not necessarily the typical attitude of people who attempt and succeed in swimming the English Channel – I know of a guy who completed it having trained as little as 25 kilometres a week. But it worked for me.

Before I knew it I had less than twelve months left to get ready for the swim. My mind was swimming – no pun intended – with all the work I had yet to do: training, preparing everything we needed, but above all, finding a way to actually be accepted into the event! Convincing people that, yes, a blind person *could* swim the English Channel was perhaps the greatest challenge of all. There was a pile of paperwork a mile high to even get the Channel Swimming Association to accept me for the swim. But in the short term, I just stuck to the plan: weekly pool swims at both Manly and Sydney Football Stadium, tethered rope swims at home, and a 4- to 5-hour ocean or lake swim every weekend.

By November, I was finally ready to face up to a true long-distance event: the New South Wales Open Water Championships at Penrith Lakes. It was a 15-kilometre event: three laps of a 5-kilometre course. In those days, there was a rule that when the first person finished, you had only so many hours to finish the event. That made my life very difficult, partly because I'm a very slow, one-pace swimmer, but also because I was up against then-world champion Grant Robinson. As much admiration as I have for him, I would curse under my breath whenever he turned up at the start line! The pressure of not only having to swim 15 kilometres, but having to do it within a narrow time limit, really got to me. At times it seemed as if I would never actually get to finish a race. They've since changed the rules, thankfully.

It was a beautiful, calm day and with Brooke and Ian set to kayak by my side, I was feeling good. Brooke is a great kayaker and we always work so smoothly together. I also love having her with me because of all my team she's probably the one that is most concerned not just with how I'm performing but with how I'm coping personally. She's constantly asking how I'm going and what I need, and always trying to find new ways to make things easier for me. She'd been the brains behind the whistle system we'd devised to tell me when I needed to veer: one long blast meant left and two short ones meant right. But I had no delusions: I knew the minute we set off that I would spend the race well behind the pack. By the time I reached the 10-kilometre mark, everyone else had finished and the presentations were about to start. One of the organisers told Ian it was time to pull me out. But Ian wasn't having any of it.

'This bloke's trying to swim the English Channel,' Ian said. 'You have to let him complete the course.' I wasn't there to hear his full speech, but being a lawyer, once he hit his stride there was no stopping him! From what I gather, a few coarse words were exchanged. Anyway, whatever he said, it worked. The timekeeper stayed on as I completed the final 5 kilometres, and I arrived at the shore to a modest welcoming party of Ian, Brooke, the timekeeper, and my mother! It was a surreal moment, but a beautiful one. I felt such a pure sense of happiness as the four of us – unimpressed timekeeper not included – stood there laughing.

In the end my time was about 5 hours. Ian and Brooke were very happy with how I'd swum. Myself, I was just thrilled to have finally finished a long-distance event! Penrith Lakes was never going to be anything like the English Channel, but it felt so good to have completed it comfortably with the whistle system working well. I was on a high for days afterwards. I think that day signified the beginning of a change in management of these kinds of events, to allow all competitors to complete the course. It was a great day for me personally and a great day for swimming. I was one step closer to completing the English Channel.

New Year's Day 1998, I made a resolution. I would attempt the English Channel on 19 July – exactly two hundred days away. Two hundred days to keep my mind on the job, to keep up not only the physical training but also the mental training. I entered every event I could find, pushing myself to my absolute limits and then some. It's the only way you ever really get better.

February arrived, and with it the 15-kilometre Tasmanian State Open Water Championships at Lake Trevallyn in Launceston. It was a Grand Prix event, which meant all the great swimmers around Australia would be there. I couldn't wait to get out there with them. But the scene when my mother and I arrived at Lake Trevallyn at 8 am was bleak. A lone woman turned to greet me, her face sullen. Our event had been removed from the Grand Prix program, and it seemed as if she and I were the only ones that hadn't been informed. We'd still be allowed to complete the swim, for what it was worth. But the opportunity I'd come all this way for, the opportunity to compete against Australia's best, had been snatched from me. And with it my sense of excitement.

But it wasn't going to stop us swimming. We set off on the first of fifteen laps and despite my disappointment I was feeling good. The water was a comfortable 15 degrees, and I was confident I could finish within 5 hours. Sadly, I wouldn't get the chance. At about the 4-hour mark, the woman finished the course and the organisers decided I was too far behind to let me finish.

This was my first big training swim for the Channel. Conditions were good, and I'd been feeling strong, swimming straight, and keeping my concentration. Everything was going to plan. And they pulled me out with three laps to go. I kept quiet, but inside I was fuming. As I trudged back to the change rooms, my mother could see how dejected I felt.

As we sat through the endless presentations, all I could think was completing, I could be out there finishing the last 3 kilometres right now. In my mind's eye I saw myself completing the event, feeling the immense sense of satisfaction that would have come with it. But it wasn't to be. Finally, an hour and a half later, it was announced that I had won the men's Tasmanian State Open Championship. It was an empty victory. At the end of the presentation, the few remaining people trickled away and it was just me and my mother, alone on the grass beside the lake. We'd come all that way, taken time off work, and this was how it ended.

At the airport on the way home, the father of one of the other swimmers came over and congratulated me. 'That was a joke, what happened to you,' he said, 'and I'd like to apologise on behalf of the organising committee.' I'm not sure the organising committee would have endorsed that, but it was nice to know that at least someone recognised the effort I'd put in. Someone understood what I was going through. In the end, as tough as the experience was, I think it was the best motivator I could have had. I said to myself, I'm going to show these people. I'm going to go out there, and I'm going to swim the English Channel. And on the worst days, that's what kept me going.

Only three weeks later, I would take my swimming to the next level: the 22-kilometre Perth to Rottnest Island swim. Even though it's only half the distance of the English Channel, it has very similar conditions and it's one of the best swims you can do leading up to the Channel. It would be a real test, and a key part of my preparation. I was raring to get out there.

At 3 am the dreaded alarm sounded and we all dragged ourselves bleary-eyed out of bed. Brooke and the boat pilot headed off to wait for us in the water, while Narelle and I headed down to the beach. The water looked intimidating. There wasn't much wind, but 7-foot cross swells were rolling towards us with no sign of letting up. But that's the way of the Indian Ocean – it can stir up anything, from the most benign conditions to the most treacherous. It was going to be an interesting swim.

Finally, 5.30 arrived. It was time to start. I felt like a bundle of nerves, but it was all in my head. I knew I was prepared. As soon as we got in the water the swells started sweeping my body up and down. And as if that weren't bad enough, I kept getting these little stinging sensations all over my body, sometimes in quite unfortunate areas! It's probably a good thing I couldn't talk, because the words that were coming to mind weren't particularly savoury. But at least I was swimming well – or so I thought. As it turned out, I *was* swimming well – just in the wrong direction! Fortunately an inflatable boat stopped me and I managed to find my way back to my boat. I'd been noticing my eyesight going sharply downhill lately, but this hammered it home – what little side vision I used to have was gone, and I was completely reliant on my team. There was no 'I' anymore

– from here on out, if I didn't pay attention to what my team was telling me, I wasn't going anywhere.

For the next 7 hours or so we rolled with the cross swells. Up and down, back and forth. I shouldn't have been surprised when I started vomiting. Some genius said, 'He's vomited', and I felt like saying, 'Thanks for the update!' As it turned out a good spew was just what I needed, and I quickly got back on track. But the next few strokes were nervous as I willed the water to wash the vomit away from me, not back towards my mouth! Thankfully the swells worked in my favour.

Poor old Brooke wasn't so lucky. She'd been out in the boat since 3.30 am bobbing up and down, and the nausea had long since got the better of her. She put on a brave face, but it got to the point where if she wasn't blowing the whistle, she was vomiting. It wasn't exactly conducive to a good kayaking performance, but Narelle picked up the slack. When we got within 5 kilometres of shore, a ship came out and took her to join the leagues of people being treated by the Red Cross.

Finally, the shore was in sight. The night before, we'd been advised at the briefing that the best shot was to swim to the southern end of Rottnest Island. And that would have been all very well, if it weren't for the strong southerly current. The swimmers whose teams had GPS were able to identify that current and swim to the northern side accordingly. Unfortunately, I wasn't one of those swimmers. The end of the swim was a painful battle against the current, against the wind, and against the cross swells. But when we got inside Thomson Bay, none of it mattered any more.

After 7 hours and 51 minutes of swimming, I'd made it to Rottnest Island. The swim certainly wasn't without its challenges, but I was happy with my time, and we were all feeling good – even Brooke, who seemed to have made a full recovery. I'd completed the Perth to Rottnest swim. Not only that, I'd become the first blind person to do so in history. I even got an ovation at the presentation. You couldn't wipe the smile off my face.

The swim was instrumental in our preparation for the English Channel. Even though it was only about half the distance of the

Channel, it was a long, tough swim and an important learning process. We'd used the whistles. We'd used the kayaks. We'd used the English Channel's no-touching rule, instead using a homemade 'feeding pole' to deliver my drinks and energy gels. We'd competed under English Channel conditions, and we'd done it well. It was a great success for the whole team.

But the most testing experience of all was battling those 7-foot cross swells – just ask Brooke! And when I came to do the English Channel five months later, that's the experience I would look back on during the toughest times. As hard as it got, at least I wasn't surrounded by vomit!

In mid-March, I entered the State Open 15-kilometres Championships at Manly Dam, ten laps of a triangular course. It was a sunny, calm day without much wind. You never want to say the word 'perfect', but that day was as close as it gets. I was excited to compete against elite swimmers, but it came with a caveat – once again they were enforcing that wonderful rule that prevents you from finishing if you're not back within a certain time after the first person finishes. I had my work cut out for me.

The course was marked out with buoys, and at first it seemed like it was going to be a fairly easy swim. I couldn't have been more wrong! At the far end of Manly Dam, beside the car park, one of the marking buoys I had to swim around was right up against the concrete edge. Any more than one or two people at a time, and you were done for. It was ludicrous! Once again I was reminded just how much my vision had deteriorated; with every stroke I expected to scrape my hand against the jagged concrete. For Narelle and Brooke on kayaks, it was basically impossible. Who decided to put the buoy there I don't know, but I hope they've since come to their senses!

Once again I was last to finish, and on my last lap I was acutely aware of the organisers trailing behind me picking up the buoys. The nerves spurred me on as I prayed I wouldn't be pulled out again. I got there, though I'll happily go the rest of my life never having to swim around that stupid buoy again! Still, it was another swim. Another experience under my belt. It was all about getting the kilometres up, doing as many swims as I could under English Channel conditions.

No sooner had I completed the State Open Championship than I poured myself into organising an event at the North Steyne Surf Club to raise funds for the English Channel. I would swim five laps of a 5-kilometre course we'd marked out, from North Steyne Surf Club all the way down to the end of Shelly Beach and back.

At the end of March, you'd think you'd get some pretty comfortable conditions, but no such luck. It was 38 degrees. A steamer. The UV index was off the charts and the water temperature was around 22 degrees, which wasn't ideal in terms of practising for the Channel. A bunch of my mates from the surf club were scattered across the hills above the course we'd marked out, spruiking my cause to anyone who'd listen. 'He's going to become the first blind person to swim the English Channel,' they asserted. No doubt about it, apparently!

Narelle and Brooke were out on the skis, Sticks was in the inflatable boat, and people were taking turns coming out to swim with me. Everyone doing their part to make sure we got the money we needed to achieve my dream. I got to the fifth lap thinking, obviously, that we were nearing the end. But at that moment, someone said 'If you do another lap, John Koorey's going to put in another thousand towards your swim!' John Koorey was the second Australian to swim the English Channel in 1969 and held the record for the fastest swim across Cook Strait. But more importantly, he was just a lovely, generous man. It was a no-brainer. I did the sixth lap, and even as I swam in towards North Steyne at the end, I was still feeling great. (It was only later that I felt the full force of the harsh sting of sunburn!)

I look back so fondly on that day. I was truly humbled by the generosity of not only my friends and family but also absolute strangers. I think we ended up raising around $7,000 just on the day. I was blown away. And the swim itself had been a great success. As much as I would have loved it to have been colder, doing six laps in much warmer conditions than I was used to was just another experience to add to my arsenal. Another set of conditions I now knew I could handle.

It was time to get into the nitty gritty of what I'd need to do to qualify. I had to organise my own boat and pilot, fill in a long-winded medical form, and do a 10-hour qualifying swim. This would all be submitted to the organising committee of the Channel Swimming Association.

English Channel boats and pilots aren't easy to come by. Popular pilots start booking up as far as a year in advance. The good pilots often accept a whole group of people each season to take one by one on each tide. The hope is that they'll get a chance to take everyone, but unless everything goes exactly to plan, it doesn't always turn out that way. That's why it's critical to get the number one position with your pilot. If you don't, you might not even end up getting into the water!

But if you're lucky enough, you'll find a good boat and pilot all to yourself – and that's the situation I somehow found myself in. When I contacted Alan Ruston, he offered me the first – and only – position on his boat, *The Gallivant*, and even gave me exclusive access to it for the whole six weeks leading up to the event. Captain Graham Pique had agreed to be my pilot. I'd had my medical and sent my application form across. And my qualifying swim was scheduled for the end of May. Everything was going smoothly... too smoothly!

It felt as if something had to give, and on the first of May that's exactly what happened. I got home from work excited for another weekend of training, only to learn that my pilot, Graham, had agreed without actually doing his research, and hadn't realised the extent of my visual impairment.

At the time, vision-impaired swimmers were classified into one of three categories: B1, B2, or B3. Basically, B1 was totally blind – you had to wear blacked out goggles and get tapped at the end of every lap when you were swimming. B2 was anything from zero to 2/60 vision and up to 5 degrees' visual field, and B3 was anything from 2/60 to 6/60 vision and up to 20 degrees' visual field. To put that in layman's terms, 6/60 means you can see the top letter of the eye chart from 6 metres away, and 2/60 means you can't see it until you get to 2 metres. I fell into the B2 category, and the minute Graham had found that out, he'd deemed the whole exercise too risky. He was pulling out.

The next 12 hours were a blur of phone calls. I got on the phone to six or seven other pilots asking if they would take me. I rang so many people I lost track of who I'd rung and started ringing people twice. But no luck. When midnight ticked over I decided to call it a day, get on with my training, and hope things might change over the weekend.

And change they did. Alan Ruston decided to go to bat for me. He took Graham Pique out on his boat and regaled him with the highlights of my swimming career: the Rottnest challenge, the Tasmanian Championships, the myriad swimming pool competitions – all of which I'd done in the same eyesight category I was in now. It took a lot of convincing, but Alan finally wore Graham down. When I found out on Monday that Graham had decided to be my pilot after all, the tension of the weekend evaporated. We were back on track. With the big swim now only a couple of months away, I went in search of inspiration. And I knew where to find it – at the home of the great man, Des Renford. He was remarkably patient with me as we went through his old certificates and photos. I must have sat there with him for at least three or four hours, questioning him on the finer details of the English Channel. How did he get through it? What would it all end up costing? Where should I stay? How did the tides affect him? Should I go for spring tide or neap?

Those are the two types of tide in the English Channel. As I found out, the difference between low tide and high tide is 12 feet during neap tides versus 25 during spring tides. Spring tides are great in that they give you a bit of an extra push, but they leave very little room for error, and unless you're fast enough to stay ahead of the tide you can easily find yourself way off course. As a slow one-pacer, I preferred the neap tide. At least I knew if I made an error somewhere along the way I could probably get out of it!

Catching up with Des was just the motivation I needed as my swim approached. As we parted, he called after me, 'If you ever need any help, just give me a call!' His words remained fresh in my mind when, three days later, the Channel Swimming Association issued a directive preventing blind or deaf people from swimming the English Channel. I still remember the moment I heard the news. My legs almost refused to support me as I collapsed on the couch, despondent. I'd only just recovered from the stress of nearly losing my pilot, and now this. The pressure was starting to get the better of me. I really don't know what I would have done if it weren't for Des. I got straight on the phone and explained the situation, and I felt calmer just speaking to him. 'Don't let it worry you,' he said. 'We'll work on it!' He was a real pillar of strength for me, and I will be forever grateful.

Meanwhile, halfway across the world, the Channel Swimming Association was deep in deliberation over my application. In theory I guess it should have been a pretty straightforward decision, but they didn't count on Graham Pique, Alan Ruston and Des Renford, who were all in my court, pushing for my inclusion. After four long hours they finally yielded. I would be allowed to do the swim.

When Des gave me the news that night, it was as if a massive weight had been lifted from my chest. I was barely even listening as he reeled off the requirements for my inclusion in the swim – there had to be a lifeguard and a doctor on board the boat, and I had to prove in advance that I could successfully swim beside a boat. But none of that mattered. What mattered was that the swim was back on. My dream was still alive.

The great Des Renford, nineteen-time English Channel champion, had put his neck on the line. He never said as much, he was too much of a gentleman, but I knew his reputation was at stake. All for some blind guy that he'd only met a few times and had never even seen train, let alone complete an event. Yet here he was, risking everything. It's just who he was.

May had been a long month, and it wasn't over yet. On the very last day of the month, I fronted up for my 10-hour qualifying swim at Penrith Lakes. The water temperature was about 13 degrees, within the 15-degree limit imposed by the Channel Swimming

Association. And the conditions couldn't have been better – sunny and still. I was in the water by 7 am, adorned with cap, goggles, Speedos, and a generous coating of lanolin for insulation. Of course, the swim wasn't actually a great indicator of how I'd fare in the English Channel, where I'd be tossed around by waves for the entire 10 hours. But I would prove I could hack the cold, and that's all the Channel Swimming Association was looking for.

Narelle came out and took me around the course for 10 hours, whistling to me, feeding me, and egging me on. For the first 5 hours I could feel how strongly I was swimming, and I felt confident. The next three were more of a struggle – not physically as much as mentally. But by the 8-hour mark I finally felt as if the end was in sight. I divided the remaining time into manageable little half-hour slots, and just put my head down and smashed them out one by one.

After 10 hours and 6 minutes, I crawled up the finishing ramp in the dark. Narelle and my mother, who had come down to see me finish, stood together regarding me in a way that seemed to say, 'This bloke really is a madman.' And to anyone watching, I must have looked defeated. But inside, I was victorious. I'd jumped the final hurdle. I had qualified, and I was so close to completing the English Channel I could taste it.

I felt as if some sort of celebration was in order, but instead I spent the next hour sitting greased up on sheets of newspaper in my mother's car, and the three after that madly trying to scrub the lanolin off! But despite the fairly undistinguished end to the day, I went to bed a satisfied man. The trials and tribulations of May were over, and tomorrow marked a new month.

In June Manly Dam became like a second home to me as my training kicked into high gear. When I wasn't doing radio interviews or photo shoots, I was in the dam. When I look back on it now it's all kind of melded together in my memory – all except for one particular session. A session I'd teed up with the great Murray Rose. Dad, Tony, and I were up at the crack of dawn to meet Murray at Cranbrook pool to train for the swim I had planned for that afternoon – from Collaroy Beach down to Shelly Beach and back to North Steyne. The training session itself was nothing special, I guess – but the company sure was.

I admired Murray enormously, not just for his swimming achievements – though they are undeniably impressive – but for his attitude to the game. At the 1956 Olympics, after winning the 1500-metres freestyle, he embraced the Japanese runner-up across the lane of the pool. It was a beautiful moment, because that day – 7 December 1956 – was the fifteenth anniversary of the attack on Pearl Harbor. Two men from two countries on opposite sides of the war had let go of past conflicts and come together as friends. It exemplified the Olympic spirit that I hold so highly. But even more than that, I admired Murray for his willingness to help others, infinite patience, and dedication to charity. Murray Rose was a Patron of the Rainbow Club – a charity for which I am now an Ambassador – from 2000 right up until his death in 2012.

The Rainbow Club teaches children with disabilities to swim to their capabilities, whether that's swimming out in the ocean, swimming a single lap, or even just treading water in the shallows. It's a beautiful thing when parents see their disabled children swimming out in the ocean for the first time – an opportunity that, without the Rainbow Club, they would never have had. And Murray did more for the Rainbow Club than anyone. In 2009, he spearheaded the first ever 'Murray Rose Malabar Magic' ocean swim for them – the only open-water swim in New South Wales that welcomes disabled people. It is his greatest legacy.

When I arrived at Collaroy Beach I was already buggered, after working my butt off to impress Murray Rose! Narelle, Sticks, and Brooke were unsympathetic, but then they didn't know what I'd been up to that morning. And I saw no reason to tell them. Somehow, keeping the session a secret seemed to make it even more special. In fact, until the publication of this book, the four of us – me, Dad, Tony, and Murray – were the only people in the world who knew that training session ever even happened.

So I kept my mouth shut and my head down and managed to push myself through the muscle pain and the headache to get myself back to North Steyne just as dusk was falling. Suffice to say I wasn't feeling my best by the end of the swim. But that was all about to turn around. Dad had turned up to see me finish the swim and pick me up. As we met, he gave me a firm pat on the back and said, 'Gee you looked strong out there!' I didn't see fit to argue that actually, this afternoon I was in the worst form I could remember. Anyway, it was beside the point. What mattered was that I could hear in his voice that something had changed in the way he saw me. I knew from that moment that I had finally convinced my father that, yes, his son *could* swim the English Channel.

And just knowing that changed the way I saw myself as well. I just thought, yeah, this *is* possible. I mean, of course I knew it was possible – I couldn't have reached to this point without that belief – but Dad's faith in me had brought a new quality to my approach. I wasn't just going to attempt the English Channel. I was going to complete it.

## Chapter 2
## Crossing the channel

After twelve months of paperwork and training, not to mention more than our fair share of drama, we were finally ready to go. As we waited for our flight, Sticks, Narelle, Brooke and I barely said a word to each other. It all just felt so surreal, I think we were stunned into silence. But I distinctly remember thinking to myself, the next time I walk through this airport I bloody hope I will have swum the English Channel.

Our accommodation at Kingsdown Park called itself a chalet, but I suspect the owners have never looked up the definition of the word. On the first night, we arrived in the pouring rain to a complete blackout. Here we go, I thought. Let the fun begin! A couple of minutes later the lights came back on – well, all except ours. Narelle foraged around until she found a mysterious box with a coin slot, deposited a one-pound coin, and what do you know, on came the lights. I couldn't believe it. We'd paid for the house, and now we were paying just for the privilege of electricity.

After all the rigmarole I was ready for a hot shower. Nope – cold water only, apparently. Narelle heard my struggles and shouted, 'Did you pull the cord on the left-hand side?' A cord-operated shower. Genius. The fun and games continued at breakfast, where we needed a sentry for the toast to make sure it didn't set off the smoke alarm, which was strategically placed directly above the toaster. So I wouldn't say it was a fabulous place, but it was a place to sleep, and it left us with some very funny memories.

As part of my training, Narelle had organised for me to go down to Dover Harbour to swim with Alison and Freda Streeter. Alison Streeter had swum the English Channel forty-three times, and her mother Freda had led hundreds of swimmers to victory in the English Channel swim as the lead trainer down at Dover Harbour. We got there just after 10 am and the minute I set foot on the beach Freda was already having a go at me. 'You're 5 minutes late. Get on with it!' I sensed that she wasn't the sort of woman you wanted to argue with! So I got in and I swam between Alison and her mate Chris, a New Zealand swimmer who had also attempted the English Channel. We didn't have the whistles or the loudhailer, so Alison and Chris basically acted as bumpers to keep me in line!

Afterwards, we all went back for lunch at Freda's place. I was surrounded by people who had either attempted the English Channel or were about to. It was a pretty special atmosphere, and I tried to make the most of it by chatting to as many people as I could. I was particularly inspired by a woman who had unsuccessfully attempted the channel once before and was having another go this year. That, I think, encapsulates the spirit of the channel – it's not about whether you win or lose, it's about that fighting spirit. I was thrilled when I found out that she had completed it.

Before I knew it, there were only four days left before the swim. It was time to go out and satisfy the Channel Swimming Association's final condition – to prove I could swim successfully beside a boat for one hour. It was something I'd done a million times before, but never with this kind of pressure. This was the moment of truth. My entire swim depended on the next hour.

We took the *Gallivant* out on Dover Harbour: me, Graham Pique, Alan Ruston, and all my crew. 'All right!' Graham's voice boomed out over the water. 'Lather up! Imagine you're really swimming the English Channel today. Let's do this!' This was our chance to prove ourselves and we didn't plan to cut any corners. Narelle directed me up and back, left and right, even in circles with the loudhailer. Forty minutes had gone by when Graham suddenly called it off. 'Get him out!' he ordered. My initial response was panic. Everything seemed to have been going well, but this was totally unexpected.

'Why?' Narelle demanded.

'I don't need to see any more', he beamed. 'That's already the best thing I've ever seen!'

Graham was particularly impressed with our feeding pole. We'd designed it ourselves: a long pole with two ropes attached, one for the open-end syringe, which my carbohydrate fuel went in, and one for the water bowl. He couldn't stop raving about it! People's first reaction when they saw our pole was often to laugh. And I have to admit, it must have looked pretty comical. But when they saw it in use, it shut them up! Under the rules of swimming the English Channel, you can't touch the boat or anyone on it. So for a blind person who relies completely on sound and feel, directing and feeding was always going to be a momentous challenge. But the pole, as silly as it may have looked, was the perfect solution. In fact, after the English Channel swim was over, quite a few people ended up asking for a closer look in order to use it as a basis for their own designs.

I like to think that we opened the minds of the organising committee a little bit. Their rules tend to be very black and white; thinking outside the box isn't their strength. But we showed them that you can get around that box. Just because you can't see doesn't have to mean you can't achieve the same things through other means. With a loudhailer, a feeding pole, and a bit of determination, you could communicate and perform just as well as a sighted person.

Graham slapped me on the back. 'Mate! That was bloody fantastic. Wild horses couldn't stop me from taking you across the English Channel now. I'd be honoured.' I felt a little giddy, teetering on the edge of a dream. But the next thing he said brought me crashing back down to earth. 'You'd better get going. You're up tomorrow morning at 4 am.'

It was on! I raced back to the chalet, downed as much pasta and potatoes as my belly could hold, and was in bed by 9 pm. My team would get everything prepared. But just as I started to drift off, Graham Pique ran through the door, breathing heavily. 'Sorry, mate,' he said, 'the conditions are pretty terrible out there. It's not going to happen tomorrow.' Great. Narelle poked her head around the door and said, 'If you hurry you'll catch Sticks before he goes on his walk. You just stuffed yourself with an English Channel's worth of food. Better walk some of it off!'

When we came back Narelle looked concerned. 'You look ill', she said.

'I'm not going to lie, I'm scared out of my mind!' I admitted. 'Twelve months of training and it all comes down to this.' But what Narelle said next put me at ease.

'Come on James! You *are* going to swim the English Channel. We all know it. Why else would we come all this way?' I felt the weight on my chest lift a little. 'You've proved you can do it. We believe it, your family believes it. The whole goddamn country believes it! But most importantly, if you're honest with yourself, *you* believe it.' I could always trust Narelle to know the right thing to say. 'Just remember,' she said, looking me directly in the eye. 'I wouldn't let you do this if I didn't know you were up to it.'

Narelle's words spurred me on, and I'd never felt more ready. But then, it wasn't up to me. We spent the next day waiting. And the next, and the one after that. I was at a loss as to what I should do with myself. When you're waiting to swim the English Channel you can't train heavily, because you never know when your pilot will come around the corner and tell you you're up.

And finally, he did. The conditions looked good for the next morning. All that was left was to get a good night's sleep. As I drifted off, my mind was cast back to a stormy March night earlier that year. I had dreamed that I would swim the English Channel. It would take me 14 hours and 46 minutes, and I would do it on 20 July, the anniversary of man landing on the moon. I call it a dream, but at the time I remember thinking it was a nightmare! It was all just so specific, and at the time the enormity of the challenge felt almost too much to bear. Seriously, what were the chances everything would align just like that? Could it really hold four months later?

There was no way to know. But tomorrow I would find out once and for all.

I got up at 5 am feeling apprehensive as hell. I could barely keep the cornflakes on my spoon as I battled to control my trembling hands. We drove down to the harbour, all of us jammed in between the pole, the loudhailer, and the rest of our gear. Normally we would have had a laugh about it, but we were too distracted to even notice. Every one of us had our mind on the job. When we got to Dover Harbour, it was sunny, with virtually no wind. The water temperature was 17 degrees – unheard of in July. The day before, there'd been five crossings from five starts, so spirits were high. Graham came out and said, 'Brace yourselves, everyone! This is happening!' I think my heart skipped a beat. 'Here goes nothing,' I muttered under my breath.

As I walked through the gate at Dover Harbour, I promised myself, 'The next time I walk through this gate, I will have swum the English Channel.' I only hoped I could keep that promise. We got into the boat and headed around into Shakespeare's Beach, where the swim would begin. I took a deep breath of salty ocean air. It was finally happening. I had a team I trusted implicitly – Sticks, Brooke, Narelle, and Graham. We had a doctor on board. And Norm Trustee, a man who had swum the Channel twice himself, was there as my observer, to log the details of the swim. We were set.

As we approached Shakespeare's Beach, I was teetering on the back of the boat, battling to stay upright as I applied Vaseline to my body as insulation. About a hundred metres from the beach, they dropped me in the water and I swam to shore, where I would officially start the swim. Here I was, totally alone on Shakespeare's Beach. Behind me was the statue of Captain Matthew Webb, the first person to swim the English Channel in 1875, and in front of me was nothing but ocean. It was 8 am on 19 July 1998. The first day of the rest of my life.

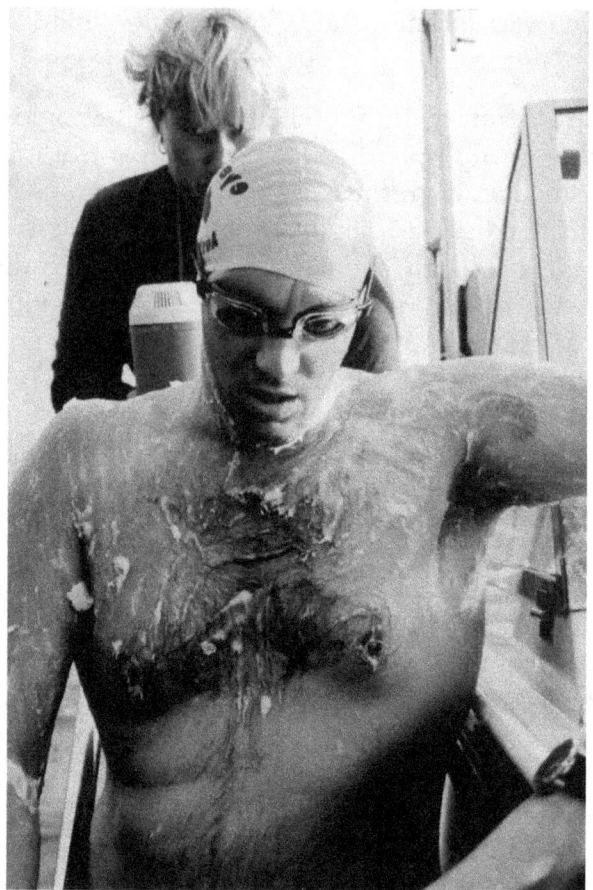
Narelle Simpson applying Vaseline

As I put my foot in the water, I tried not to think about what a long day I had ahead of me. Instead, I focused on why I was here. 'Let's do this for my family,' I told myself. 'Let's do this for Australia.'

The first hour of any long-distance swim you're always a bit hyped up, and you have to really knuckle down to let yourself get into a rhythm. For me, that means concentrating on the loudhailer, because the more you swerve, the further you ultimately have to swim. For the first hour, that was my mantra. *Listen. Don't swerve. Listen. Don't swerve.* The loudhailer became my guiding light. My compass.

And things went well. I don't normally take an overly optimistic approach to my swims. I do as much training as I can and I always put in my best effort, but beyond that I don't make any promises, to myself or to anyone else. But this swim was different. It's one of the only swims I've ever done where I somehow just knew, right from the word go, that I was going to complete it. I felt as if I could have swum all day; I was just in the zone, both mentally and physically. Everything was going right.

The first feed showcased the pole in all its majesty – taking the carb gel from the syringe and the water from the bottle was gloriously straightforward. The second feed didn't go quite so smoothly. Sticks mistimed the delivery of the pole and smacked me in the head! But maybe it was a good thing. It seemed to knock some sense into me, literally, because after I shook it off I found myself paying better attention to my team's instructions at each feed. Often you sort of brush off instructions because you're too focused on your own personal swim. I'm definitely guilty of that. But not today. I took the instructions, I put my head down, and I just continued swimming. We were still very much at the beginning of a very long day.

At the 5-hour mark a seagull appeared, and she would follow the boat for the next 7 hours. I don't consider myself a spiritual person, but to this day I believe that seagull was my Granny, there to support her grandson. In fact, any time a seagull hovers around in one of my swims I believe it's her spirit coming to say, 'Well done mate. You've done me proud.' When she came to me that first time, I just knew. Before her death in 1991, my grandmother on my mother's side was a very important figure in my life. She was a bit of a sporting icon and played a big part in fostering my love for sport.

Multiple times over the years, right when I've needed her most, she's hovered with me, sometimes for many minutes – or, in this case, hours – at a time. I've told people about it over the years, and nobody has ever experienced anything like it. It can't be coincidence. Of course, cynics would say the seagull appeared at the 5-hour mark because the guys were making bacon and eggs in the boat, and maybe they're right! But either way, that seagull kept me going. While everyone aboard enjoyed the feast, I just slurped up my bland, so-called 'chocolate' carbohydrate gel and kept on swimming.

Halfway through, about the eighth hour, Brooke started reading me messages from friends and family, and it really spurred me on. The support was great, but as much as anything I was just grateful to have something else to think about! I've said it before and I'll say it again: it's a mental game. A constant effort not to let the boredom get the better of me, to keep my mind on anything but what I'm doing. The messages were a welcome distraction for me, but I can't say the same for Norm. The role of the observer is to record every last detail of the swim – including every single thing that gets said. I felt sorry for the poor guy, frantically scrawling down message after message!

At the 10-hour mark, I asked Narelle where I was. 'Halfway!' she reported. My heart sunk. It looked like it was going to be a 20-hour swim. But lo and behold, only about 20 minutes later, Sticks said over the loudhailer, 'You beauty! We're more than three-quarters of the way to France!' At the next drink break, I couldn't stop smiling. I didn't say anything at the time, but I remember exactly what I was thinking: I'm swimming better than Grant Hackett today. Better than Ian Thorpe. A bit of hyperbole perhaps, but you have to allow yourself that when you realise you've swum 11 kilometres in 20 minutes. Narelle said, 'You weren't meant to hear that,' and I replied, 'You shouldn't say it over the loudhailer then!'

About the 11-hour mark, I got so desperate that I started doing tax calculations (I work for the Australian Tax Office). I did two calculations, and got neither right, but they wasted 15 minutes and that's all I was after! At the 12-hour mark, Narelle yelled, 'Sprint for the next 500 metres!' No explanation. Just sprint. I trusted Narelle enough to do as I was told. I didn't know it at the time, but I was approaching a sand bank. If I got over it, it would only be another hour or two's swim to France. But if I didn't, the changing tide would stretch the swim out by another 6 hours. I made it, and from that point on, though I didn't know it, I was in sight of victory.

An hour and a half later, my arm hit something. It wasn't a lobster pot, it wasn't a shark, and it wasn't a rock. It was the sand of Strouanne Beach. I got to my feet, and walked through the waves in a bit of a daze. Was this real? Had I really swum that far? Mum was waiting on the shore, and she started to approach me. I felt terrible barking at her to go away, but it wasn't official yet and there was no way I was jeopardising that! 'Don't touch me!' I ordered. She seemed a little hurt at first but I think she understood. Under the rules of the English Channel, you must get onto dry land without anyone touching you and the observer must officialise the swim. So for a minute everybody just stood there, unsure of what to do.

But then my mother broke out in song, belting out the Australian national anthem followed in quick succession by 'God Save the Queen' and 'Waltzing Matilda'. She wasn't about to let the fact she'd been born in Kenya get in the way of her patriotism! Two men had come down to see what all the commotion was about, and when she ran out of songs to sing herself she turned to them and said, 'You're from France. Sing "La Marseillaise"!' It turned out they were from Belgium, but they took it in good humour and sang the Belgian national anthem instead. Mum was really scraping the bottom of the barrel now. She started reciting the Lord's Prayer, but got halfway through and forgot the rest.

But while discordant voices rang out around me, there was only one song running through my head. The first few lines of 'Stand by Me' summed up the swim so perfectly it was as if they had been written just for the occasion. The moon was high as I gazed around at my team and my mother, the people that had been there for me throughout the struggle to get where I was. And then came the moment we had all been waiting for.

It was official, Norm announced. I'd successfully swum the English Channel. It was 6.50 am Australian Eastern Time on 20 July 1998 – the 29th anniversary of man landing on the moon. I hadn't realised the massive weight I'd been carrying on my shoulders until this moment, when it all fell away. I felt as if I could float off at any moment. I turned to my mother in the golden light, and the emotion between us was palpable. All she said was my name, but that one word contained all the love and pride in the world. Our instinct was to embrace, but of course the layers of Vaseline and sunscreen put paid to that idea. Instead, we shook hands.

My mother died only a few weeks before I sat down to write this, and when I think about the bond we shared, this is a moment that endures in my memory. That shake of the hand, that one transient moment, represents everything that was wonderful about our relationship. Her support, her love, her understanding. I couldn't have wished for anyone else to be the first person I touched following the greatest achievement of my life.

And I only had one person in mind as the second. But she was one step ahead of me, as usual! I barely even had time to think before Narelle planted a massive bear hug on me. My legs felt like jelly and she practically bowled me over, but I didn't care. As I stood there shaking in her arms, I could hardly grasp what was happening. I just couldn't believe it. I had swum the English Channel.

Eventually the practicalities had to take over, and we got in a little inflatable boat to get back to the main boat. A simple task, and something I'd done literally hundreds of times. But I could hardly get in. It was as if my muscles had gone on strike as my legs trembled like leaves. Getting from the inflatable boat onto the main boat was just as mammoth a task. Normally it would have been frustrating, but not today. Today it only cemented the momentousness of what I had just achieved.

I sat there just trying to absorb it all. They tell you swimming the English Channel will make you spew, and I sure felt like it, but thankfully I managed to get some food into me – real, solid food! – and the nausea subsided but for a few remaining butterflies. I crossed my fingers and asked Norm what my time was. Thirteen hours and fifty minutes. My aim was to break 14 hours, and I'd done it with just 10 minutes to spare. I felt as if I would burst with pride.

And I wasn't the only one. One other Australian had swum today: Sean Harris, a leg amputee. And he'd done it in 9 hours and 52 minutes. To break 10 hours is outstanding. What a great day for disabled sport in Australia. A one-leg amputee and a blind man, both Australian, had both swum the English Channel, both on their first attempt, and both on the one day.

They say you should never dry someone thoroughly after the English Channel because the salt makes your skin so dry and fragile it will just peel off. I wasn't particularly keen to put that advice to the test, so I was patted down and then I got cosy in some warm clothes and a beanie. There was a bed on the boat, and God it felt good to lie down! I fell asleep for 2 or 3 hours and by the time I woke up we were almost back. It stung a little to realise that after 13 arduous hours and 50 painful minutes, I was back where I started within only 3 hours 30! My neck, back, and shoulders were killing me and my stomach was rumbling like thunder, but I'd warmed up and I was starting to recover. And getting on the phone to my dad, my brother and my sister really lifted my spirits.

We got back to Dover and lumbered off the boat. Narelle swayed back and forth looking as if she could tip over at any moment. After standing on the boat for the entire day with the loudhailer, the poor thing was having trouble adjusting to the feeling of standing on solid ground! I couldn't help ribbing her a little bit but made sure I put my arms on her shoulders to steady her. By now it was 2 am, so we were surprised (and flattered!) to find a reporter from the Australian Associated Press waiting to take our picture. As we walked back through the gate to Dover Harbour, I remembered the moment long ago – no, wait, only the day before – that I had made a promise to myself. Now I had kept that promise. I shut the gate behind me, and with it an entire chapter of my life.

We crammed back into the car, this time relaxed enough to see the funny side of how crushed we felt! It was a lot of fun, mostly because I was the one that managed to get the front seat and avoid the worst of it. When we got back to the chalet my legs still hadn't regained full function and I needed help just to stay upright in the shower, let alone get all the Vaseline off! I was all over the shop. Eventually, a few minutes shy of 3 am, I made it into bed. I had the cassette tape of Elton John's 'Your Song' on repeat, trying in vain to get to sleep. I don't know if it was the excitement, the relief, the pain, or a combination of all three, but no matter how exhausted I was it seemed as if sleep would never find me.

Of course, it didn't help that my body was also frantically trying to eliminate the I-don't-know-how-many litres of sea water I'd gulped over the course of the day.

I eventually did get to sleep, and by the time I woke the next morning everyone was already up. I was still barely with it and struggling to operate my limbs, but everyone else seemed to somehow be in power mode! Brooke kindly volunteered to give me a massage, while Narelle and Sticks took turns running back and forth from the main office to bring me the myriad faxes of congratulations that kept feeding through. I particularly treasured a heartfelt message from Murray Rose, which only sweetened the memory of our secret swim back in June. Later that morning we went to the bar, convinced the bartender that my odd gait was a result of pain not inebriation, and finally got to have a few celebratory drinks.

That night the whole team went down and played trivia at a local pub. We didn't do particularly well but it was nice just to do something normal for a change. That night, there was a massive storm, and I said to Mum, 'I think Granny's sending her congratulations! It's not every day you get an electrical storm in England!' There's nothing like a life-changing achievement to bring out your sentimental side. On the way out Graham Pique said to the bouncer, 'Couldn't you put the lights on so the blind guy can see where the puddle is?' He still hasn't quite lived that one down.

Even by the Tuesday morning, it still hadn't fully sunk in that I had actually swum the English Channel. It's funny the things that end up affecting you, because that afternoon I was standing outside the chalets when a kid on his bike stopped and asked me, 'Are you a swimmer?'

'Yeah, I am.'

'Did you swim the English Channel?'

'Yeah, I did.'

'Well done.'

Not the most effusive congratulations ever, but for some reason it just got me. And that's when it came to me, I mean *really* came to me. I thought, 'Yeah. I *have* swum the English Channel.' It was a simple moment, but then the greatest moments usually are.

The English Channel is the Holy Grail for open-water swimmers. It's the mecca of swimming and, like the holy city, it welcomes all those who believe. It doesn't discriminate. No matter how good a swimmer you are, whether you're an Olympian, an amputee, blind, in a wheelchair, or just your average guy, you can have a crack. If you want to swim the English Channel, all you have to do is go out and train for it. Of course, a large part of whether you get there on the day comes down to luck, and luck fell in my favour on the day. But that doesn't lessen the achievement. When you swim the English Channel, you're a somebody. On 19 July I was a nobody, and on 20 July I was a somebody.

The English Channel is the ultimate test – the 12% success rate can attest to that. They say it's equivalent to climbing Mount Everest. One bloke attempted it twenty-two times, and failed twenty-two times. It sure puts Des Renford's achievements into perspective. To succeed nineteen times from nineteen starts is an absolutely outstanding achievement in itself. But that's not even the best part. In 1980, just days before his fifty-third birthday, Des completed three single crossings of the English Channel in fifteen days. He did it with no GPS, no doctor, no physio, no masseur. Just him. At the time nobody else had even come close to that achievement.

When I wrote the first draft of this book, I wrote that Des' feat would never be matched, and I truly believed it. But now I eat my words, because in 2016, at the age of thirty-one, Chloë McCardel became the first person in history to complete three single crossings of the English Channel in *one week*. It's beyond impressive. It's one of the most incredible feats in history. I would never try to detract from what she has achieved, but I do want to say that it in no way reduces my admiration for Des. I was twenty-five years younger than Des when I did my English Channel swim, and there's not a hope in Hades that I could have swum again four days later. In fact, I don't think I'd ever be able to do it again. You know, I don't particularly like the word champion. I never have. It's used too much, too easily, too flippantly. People are ready to call horses, dogs, even cats champions. Come on, let's at least restrict it to humans! There are very few people I would call a champion. But Des is one of them.

Being good at something doesn't make you a champion. Even being the best at something doesn't make you a champion. At least, not in the sense that I use the word. If I call someone a champion, it means I consider them a champion as a person. Someone who has a whole range of positive traits, and who actually puts in the effort to use those traits to make the world a better place. Altruism, resilience, commitment, dedication, sportsmanship. Des Renford and Nelson Mandela are the first names to spring to mind, and they are people I have always looked up to. But another less-recognised champion is Tanzanian marathon runner John Stephen Akhwari.

In a Mexico City marathon, Akhwari cramped up due to the high altitude. At the 19-kilometre point he fell badly, dislocating his knee and hitting his shoulder hard. But he kept running, and finished over an hour after the winner. The sun had set, and there were only a few thousand people left in the stadium. The winner of that race wasn't the champion. Akhwari was.

When he was asked by a reporter why didn't he give it away, he said, 'My country did not send me 5,000 miles to start the race; they sent me 5,000 miles to finish the race.' That quote makes my skin tingle. It encapsulates my entire marathon-swimming career. It's never been about winning; it's always just been about finishing. And a good thing, too, because at my pace I would never have had a chance! Whenever I'm struggling, that quote gives me the energy to push on.

When people say I'm a champion, I shy away from it. I've tried to be a good person, to be guided by my morals, to play by the rules. On 20 July 1998, I achieved something amazing. But that's not enough to merit the title of 'champion'. I've had a lot of luck and I've been surrounded by amazing people the whole way. The victory of crossing the English Channel was as much theirs as it was mine.

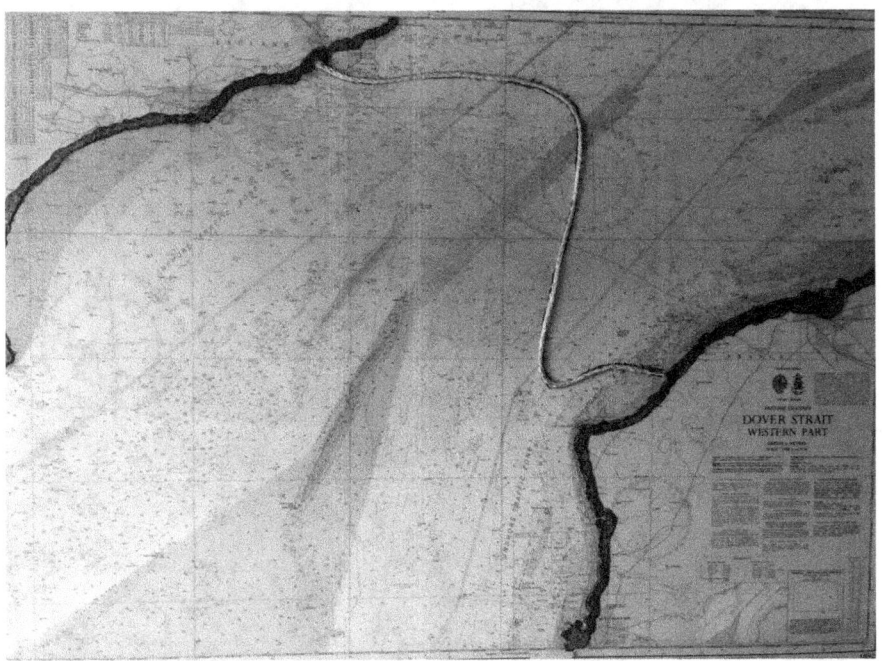
Actual swim route across the English Channel

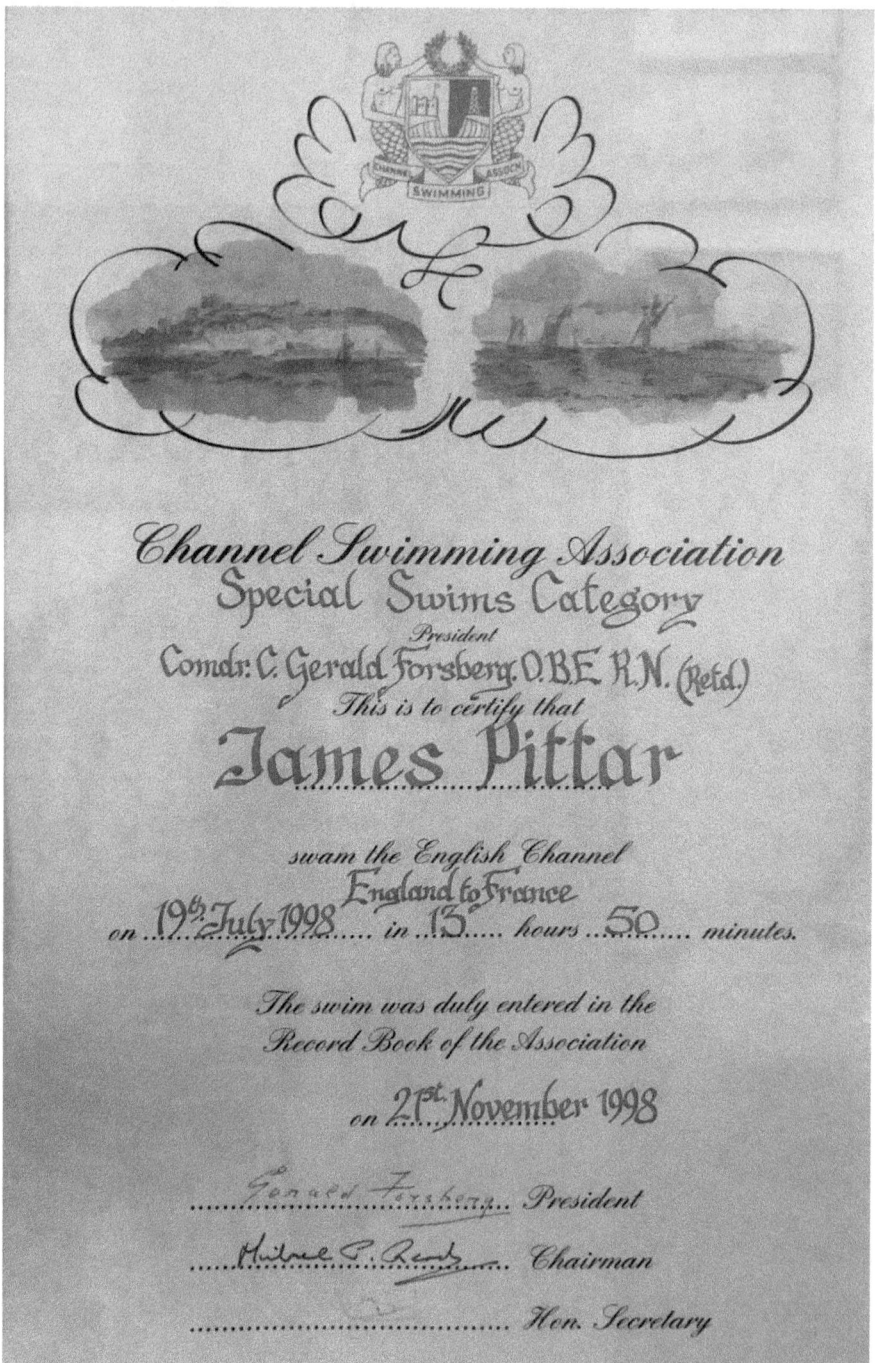

Certificate from Channel Swimming Association

## Chapter 3
## My early life

Of course, none of it could ever have happened without my wonderful mother and father. Mum and Dad's meeting was unlikely in a lot of ways – Mum was born in Kenya and raised in England, Dad born and raised in Australia. They met when Dad, an ophthalmologist, started working as a registrar at The Royal Eye Hospital in London. As fate would have it, Mum was working at the same hospital as an orthoptist – an eye movement specialist. They fell in love quickly and married in 1964 in Scotland.

I was born Richard Robert Pittar at 11 pm on 5 October 1969. But after six months, my parents decided I didn't look like a Richard. Apparently, I looked like a James. And so my name was officially changed. Right from birth, the word 'ordinary' was never going to apply! I had the best possible start in life. I was born into family of loving parents, a brother Tony and a sister Buffy, a cocker spaniel called Leo, and two Burmese cats called Rangoon and Simba. We lived in a beautiful big house in the leafy north-shore Sydney suburb of Killara, and until I met my wife I never lived anywhere else. Why would I? It had everything. Masses of living space – it was originally built as two separate flats, so it had six or seven bedrooms, two bathrooms, and two kitchens. A big tree for us all to climb, and a beautiful grass tennis court that got used to within an inch of its life – and not just for tennis, but for football, cricket, and any other sport we could dream up. One day my brother brought home some chickens and we ended up with a chicken coop as well. We loved having the fresh eggs, but

Dad wasn't as enthused about the mess they made on his tennis court! Fortuitously, we eventually added a swimming pool to the list. Behind the backyard were the beautiful Swain Gardens, set in a valley complete with a creek, swathes of trees and clusters of vibrant wildflowers. Needless to say, our birthday parties at the house were the envy of all the kids in town.

I was born in perfect health – eyesight included – but at the age of two, I developed epilepsy. The first couple of medications didn't do much, but the third one seemed to control it. The seizures persisted until I was three and a half, and I was finally allowed to stop taking my daily medication when I was seven. And I've never had a seizure since. It's not lost on me how very lucky that is – if the seizures had persisted, I would barely have been allowed to get in the pool, let alone build a swimming career.

We lived across the road from our greatest friends: Chris and Jane Chown and their kids, Roland, Annabel and Alexia. Roly was born exactly 364 days after me, meaning we have the same age for just one day of the year. We realised this when we first met at his fourth birthday, and at that age it was as good a basis for a friendship as any! We were inseparable for a while, always having sleepovers at each other's houses. And it ended up being one of those rare early childhood friendships that actually stands the test of time. Even today we live in adjacent suburbs and I'm Godfather to his first child.

When Roly and I were six or seven and my brother was ten, the *Sun-Herald* newspaper ran a 'Tibby the Lion' promotion – some character they'd dreamed up to make kids hound their parents to buy the paper! Every newspaper had a little Tibby sticker attached to the front page, and if you collected enough, you'd get a massive Tibby sticker. Tony convinced Roly and me to go on a mission to collect as many of these things as we could. Whatever it took!

And so, one Sunday morning, the two of us went out in nothing but our dressing gowns at about 6 in the morning. We went to each house in turn, scouting people's yards for their newspapers, tearing off the plastic wrapping, taking the Tibby stickers, and getting out of there as quickly and stealthily as we knew how! There were a few close calls, but I tend to think even if people had seen us they would have been too struck by disbelief to do anything about it! It must have been quite an image, these two dressing-gown-clad would-be thieves pillaging their newspapers.

We took home a haul of about a hundred stickers, and Tony was absolutely delighted. He traded them in for a bunch of massive Tibby stickers. He'd worked out the scheme, he'd sent us into battle, and now he was enjoying the glory. It didn't really seem fair, but we were the idiots that agreed to it! I guess it goes with the title of younger brother – this misplaced sense of duty to your elders that does nothing but get you in trouble. But when all was said and done, we had a lot of fun.

When I was seven, Dad decided we were getting a pool. When Dad got an idea, he saw it through, and he saw it through fast. Unfortunately, I don't think he'd thought through the timing, because he had it built in May – the beginning of winter. For six months, it seemed as if it would be no more than a burden to clean! But Dad had an idea. This'll be interesting, I thought. Whenever Dad proclaimed that he had an idea, you cringed. When his face lit up like that, it was time to run for cover!

The next day, Dad came home with twenty trout. He tipped them into the pool, and we had our own personal trout farm for the next six months. It was an ingenious idea… in theory! The concept of sitting in your own backyard with a fishing rod in hand was quite novel and exciting. Roly loved it; he came over all the time with all his fishing gear. He was always very into fishing. Personally, I don't see the appeal, but Roly seemed to derive a great deal of pleasure just from sitting there waiting for a fish to bite. A good thing, too, because the trout in the pool weren't in the habit of biting.

November came around, and we were ready to use the pool for its actual purpose. Tony's birthday party became a competition to see who could get the fish out. To date, we had caught a grand total of two fish. Eighteen to go. It took all afternoon to catch a single fish (and not without the help of the tennis net!). The other seventeen, unfortunately, suffered death by chlorination the next day. Dad's pool filter didn't survive it, and in the end we had no choice but to replace it. But it was good fun. And filter or no filter, it was a good investment in the end.

That summer we were in the pool almost as often as we were out of it. I've used it many times in training for my marathon swims, but I will always remember it not as the pool that got me across the English Channel, but the pool that got me to victory over my dad! All the kids said that no one could ever beat my dad, and he agreed. I think he was secretly pretty proud of his reputation among the under-tens. But to his credit, even in his early forties he was still good enough to beat his kids. Of course, as we got older and stronger, and he got older and weaker, the day inevitably came that one of us beat him. But when we were really young, that never crossed our minds. He was a local legend, and that was that.

When Sunday would come around, the pool would be abandoned for the beach. From the age of seven, every Sunday morning was the same story: we'd go to Freshwater Beach, have a surf – Dad loved his body surfing – and on the way home, get an ice cream at the local shops. That was the ritual, and we didn't dream of breaking it. I loved going to the beach every weekend, though it was a shaky beginning. At first, every time a wave would break I would run away petrified, shouting at it to leave me alone! My brother, on the other hand, was a born surfer. He loved it from the moment he set foot in the water.

Every summer from the age of about five to twelve, we would go to Lord Howe Island. What a place. Every year we went to the same place, but it never got old. The roads were covered with children instead of cars and you were hard pressed to find a piece of litter on the whole island. That's what it was like. It was all about relaxing and doing whatever made you happy, but respecting the beauty of the place and giving it due care as well. It's still regarded as one of the most eco-conscious holiday destinations in the world. Of course, as children that wasn't a priority. All we cared about was what kind of excitement and mischief we could get up to!

And the possibilities were virtually endless. Cycling, swimming, surfing, fishing, windsurfing, snorkelling. Sometimes we'd hire a boat and take it out to Rabbit Island or Ball's Pyramid, an ancient volcano remnant. Every Friday night, Milky Way Villas put on their famous 'Fish Fry'.

Then there were the walks. Every year Mum would make us to do some terrible walk or other, to the King's Lookout, Mount Eliza, or whatever destination took her fancy. She loved walking, and wasn't about to let the fact that the rest of us didn't stop her from dragging us with her.

When I was seven or eight, we came upon Neville Wran, the Premier of New South Wales, playing tennis with his wife at our resort. I ran out from the trees just as Mr Wran had hit the ball and yelled, 'Bad shot, Mr Wran!' at the top of my voice. I'd been having an argument with Buffy and I guess it was my way of venting my frustration, but what a way to do it! Of course, I didn't know what 'Premier' even meant at the time, I must have just seen his face on TV or something. Either way, my parents were highly embarrassed!

In February 1975, at five years old, I started at Newington Prep School in Lindfield, just across the valley. The school was incredible. With Swain Reserve stretching out behind it, at break time all you had to do was wander down to the back of the grounds and you felt as if you were deep in the bush. We had a pool and tennis courts on campus, plus the beautiful Koola Park just down the road for sporting events, with cricket, soccer and rugby grounds. There were go-kart and swimming competitions each year. All within ten minutes of my backyard! They really were such fun times. If only you could go back and explain to your younger self just how great and important these times are. But you never fully appreciate the best times of your life until they're over.

I'd leave home at 8.50 am, walk across the valley, jump over the stone wall at the back of Newington, and meander up to the classroom with a couple of minutes to spare. At the end of the day, I was home by 3.10 pm. Those were the good old days. School would finish, and before I knew it I'd be in the backyard playing with my friends, while Mum fixed us some drinks and snacks. Mum was always there for us full time, and I only wish I'd recognised at the time what an incredible luxury that was.

She was the most present and encouraging mother anyone could have wished for. I'm sure plenty of stay-at-home parents long for the different satisfactions and achievements of working life, but even though she came from a professional career, that was never Mum. She loved every minute of raising us, and we always knew there was nowhere she'd rather be. It made an enormous difference, and of course I have Dad to thank for that as well, because without his income to support us all, she could never have done it.

Just as my wife Jenny and I could never have done it. Annica was in childcare a fair bit through her first three or four years of life, and even since she's been at school we still rely on after-school care. Some days we're apart from 7 am to 6 pm. It's the routine, we're used to it, and we still enjoy a beautiful relationship with her. But it's a far cry from my own childhood. I was home from school in 5 minutes, and there was Mum waiting for me. It's incredibly rare to have that these days, and easy to forget how good we really had it.

That being said, Mum did go back home to Africa and England fairly regularly to see her family and friends, leaving Dad and the three of us kids to fend for ourselves. When I was about seven, we got a babysitter to help us. But she was a real talker, and Dad soon reached the end of his tether. He rounded us up and said, 'Right. We're going out tonight.' An hour later, there we all were – seven, nine and eleven years old – absorbing a frenzy like nothing we had ever seen before: the 1977 Abba concert. Everyone said, 'What a hip dad.' If they only knew the backstory! It absolutely poured with rain, and the only thing I could really see at my height was the fireworks at the end. Still, it was an incredible experience and one not many seven-year-olds would be able to boast!

Meanwhile at school I was making so many great friends. Friends that would stand the test of time. By the time I went to school I already knew Mark Johnson, a kid that lived just around the corner, and very early on we met a boy called Dean Reeves and immediately hit it off. An enduring friendship bloomed between the three of us. To this day, we remain the best of friends, and they have been some of the most influential people in my life. Their irrepressible optimism and never-say-die attitude rubbed off on me in a big way, and when my eyesight started to go they never let me wallow in self-pity. As far as either of them were concerned, you take what you're given, and you make it work.

In fifth grade, Dean and I sat next to each other, and one day we decided to cheat on a spelling test. Everyone was getting scores in the 20s and 30s, but Dean and I both got 47 out of 50. There was no denying it was a bit suspect, but nobody had any proof. Ask anyone else in the class about that spelling test and there's no way they'd remember it. But Dean and I will never forget. When you're an honest person, you never quite let go of these little moments of dishonesty.

Dean and I also played saxophone together, and we loved it. But our teacher Mr Holburt was always fighting an uphill battle – I don't think either of us was ever destined for a career in music. Nevertheless, Dean and I played a duet together at the end of sixth-grade Presentation Day, which was a great experience. And when I went to The Shore School I was bloody glad I knew how to play an instrument, because it was either join the orchestra or join the cadets or air training corps. Thank God for that!

We had some interesting people in our classes. One kid put a knife into a wall socket, which was exciting. Another threw an aerosol can onto the barbecue at school camp, and when it exploded all the teacher had to say was, 'Well, there's your science lesson!' (We had some interesting teachers as well!)

The one teacher that sticks in my mind was my sixth-grade teacher, Don Jackson. He had been a prisoner in World War II. We were all captivated by this fact and always wanted to hear stories about the prisoner-of-war camps, but he was always reticent – understandably so. He was small in stature, but commanded a great deal of respect and always brought out the best in all his students. It was always obvious how much he enjoyed teaching, and really, I think that's half the battle.

Newington was into sport, and we got to play six hours a week for four years. But in those days I couldn't get enough, so Dad got me involved in the Lindfield soccer club. Mark Johnson and I played together in the under-sevens with Dad as our coach. That's when we met Andrew Peken, yet another of the lifelong friends I made as a kid. Andrew was a bright kid who loved sports, who was willing to give anything a go, and we got on right from the start.

Our team didn't win a game all year, but we enjoyed it thoroughly all the same. I had to feel for Dad when Mark's dad took over for the only match he missed for the whole year, and we drew. A draw doesn't sound like a great result, but when you lose every other game for the entire year it starts to look pretty good! The story became part of the Lindfield under-sevens folklore for a good long while. Dad wasn't impressed, but he took it pretty well.

I don't have a lot of memories of my stint in soccer, but there are a couple that stick in my mind. I'll never forget the time I kicked a goal from the halfway line just before halftime. I had a good boot and a good kick, but you still never quite expect to get it through from that distance! I whooped with joy and looked around for someone to share it with. But all I got was Mark walking past saying, 'Nah, didn't count.' I turned to Dad.

'What's he talking about?' I asked.

'One of your mates was behind the goal line,' he explained. 'That means he wasn't in the field of play, which means it doesn't count.'

'You're joking?'

'Nope. Sorry mate.'

I can look back on that day and laugh now, but at the time I was crestfallen.

When my Lindfield soccer team played Newington I couldn't get my head around the fact that I was playing against my mates, people I went to school with every day. I wanted to go hard for my team, but it meant making my mates lose. My allegiance was bouncing back and forth like a ping-pong ball. With time and experience you learn to separate competition from friendship, but at the time the concept of playing to win with no regard for the opposition was very difficult for me. Of course it was. I'd spent my whole life so far playing sport purely for the fun of it. This playing-to-win thing was always going to take a bit of getting used to.

Mark Johnson and his brother Rick used to come round nearly every week and play sports on our tennis court. If we were playing rugby, we'd assign ourselves the roles of Graham Eadie or Ray Price, or if we were playing cricket we were Dennis Lillee or Greg Chappell. It was no more than a fantasy, but it gave us so much joy to get out there and pretend to be big guns! On the big grass tennis court we got the chance to hit fours and sixes, which always prompted a fair bit of excited yelling and screaming.

I think poor old Rick always felt under the pump, probably because he was. When we assigned 'teams' it almost always ended up being me and Mark versus him. I'm sure it sparked a bit of resentment, but he probably decided to cut his losses and just go with it as the smallest and youngest! The bonds you make in your early days have a quality you just don't find as you get older, and I'm so grateful to have been able to forge such strong friendships with boys that have grown into amazing, upstanding men.

In 1977, Dad and I went with Mark and Rick and their dad to our first ever game at the Sydney Cricket Ground – the rugby league preliminary final between Parramatta and the Eastern suburbs. It marked the beginning of a love affair with the SCG that has never dwindled. My love only grew when, the year after, I got to watch my rugby team, Manly, get through a replay of a knockout semi-final that eventually led them on to win the 1978 Grand Final. I've supported Manly as long as I can remember, and I always will, whether they're at the top of the ladder or the bottom.

In 1979 I went to my first ever cricket test match at the SCG – Australia versus India. And so began my second love affair, with test cricket. Sport quickly became something of an outlet for me in life – something I could always rely on, always turn to, no matter how crazy the rest of my life might have been. Way back then I couldn't have known just how big a part of my life sport would become. How many incredible opportunities it would afford me. But at the time it was bliss just to be there with my dad and my mates in the best ground in the world having a laugh and a good time.

Ever since that first match, barely a summer goes by that Mark and I and all our mates don't gather to enjoy the test and one-dayers. It's about endurance, strategy, the long game. It takes a certain type of person to be able to play five days of intense cricket only to have it end in a draw. But then that draw could be the result that wins you the series. There's no other sport quite like it.

I feel lucky that I got to fall in love with cricket while I could still see. Now that my sight is gone the experience is different, of course, but I don't love it any less. I've always loved listening to sport, and there's no better game to listen to as a blind person than cricket. In fact, an Australia versus England match – the holy grail of test cricket – is the only thing in the world I'm willing to get up at 2 am for. I don't care who's good and who's not, I only care who's playing. English and Australian commentators are some of the best in the world, and their descriptions are brilliant. I would hate to think how many hours I've spent listening to sport since 1977! Probably as many as the number of kilometres I've swum.

Dad is the exact same way, but for him the greatest sport in the world is golf. He loves watching games on TV, but the ads make him furious. So to get around it, Dad never watches games live. For as long as I can remember, he has always taped all his sports (and anyone who walks into his house or his ophthalmology practice in the meantime receives the bellowed greeting, 'Don't tell me the result of the match!'). Fast-forwarding the ads is the only way he can get through the match without frustration. No joke, a few months ago the fast-forward button actually fell off his remote control! Many nights Mum and I would sit there just waiting for him to get through his tape so we could finally talk about the result.

In 1980, when I was almost eleven, Mum took us to visit her mother and brother in England. Granny had come out and spent a couple of weeks with us at Lord Howe Island when I was six, but this was the first time I really got a chance to get to know her. It didn't take long. Our shared deep love of sport created an unbreakable bond between us. She was the captain of the England hockey team in her day, not to mention playing lacrosse and tennis at a national level. Even into her seventies and eighties, she was still out there playing golf every week. She was always banging on about how great sport was and what an important role it had played throughout her life. I was only young, but I already knew what she was talking about. Like her, I didn't just love playing sport, I loved everything about it. I loved watching it, I loved seeing other people play, I loved the way it brightened people's lives.

Granny was an outstanding sportsperson, but more importantly, she had such an admirable attitude to sport. It's probably the greatest asset I gained from her – sportsmanship, no matter what the circumstances. And she never gave in to the bitter spiral some old people fall into. Right up to her death, she retained the same incredible outlook. She was an amazing role model for me, maybe more so than anyone else in my life, and she gave me everything I could ever have wanted from a grandmother. It was her greatest legacy.

On the other side of the equation, Dad's mother, Frances, lived only 20 minutes away and used to come over every Sunday for breakfast. She was the polar opposite of Granny. She had no interest whatsoever in sport (yet somehow both her sons found their way into it). She preferred just to spend all day smoking and watching TV. I couldn't understand it. And, though neither of us intended it, that divide cost us our relationship. I never felt at ease with her. I would often find myself thinking how unfair it was that my maternal grandmother, the archetypal sportswoman, lived 12,000 miles away while my paternal grandmother was right here with us every weekend and couldn't even muster the motivation to watch a single game with me.

One time I showed her my cricket ball and she barely even reacted. You can't control what you do and don't like, but you can control your actions. How much effort would it have taken to feign interest for a second, and maybe feel some sense of connection to her grandson for once? If it had been Granny on the other end of that exchange, she would have been out there putting up the stumps and saying, 'What are we waiting for?' It was hard to accept, but we were too different to ever really build a relationship. But what I missed out on with her was more than made up by the incredible connection I shared with Granny.

In this day and age, I believe sport is the greatest leveller. It's the one thing that brings people of ability and disability, and every creed and colour together for a common purpose, no matter what their history. It breaks down the barriers because it's something everyone understands. Something everyone can enjoy. And Granny is the one that instilled that belief.

Granny understood the importance of inclusion and acceptance, and one thing's for sure, she definitely passed it on to Mum. From about the age of ten right through to about eighteen, my mother was constantly offering up rooms in our house for people to stay. It epitomises her generosity, though she would never acknowledge it – 'it's what anyone would do', she used to say. She had a lot of friends in England and Africa, and whenever one of their children decided to come to Australia for a gap year she was straight on the phone offering to welcome them. It was sort of an unwritten law that all these kids would spend their first night with us – 'just until they found their feet'. But it wasn't uncommon for that 'first night' to stretch into a week, a month, or more! Mum never resented it. In fact, the longer they stayed, the happier she was. We had a saying: 'Come and have dinner at the Pittars'. Stay the night. Then why not stay the week? Better still, two weeks, two months, or four months!' Most of our visitors were interesting, some were a bit special and a few were absolute shockers!

I remember one guy that came to stay whose name was so long I struggled to remember it. And he lived up to his illustrious name, with a pompous English accent and a constant look of surprise at the things we got up to. He had a real holier-than-thou attitude. It didn't help that he arrived on one of our 'firecracker nights'! The poor old bloke got thrown in the deep end there.

Another young man came to stay for 'a couple of weeks', and for months he never seemed to bother attempting to leave. Only about a week after we finally sent him on his way, his mother wrote to us and said, 'Where is he?' For the first time in about six months, we didn't know! He did eventually get home.

Then there was the professor of the first foot of the ocean – yes, you are reading correctly, and no, I don't know what that means

– and his son, who was hoping to get a grant to study butterfly eyes. To this day, I've never heard of two more specific professions. They were characters all right.

You just had to endure these people; you had no choice but to sit at the dinner table and try to converse with them. We worked out along the way that when Dad was sick of our guests, he would say, 'I'd better get off to bed, I've got a big operation to do tomorrow. Goodnight.' Then he was out of the room like a shot, leaving Mum and all of us there with whoever it was that had gotten his goat. It was hard not to laugh when he said it, and sometimes a nudge under the table was all it took for a giggle to slip out.

One time on a flight to Australia Mum gave her address to two Swedish backpackers, and they came back and pitched their tent on the tennis court. They were bashing the pegs with real gusto; I think they couldn't believe their luck! It didn't last too long though. The minute Dad got home from work, they were shafted off to the local caravan park. Dad was very tolerant of Mum's constant desire to provide for people, but when it happened with complete strangers, without his prior knowledge, and involved damage to his property, it stretched his patience that little bit too far!

Every time someone new came to stay, we would think, here we go again! Another dinner, another person. But now I realise it was all one big lesson. And it's one of the greatest things my mother taught me. Her embracing attitude to people of all backgrounds is one of the most important qualities any parent could impart. And you have to be able to converse with all sorts in life. From a very young age I understood how to be around people older than me, how to talk to them, how to show them respect – even when I didn't like them. I learned what to ask and what not to ask, how to keep the chat going. And that gave me a great grounding in life. I begrudged it at the time but looking back on it, it was an invaluable crash course in communication. It's something that still helps me every day.

And it was a conscious choice on their part to deliver this lesson, and to build my confidence in applying it. One time they brought back this couple and Dad said, 'She's not a great talker. She seems like a bit of a hard nut to crack. So I'm putting her next to you because I know if anyone can bring her out of her shell, it's you.' Despite the fact that Mum was always the one who was more present, Dad was just as instrumental in bringing me up to become a strong, resilient, and kind adult. He was both wise and optimistic – a combination that's not all that easy to come by. I look back very fondly on all the stories Dad used to tell me about his life – the good times at uni, swimming at Bondi Beach, playing golf, living in Wimbledon. He had so many funny stories and beautiful memories to share, and in retrospect I think that's what I've always tried to emulate in my own life. When and if I had my own children, I wanted to be able to have the same myriad of lovely life stories to pass on to them. And I'm so proud to be able to say I'm giving Annica that same wonderful experience my dad gave to me.

I truly can't fault my upbringing in Killara. Living the carefree lifestyle embodied by the seventies and eighties, never having to think about money, having my school and most of my friends literally within a few hundred metres, playing every sport I could dream of with my mates. And it didn't occur to me at the time, but having a tennis court, a climbing tree and a swimming pool in your yard was hardly par for the course. It was a good life. An easy life. But it wouldn't be long before I'd be thrown my first real challenge.

## Chapter 4
# High school

When I left Newington, I went from this wonderful, secure bush school with only one hundred and fifty local kids to a huge school with over a thousand boys from all over the world. Gone was the 5-minute walk to school, playtime in the bushland, games of cricket just down the street. It was a massive transition, and one I wasn't altogether ready for.

I'd been a little hell-raiser for basically my entire childhood, and unfortunately I still hadn't grown out of the temper tantrums. I'm told I used to headbutt the table, scream my lungs out, and smack myself against everything. I would always rise, too, when people egged me on, something my brother and sister took great joy in doing. So my parents were now faced with spending the whole eight weeks of holidays before I went to Shore School trying to teach me judgment and self-control. They laid it out clear and simple. 'At Newington you were the best cricket bowler, you kicked a good haul of goals in soccer, and you were even all right at rugby – out of only thirty kids, that is. But you're not in Kansas anymore. Your year level is going to be bigger than all of Newington, and you're going to encounter boys who are fifty times better than you. Things are going to happen that will test you, and you have to be ready for that. You won't last a second if you don't learn to control that temper.'

That summer we went to Lord Howe Island as usual, but the training didn't stop. Every day, Mum and Dad would come up with a new scenario designed to teach me some kind of lesson. One afternoon Mum said, 'Right, who wants to go back and get a tennis ball for us to play a game?' In characteristic style, I said, 'Not me!' I didn't want to ride all the way to the resort and back just for a stupid ball. But Dad said, 'Off you go', and I begrudgingly did it. I knew it wasn't about the tennis ball. It was about learning that sometimes, you just have to do what you're told. I hated it, but it was the best thing they could have done for me. I learned to fend for myself, and to pick my battles. Mum and Dad were so attuned to what I needed, and I'm forever grateful for how well they prepared me.

At thirteen years of age, I arrived at the school gates with six other petrified kids from Newington, Mark Johnson included. The huge buildings loomed ahead, dark and intimidating. I felt insignificant. All at once, I realised how sheltered my existence had been up to that moment. And looking around at the others' faces, it was clear they felt the same. My God, I thought, I'm out of my depth here. Having Mark by my side and my brother in year ten was of some comfort, but still the fear weighed on me. The first week was thirty-odd degrees every day, and sweating up a storm inside trousers, a long-sleeved shirt, a tie, a coat, and a boater didn't help my anxiety. It was torture.

Without Mark, I would have been lost. He's been one of my best friends all my life, though I know I'm not the only one who calls him that – he's been best man at *seven* weddings! We have a running joke that if Mark doesn't get asked to be a groomsman at a wedding, something's wrong. He attracts friends like a magnet, and if you stick with Mark you get to meet all sorts of people. He's a wonderful, friendly man with a reputation to match.

Thanks to my thoughtful, forward-thinking parents, I did know a couple of other people in my class. Knowing classes were organised in alphabetical order, they had organised a barbecue the week before school started with my under-sevens mate Andrew Peken and another kid called Stuart Parker. I eventually built some good friendships of course, but it was slow going.

Having my brother Tony at the school was a blessing and a curse. He tried to be supportive and it was handy that I knew some of his friends, but it probably held me back a little in forming my own friendships. And from the very beginning I felt as if I was constantly in his shadow. Tony was a great athlete and everyone knew who he was. In 1984, he and another kid competed in a high-jump contest that went on for almost an hour. They just kept matching each other jump for jump. When the buses arrived, parents and teachers tried in vain to bundle everyone out of there, but they couldn't drag our eyes away from this incredible match. Unfortunately, Tony lost right at the end, but by then who won was beside the point.

My self-confidence took a heavy blow in those first few weeks. The teachers all seemed to favour the kids who had been at Shore Prep School, and trying to get into any of the sports teams was hard work. It was a totally different ball game compared with Newington. Suddenly I'd gone from the top rugby team to the bottom. I now played rugby because I had to, certainly not because I was any good. Oh, the humiliation the day we lost 98–0! I quickly discovered that I wasn't quite the cricketing phenomenon I thought I was, either, as I dropped down to the sixth cricket team.

I ended up loving the school, but it took me a long time to get into. I was grateful that Shore operated with three thirteen-week terms rather than the current four nine-week terms, because it gave us all a proper chance to get into the routine, to understand the system, to get to know people. That was critical. If I'd only had nine weeks I know I would have struggled. But as it was, by the end of the term Mark and I had started to build some solid friendships.

I took to walking most of the way home from the station with Peter Duncan, a kid who was somehow simultaneously the smartest, the craziest and the funniest person in the class. He was one of those people who is willing to give everything a go, seemingly with no fear of failure, and I loved that when I was around him a little bit of that attitude rubbed off on me. And of course he shared that all-important love of sport. No matter what the conditions or how he was feeling, you could count on Pete to show up and give his all in any and every sport.

In Ancient History class I met James Shellshear. As much as we gave our teacher a bit of grief – James does the best impersonations

I've ever seen – we loved that class. He was the one that seemed to share the same passion I felt for it. Even after class was over, we would often sit down on the oval and wax lyrical about Greek or Roman history. But when James started up about his other great love, English, it was time to go home. The 'great' poets John Donne and William Blake were of absolutely no interest to me! So little has changed over the years. These days James actually teaches high-school English and History.

At the end of year seven we had a school camping trip at Galston, and that's where my friendship with James really started to grow. We still reminisce sometimes about sitting in the pool, having an extended debate about the 1982–83 Ashes series. Allan Border was the best. No, Geoff Lawson was the best! A stupid, pointless, wonderful debate. The rest of my memories of that camp are not so fond. We had to do this massive walk to a campsite then back in the morning. I just hated it. I hated walking, I hated camping, and I sure as hell hated the combination of the two! But, as my parents had taught me the previous summer, I sucked it up and got it done. It was the sort of camp that revealed people's true selves, and while I didn't shine, I didn't fall apart either. I was proud to know that I had grown. I had changed. I wasn't that temper-tantrum-throwing kid any more.

In year eight I began to realise my eyesight was starting to go. When I was about ten years old, just going into fifth grade, I had found that I was starting to have trouble seeing clearly at night. I didn't know it at the time, but the eye disease that would ultimately claim my vision was beginning to set in. Now, things were really starting to go downhill. I had to sit on the sunny side of the classroom just to be able to read.

I found out I had an eye disease called retinitis pigmentosa, which gradually destroys the retina. Any other parents might have despaired at the direness of the situation. Not my parents. They got stuck into the practicalities, finding machines and technology that would help me get by in the classroom. Taking me to Vision Australia, the Royal Blind Society, Retina Australia, anyone that might be able to help. Getting me involved with groups. At the time I remember wondering why they weren't more rattled, but in retrospect I understand it was just their way of dealing with it. Dad in particular I think took it much harder than he let on. He was fiercely protective of all his kids and to have something like this happen to me, something completely out of his control, was a lot to take.

But pessimism was off the table. I'll never forget my mother saying, 'You are so lucky to live in Australia where you have bright light and good conditions all year round, not like in England where it's constantly bloody cloudy and crappy. You're so lucky.' I sure didn't feel it. The whole thing came at a very hard time for me, right when I was going through puberty and trying to find myself. I was a very disgruntled, unhappy young person for a few years.

I regressed to my temper tantrums – well, maybe tantrums isn't the right word, but I certainly wasn't very pleasant to my parents. They deserved so much more; I was so fortunate that Mum and Dad were in the eye business and took charge of my situation. Not to mention the fact that our family had the money to be *able* to tackle this problem. But when you find out in your teens that you're going blind, it's hard to react calmly. Would I still be accepted by my friends? How was I going to get by without my beloved sport? Was I going to end up having to carry a cane? What use is someone who can't read? What was going to happen to me?

If there's one good thing that came out of the whole sordid situation, it's that I found out who my real friends were. Who stood up, and who stood down. All the people that mattered stood by me; Mark Johnson, Dean Reeves, Pete Duncan and James Shellshear, in particular. I still got accepted. I still got invited to everything, even if everyone knew I couldn't do it. My vision loss was a non-event to all of them. They never treated me one bit differently.

Year eight was just all about getting through, trying to work out how to get around the problem of my eyesight failing. The next couple of years were one big question mark. Discovering Surf Life Saving at the end of year eight was a Godsend. Finally, something I could do, something to look forward to each week. I enjoyed being in the water, of course, but as much as that I enjoyed finding a way to put my mind to good use without having to be able to read or write. There was a lot of memorising procedures and figures, and fortunately I had inherited Dad's excellent memory. It was as if I had found my calling.

I'd signed up to do the scoring in cricket in year seven, which I loved, and I ended up doing it for four or five years. But once I got my start in Surf Life Saving, hanging out on the boundary started to seem kind of boring. When I joined Surf Life Saving in October 1983, there were only fourteen or fifteen of us gathering on the beach for three hours each weekend. It wasn't even really considered a sport. Everyone wanted to do the big-name sports – cricket, rowing. Well, how things change! Not long before, Kellogg's had founded its Nutri-Grain Iron Man competition. It hadn't quite caught on yet, but it wouldn't be long before Surf Life Saving became the most coveted sport at Shore. By 2003, twenty years later, 400 boys at Shore were competing for spots in Surf Life Saving and the list for cricket was all but empty. What a difference twenty years can make!

Orchestra camp was another activity that went against the grain, but turned out to be one of the best decisions I could have made. The rest of my friends went off to cadet camp, and it was forty-plus degrees every day. They'd come back and ask how orchestra camp was going. I took great pleasure in saying, 'Oh, we played in all the nursing homes. The air conditioning was fantastic!' The next year, cadet camp was a complete mud-heap and I got to gloat again. 'We had a great time. Nursing homes might not smell that great, but they sure are dry!'

By year nine my eyesight had deteriorated further, and there was no denying it any more – I was going blind. It was decision time. At the start of the year, Mum went to the headmaster, 'Jika' Travers, and said, 'What are we going to do with James? Should he stay at this school? Or should we put him in a blind school?'

Jika turned to my parents and said, 'Does he enjoy coming to this school?'

'Yes.'

'Does he like this school?'

'Yes.'

'Does he have lots of good friends?'

'Yes.'

'Well, then, why wouldn't he stay? God never intended to make everyone equal. He stays.'

What a quote. What a decision. What a man. I have always known how important that decision was, how it shaped the way I grew up. What seemed like an impossible decision was made in a heartbeat. It was categorically the right decision and I am forever grateful. In 2000, another blind person enrolled at Shore and completed the whole six years there. I like to think it was Jika's legacy that the school would never discriminate based on sight. I vowed that the day that man died, I would be at his funeral.

Unfortunately, one sweltering day in January 1999, I had to make good on that promise. I did it not just because I said I would, but because I understood the impact his decision had on my life. The impact it continued to have. If I had left Shore and gone to a blind school, my blindness would have defined my path and I would have missed out on so many valuable life experiences. I wouldn't have achieved the things I have. I wouldn't have all my amazing friends. I may never have met my wife. I am not defined by my blindness, and I have Jika to thank for that.

As my sight gradually got worse, we tried these lever-operated contraptions that magnified the words on the page one section at a time, but it quickly became evident that wasn't going to cut it. So at the end of year nine we introduced my first reading machines into the school – one in the main classroom and one that I'd push around on a trolley. You'd put a piece of paper under the camera and it would display the entire page in large print on a little TV monitor. That's how I got through years nine to twelve at Shore. Thirty years down the track it seems totally archaic, but in 1984 it was revolutionary.

When your sight starts to go, suddenly things become much harder to find (no surprise there!). I'd always been very organised, but the more my vision deteriorated, the more I had to stick to a system. Once when I went overseas my mother thought my study looked a mess and decided to surprise me by tidying it up. But despite appearances, my papers were actually in a very specific order; I knew exactly where everything was. When I came home, she had filed all my papers into six trays, each with its own label. I'm sure it would have been the perfect system for her, but that's not how my brain – or my eyes! – worked. She'd gone to such trouble and I wanted to thank her for it, but the truth was I was angry and despondent! I had no idea where anything was anymore.

By year ten I was in the lowest class for everything, but it didn't faze me. It was what it was. Even before my eyesight started to go, academia just wasn't my thing. But Shore was a great school, with great teachers, and I always enjoyed being there. Yes, I was having a bit of trouble in the classroom, but that wasn't what bothered me. The difficulties playing sport, that was the hardest blow.

I tried not to let it stop me. In 1985, Shore introduced soccer, and I put my hand straight up. The introduction was thanks to a record four broken necks in rugby in 1984. Aghast, the parents had thrown their arms in the air and demanded that the school offer a different winter sport. And so I found myself on the soccer field. My eyesight was really starting to be a challenge. But I played fullback, where I stayed out of the throng, and my mates stepped in to help me any way they could. I lasted until halfway through year eleven before my eyesight got too bad for me to continue.

I hated English, I hated reading, and I hated poetry, but in year ten, one book transcended that. In *To Kill a Mockingbird*, a man is vilified for a crime he didn't commit in the absence of any proof whatsoever, purely because he is black. Most of the community doesn't bat an eyelid, but one man goes in to bat for him, and by the end he starts to change the minds of his opponents. It's the kind of book you can't help but be affected by, and it certainly changed my attitude. It was all about overcoming prejudice and supporting the underdog, and at the time that's just what I was – the underdog. It really resonated with me, and it shaped the way I approached my disability. I determined never to accept that I couldn't do something. Never to accept anyone telling me otherwise. And never to give up on proving people wrong. Childhood is the best time to learn these things. As people age they may become jaded and bigoted. But kids don't care about colour, creed, disabilities. It's one of the things I love most about my daughter Annica: she couldn't give a stuff about any of that. All she cares about is whether you're going to play with her! Prejudice is learned, and if we can teach children the value of tolerance and acceptance early in life, maybe we can prevent that.

There aren't a whole lot of advantages to being blind, but there is one: I always meet new people without preconceptions. I can't judge a book by its cover, because I can't even see the cover. I walk up there and have a chat to a person, and I judge them by who they are, not what they look like. If only we could all do that. Who cares if you're black or white, Christian or Muslim, disabled or not? The only thing we should care about is what people say, and what they do. That's the one and only valid way to judge someone's worth.

Before I knew it, the build-up to the HSC – the Higher School Certificate – had begun. There's no way I would have got through those couple of years without my mother. Around year nine, she had started reading all my books onto tape so I could listen to them. She would sit there munching away at her Kingston biscuits and drinking her tea with the grandfather clock chiming in the background for hour upon hour, day after day. She spent so much time studying with me, helping me get through exams. Fortunately by this stage I'd matured enough to recognise what a mammoth effort she was putting in for me and to actually express my gratitude. But even then, no matter how effusive I was, there was no way I could ever repay her for what she was doing for me. That's not to detract from Dad's contribution – he was the one out there day in, day out, making the money to keep me in a brilliant school with all the reading machines I needed.

Every day I had to work twice as hard as everyone else, carting my reading machine around, memorising everything the teachers said, listening to Mum's tapes. I can tell you, it really takes it out of you. By the end of the week I was always absolutely exhausted.

In the August holidays of year eleven, I once again got the chance to go over to Scotland with Mum for four weeks and visit Granny and Uncle Sandy. I think Sandy was glad I'd come along for the visit; for once there was another man around! Mum and Granny are both very headstrong women – it's one of the things we love most about them – but when you get them together, don't expect to win any arguments! Sandy loved sport every bit as much as the rest of us, and had this uncanny memory for it. When we went to a test match at The Oval he was reeling off the stats for every player. I remember thinking, one day I'm going to be able to do that.

We had a great time visiting all Mum's friends and exploring the beautiful districts of England. But the whole time I could still feel a shadow hanging over me. I knew we were coming back to sixteen of the hardest months of both our lives.

At the end of 1986 I had to give up scoring the cricket, and after the summer I let go of Surf Life Saving as well. From here on out, it was all about the HSC. In year twelve I did three units of modern history and two units of ancient history, and I absolutely loved it. I remember one time at about 7 in the morning, while everyone else was still trying to brush away the mental cobwebs, I was on the ball enough to correct the teacher on a date in Russian history. He was blown away. When we had to do oral presentations, I was more grateful than ever for my good memory. For a while there, I really enjoyed school.

But then things got serious. The last phase of the HSC began with two weeks of trials. The name 'trials' is sort of misleading. They were intended as preparation for the real thing in a couple of months' time, but they counted for twenty percent of the overall mark. In other words, they were damned important! I'd somehow managed to land myself with six exams in the first week and only one in the second. The timing was a nightmare. No sooner would I finish an exam than I'd be studying for the next. And not your average studying, either. Listening to tapes all night was slow work and required intense concentration. When I walked out of my final trial exam that next Friday I could finally let myself relax. I had done everything I could do. It was out of my hands.

Or was it? The next Monday we got the news that the teachers had given some boys the second day's English paper on the first day. The boys owned up straight away, but once the questions were out, there was no taking them back. So the next week we all found ourselves back in the school hall sitting another English exam. It didn't do much for the teachers' reputation and we were pretty dirty with them for a while afterwards.

I did as well as I could have hoped in the trials, and before I knew it, the end of the year had arrived – and with it the real HSC exams. I didn't care how well I did, all I cared about was walking out of that school having given every ounce of my brain, every ounce of my body, and every ounce of effort in those exams. It's a mantra I live by. If I can walk away from something knowing I gave the best effort I could give, I'm happy. But I also knew how much it had cost my parents to get me here, both financially and in terms of time and effort, and I couldn't let them down.

The school set aside a room especially for me, where a year-eleven boy would read the exams out to me and a Board of Senior School Studies representative would supervise. I used a reading machine to write my answers. They gave me extra time for all my exams, and I took it – I needed all the help I could get. But exams are hard enough when they run for the normal amount of time. When you're doubling up on that, it starts to take its toll, not just mentally but physically. And with three exams in three days to start, it would be a baptism of fire.

The first day was an absolute corker. It was 35 degrees and the room I was in had no air conditioning. The exam was English comprehension, and there are few things in life that strike fear in my heart quite like that does. I had the year-eleven kid read the comprehension to me so many times that he lost his voice and the supervisor had to get him a jug of water. It would have been amusing if it wasn't so stressful. As expected, I tanked. At least it was over, but there were plenty more where that had come from.

The Geography exam was a real test of my courage and abilities, because at the start of the day the supervisor said, 'You have to do mapping.' My heart skipped a beat. There was no way I could do that. But I shouldn't have to! I said, 'No, I've got dispensation from the Board of Senior School Studies.' I produced it from my pocket and pointed out the relevant exception, but for whatever reason she didn't seem convinced. After a few minutes of pointless arguing, she said, 'Wait here.' When she returned she reluctantly admitted I was right and handed over the alternative exam. An argument ten minutes before an exam could have been a distraction, but instead I took it as a victory, and it was just the motivation I needed to do well in the exam. I'd stood up for myself for once in my life, I'd taken on my superior, and I'd come out on top. When I finished the exam, I knew I'd nailed it, and it ended up being the best mark I got in the whole HSC.

My final exam was Modern History – my favourite – and I was hoping to do well, but much as I tried not to let my emotions and my tiredness get in the way of things, I was so burned out by then I didn't really have a choice. It didn't help that for the second half of the exam I could hear the rest of my group celebrating the end of exams in the next room while I ploughed through another half-day of extra time.

All the same, I'd done what I'd set out to do – my best. I'd done my parents justice. As I handed in that last exam the supervisor said, 'Are you happy?' When I said yes, I truly meant it. Two years of intensely hard study were over just like that. We had finally reaped the fruits of our hard work. And about time, too.

I walked out of Shore with a mixture of joy and sadness, acutely aware that it was one of the last times I would ever walk through those gates. Yes, walk. Everyone said, 'You should have been skipping! Jumping for joy! Yelling and screaming!' But I genuinely didn't have it in me. Outside I was broken. But inside I was victorious. I had finished the HSC, and I had done it blind. I'd never been more proud of myself. My celebration was muted – a game of croquet and a couple of drinks with Mum and Dad – but it was perfect. Later that year at Speech Day, I was given a prize and a standing ovation. I didn't need recognition to validate my achievements, but it was nice to receive it all the same.

Shore taught me about persistence, about relationships, about self-motivation, about survival. It gave me the friendships and the discipline to survive the real world. And it inspired me to give everything, every day, always. The discipline I learned at that school is the same discipline I have applied through my entire life. The same discipline without which I could never have swum the English Channel.

## Chapter 5
## Racing in the pool

In 1988, my first year out of school, I was doing work experience at the First Home Owners Scheme, but it was out of obligation, not desire. I was just waiting and hoping that the right path would present itself. When I was invited in August to a one-week vision-impaired sports camp at Narrabeen Academy of Sports, I didn't hesitate. I missed sport like crazy.

The sport I was most excited to get back into was soccer. But it wasn't quite as I remembered it. I can tell you, a blind game of soccer is a pretty violent affair. When you kick it as hard as you can and someone happens to be a foot in front of you, some pretty impressive bruises can result, and I was the recipient of a good few. Fair to say soccer lost some of its sheen.

Then it came time to try competitive swimming, and I took to it like a duck to... well, water. I swam more laps than I could count, and someone must have seen me, because the next thing I knew, I had the secretary of the Blind Sporting Association of New South Wales inviting me to the Blind National Swimming Championships in six months' time. All I had to do was submit some official times, and they'd enter me.

So on the first Saturday of October I went down to West Pymble swimming pool with Dad to record some times. Obviously he wasn't an official timekeeper, but it would give us an idea. We arrived at 7 am, opening time, and there wasn't a spare park for miles. There were about two hundred cars spilling out of the parking lot. Apparently we'd turned up for the Ku-ring-gai amateur swimming club. They raced there every Saturday morning from October through to March. They'd be there right up until 10 am, so we cut our losses and headed home. But as soon as we got home I realised, why avoid them when I could just join them?

The next weekend I did just that. From 1988 to 1997, the club gave me great joy. At its peak, it had 600 members. They ran 200-metre, 100-metre, and 50-metre events – sometimes as many as fifty heats – as well as medleys and the occasional novelty event, like a parent-child relay. It was a great club, and a good chance to record those times I needed. I was a bit nervous about how I'd perform, but in the end I was well under the qualifying times. I was accepted to swim in the Blind National Swimming Championships.

In March 1989, I arrived with my team and we got settled in our accommodation behind the Chandler Aquatic Centre. At nineteen years of age, I was about to receive my introduction to blind sports. For it was here that I would meet Ched Towns – one of the great champions of my career. If I hadn't met him, I may never have got into blind sports, at least not at the same level.

There were athletics and power-lifting competitions going on at the same time as the swimming, and Ched was competing in running, pentathlon and javelin. He had been involved in blind sports for a long time and he was a great man in so many ways: funny, kind, optimistic. And what an outstanding athlete. He did Hawaiian ironman contests; he competed in the 1988 Paralympics; he kayaked across Torres Strait. He was the perfect person to step in as a mentor and role model at that time in my life, and the greatest thing to come out of the championships. At a time when I was still grappling with my blindness, he taught me that blindness is only a barrier if you let it be. He proved to the world that disability didn't mean a thing.

Ched would get up every morning at 5.30 for a training run around the track, but not before running past every single thin-walled room bellowing at the top of his voice, 'Good morning Vietnam!' It would reverberate along the whole line of rooms so that no one had a chance of missing it. At the breakfast table we would sit there in tears of silent laughter as everyone cursed 'that bloody "Good morning Vietnam" thing'. No one ever worked out who was responsible.

When Ched's pentathlon came around, our roommate Ed Holicky, a sprinter, decided at the last minute that he would put his name down for the event as well, just for a laugh. Ched was cocky as hell and just brushed it off, but when it got to the last leg of the event and Ed was still giving him a run for his money, the nerves were showing even through all the sweat! Ched did eventually win, but it was damn close. Ed pushed him all the way and showed that he was a bloody good athlete as well. Sure enough, Ed went on to compete in the 1992 Paralympics. Ever the sportsman, Ched took the whole thing in characteristically good humour not that we ever expected any different. I would have loved to have seen his response if Ed had actually got up and won it though.

Ched had the same eye disease as me – retinitis pigmentosa – and it brought his aspirations of becoming a first-grade rugby league player for Penrith to a screeching halt. His dream was shattered, and I think he must have been in a state of shock, because when someone in England told him he would be cured by 3,000 bee stings a day on his temples, he signed up without hesitation. And he didn't just sign up. He actually went through with it. Every day for two months, he got 3,000 bee stings on his temples. People who knew him then say he did come back a cured man – he didn't have his eyesight, but he was ready to do anything he put his mind to; he was a great athlete. I don't dispute that the bee sting 'treatment' probably changed him. How could it not? People said he came back better, happier, funnier, more charismatic, more driven. But he didn't get to live his dream of playing rugby, did he?

You've got to maintain a healthy cynicism when it comes to these fancy professed cures. When I joined the Defaults department at the Australian Tax Office in October 1989 (I'd found my passion, but in the meantime there was the little issue of making a living!), each night I would have to wait outside for a cab. Three evenings in a row, someone from the local church came up to me to convince me God could cure my eyesight. I believe in God, but one thing's for sure, I don't believe He can cure blindness. Everyone's entitled to their beliefs, but it's not okay to go around making false promises to strangers. By the third night, I had reached the end of my tether. I did the one thing I knew was both intimidating and completely benign. I shook his hand. It was my brother who taught me to always give a firm handshake. Your handshake is someone's first impression of you. It shows what type of person you are. It shows your intentions. If you give a fishlike, slobbery, soft handshake, it shows a certain apathy, it shows that you can't commit. But a firm handshake shows conviction, a willingness to stand by your beliefs and values. It shows that you mean business, whatever that may be. So when I gave this man the firmest handshake I could, he reeled away and realised perhaps this wasn't a battle worth fighting.

The swimming was over two stormy nights. As we made our way down to the aquatic centre thunder rumbled overhead and I couldn't help but feel as if it were some sort of omen. But if it was, it was a good one. The first night, I broke a national blind record in the 400-metres freestyle and won the 50-metres freestyle; and the second night, I won both the 50-metres breaststroke and the 200-metres individual medley. But I guess I should admit that it's not quite as impressive as it sounds. There was no one else in my category!

I met three outstanding blind swimmers at the championships as well: Kingsley Bugarin, Tracey Cross, and Mandy Maywood. At the time, Kingsley Bugarin was the only Australian of any ability or gender to have swum in five consecutive Paralympic or Olympic Games – from 1984 to 2000 inclusive – and has won a total of five gold, eight silver, and six bronze medals. Vision impaired or not, that's bloody impressive. At the time he held the record for the highest Paralympic medal count. Tracey Cross won ten medals in three Paralympics, and Mandy Maywood won five medals in two Paralympics. Between the four of us, I think we won every event in our categories. Over time we developed an easy friendship, but that sense of awe at their brilliance never went away.

When Dad congratulated me on the way back to my accommodation at the end of the championships, I accepted wholeheartedly – because I agreed. Whether or not I had anyone to compete against was beside the point. I had swum better than I even knew I could, won four gold, broken a blind national record, met a whole host of inspirational blind people, and had the time of my life. Had I found my path in life? It sure felt like it. I was in the system, and on my way to a lifetime of rewarding involvement in blind sport.

When I got home, I had a sense of purpose like nothing I'd ever experienced before. I immediately started training in squads at North Sydney Pool, but their organisation was terrible and they were squeezing twenty-five people to a lane. I couldn't stand it anymore. So in 1990 I decided to leave North Sydney for the Ryde Carlile Swimming School, where I met Ian MacDowell-Jones. He would become my coach for the next three-and-a-half years, finally giving some structure to my training routine.

My first event with Ian was the 1990 National Blind Championships in Melbourne, in January. It was the forerunner for the World Championships for the Disabled, to be held in Assen, the Netherlands in July 1990. I entered the 400-metres freestyle, the 50-metres freestyle, the medley, and a couple of relays, and again I won my category in all my events. I made some good times and I knew there was a chance the World Championships might be on the cards.

When I finally got the call in February to say I'd been selected to represent Australia, I was absolutely over the moon. It was an honour to have been selected. I couldn't get my head around the fact I was actually getting to represent my country in sport. When I told my family, I learned that my selection made it four consecutive generations of my family to have represented their country. My mother represented Scotland in squash and junior tennis; my grandmother represented England in hockey, lacrosse, and tennis; and my great aunt won two medals for England in tennis at the Olympic Games. What an amazing record – and I'd added to it without even realising its existence.

When I was a kid I used to dream of representing Australia in cricket and football, but when I lost my eyesight I put it out of my mind because I believed it would never happen. I couldn't decide what hurt more – hearing stories from Mum and Granny about representing their country and what a thrill that was, or not hearing them and knowing it was because they were trying to protect my feelings. But that was all in the past now. I'd never been happier to prove myself wrong.

On 8 July 1990, I arrived at the airport wearing an Australian uniform for the very first time. I felt as if everyone was looking at me, but in the very best way. I *hoped* they were looking at me. I was representing my country, and I wanted everybody to know it! The World Championships for the Disabled included not only blind athletes, but also those with cerebral palsy, amputees, and those in wheelchairs. I travelled with a group of cerebral palsy swimmers. We touched down in Amsterdam the next day, then took a 3-hour drive up to Assen.

We stayed in a dormitory-style wing of an old army barracks with ten beds and a couple of lockers. It was pretty basic accommodation and I saw a few turned-up noses, but I couldn't have cared less. I was having the time of my life already. We would spend a lot of time in the barracks over the following two weeks, all the guys just hanging out having a chat. There was a dining tent where you could get a feed any time of day, and even an ice-creamery. It was brilliantly organised and the staff were always up for a laugh.

We kicked off with what they call 'classification re-testing'. We all had a classification already, but in international competitions they always do a standardised re-classification, just to keep things fair. For the blind it's a simple on-land test, but the guys with cerebral palsy were up for not only a land test but a water test as well. In cerebral palsy they've also got different classifications for the different events, so it was a very complicated process. But it had to be done.

As boring as the formalities were for the seasoned competitors, it was all new and exciting to me. I was absolutely pumped. I'd never felt more ready in my life. It was unfortunate, really, because it was still five days until the games actually started, and even then my events weren't on until the last four days of the competition. I was left to try in vain to curb my enthusiasm as I sat and watched the rest of my team do their thing. We did take a day trip to Amsterdam in the meantime and had a bit of fun doing a canal tour and wandering around the city. The tour was particularly good because it came with descriptions. I might not have been able to actually see the smallest house in Europe, but at least I could imagine it! The one thing I regret – and I'm not a man with a lot of regrets – is that when we were given the opportunity to spend a day with a family in Amsterdam, none of us took it up. I wish we had because the Dutch are such lovely people. Beautiful people who are incredibly generous with their time and hospitality. I think I would have gotten a lot out of it, but I missed my chance and that's that.

The day of the Opening Ceremony finally came around. Until now, I'd been riding high on the *prospect* of representing my country. But tonight, it was actually happening. When the Games were declared open, I would become an official representative of Australia. What a thrill. As we waited for the order to march into the stadium, I could barely contain myself. Fortunately, we only had to wait for one country – Argentina – before our turn. Nothing could have prepared me for the roar of clapping and cheering that awaited. Rarely have I felt as important – yet humble, too – as I did waving to those adoring masses (well, that's how I framed them in my mind!).

When The Netherlands national anthem came on, the leagues of spectators behind us all sang as one. It's a beautiful anthem and it was a truly touching moment. Right at the end a choir sang 'We Are the World', the song Bob Geldof used in 1985 to raise money for starving Africans. The emotion I'd felt upon hearing the anthem rose up again tenfold, and it's a song I will always fondly associate with the event.

Now it was down to the competition. My first event was the 400-metres freestyle. There were no heats – it was straight into the final. While I waited in the marshalling area, the B1 women's 400-metres freestyle was going on. In her first ever international event, the great Tracey Cross led from start to finish. But I didn't have time to feel happy for her. The pressure was now squarely upon me, and the butterflies were starting to set in.

From the moment I hit the water, the swim just didn't work. I made the mistake of trying to please the coach by doing the tumble turns he'd tried to teach me in the lead-up to the event. He thought it would make me quicker. It didn't. Maybe with time it would have, but right before a comp wasn't the time to start changing things up. When I touched the wall, the band stopped playing, and I knew what that meant. I had finished last. I should have stuck to my original plan, though ultimately it probably wouldn't have made much difference. It was an appalling swim and I was devastated. I never thought I'd win, but to get absolutely flogged was embarrassing. I traipsed to the changing rooms feeling very disappointed with myself.

I learned that you should never change your plan. Go in and do what you set out to do, and don't take advice from a coach you've only just met. Coaches come and go, but nobody knows your style as well as you. This coach had never even seen me swim before! He was very black and white in his methods, and seemed to think that the best way to motivate us was to have a go at us for never measuring up to his standards. I appreciate his trying to do new things with me, but the World Championships wasn't the place to do it.

My parents had come to see me swim, which meant a lot to me, and I was ashamed that my first world event had to go down like this. They did their best to console me, but in a way it almost made me feel worse. I felt that I'd let them down. I got back to my room still feeling completely dejected, almost in tears. I was having a massage when one of the other swimmers came in and asked how I did. 'Terrible', I said bluntly. She said, 'Don't do that to yourself. You represented Australia, and you did the best you could. You've got nothing to feel bad about. Chin up! You've got another event tomorrow.' She was right. Her words gave me the motivation to get myself up and focus forward.

I got up the next day and swam in a 50-metres freestyle heat. I didn't make the final, but I was close, and it didn't bother me one way or the other anyway. All that mattered was that I felt proud of the way I'd swum. My parents came out and said, 'Well done', and it was nice to be able to agree with them this time! My mood picked up just in time for the Closing Ceremony. It was a spectacular night with incredible fireworks and plenty of drinks, dancing and shenanigans.

Maybe I hadn't swum quite as well as I would have liked, but for the first time in my life, I had represented Australia. I had fulfilled one of my earliest dreams, and contributed to my family's long history of sporting success. And no one could take that away from me.

Rather than fly across the globe then straight back home again, I'd decided to follow the championships up with a holiday. So after the closing ceremony I flew to Germany to meet up with my old school mate Dean Reeves. He'd been living there for about eight months but we still chatted regularly. When I first arrived I was exhausted from the physical exertion and emotional rollercoaster of the previous few days, and Dean had the misfortune of being on the receiving end of my tiredness. But I warmed into the trip, got a few drinks in me, and it wasn't long before I was having a wonderful time.

The first night I was there Dean's friend Frank's father was holding his fiftieth birthday in an opulent castle in Nuremberg. We sped down the autobahn at 200 kilometres per hour with the sunroof down, and it was gloriously liberating. We did the 160 kilometres from Munich to Nuremberg in 50 minutes flat. It seemed like light speed to me, but it was nothing by German standards. Even at our hire car's limit of 200 kilometres per hour, we were getting overtaken every few seconds. Dean's mate Mandy spent almost the whole journey fighting a losing battle to try to control her hair. I wish I'd had a camera to capture her 'do at the end!

We arrived at the castle to one of the most extravagant and unusual dinners of my life. Entrées were served on the first floor, mains on the second, and dessert on the third. Frank's father spoke for 50 minutes in German. Dean translated for a while, but when it became obvious the speech wasn't ending any time soon we gave up.

We stayed with Frank and his family, and we decided that in exchange for their kindness and hospitality, we'd make dinner for them. We wanted to make an Aussie classic and settled on lamb –

and three bottles of wine, naturally. When we got to the counter to buy the leg of lamb and the price came up on the screen we stood there for a second squinting. That couldn't be right. Could we have made a mistake in converting currency? We hadn't. It cost 64 Aussie dollars for a leg of lamb. I hope the cashier couldn't speak English because we all let slip a few choice words. If this was what the lamb cost, how much would the wine set us back? As it turned out, 12 dollars total. I said to Dean, 'There's something wrong with this place.' At dinner we joked that every bite was worth at least a few dollars, and the estimate probably wasn't far off!

We spent a good deal of time just hanging out relaxing in beer gardens. I remember sitting out at The Sea Garden, a lakeside beer garden, enjoying a few litre stein beers while the sun went down on a stunning evening in Germany. It was just magnificent. One thing for sure, Germany loves its beer. Just have a look at their vending machines! Indeed, why spend your coins on a soft drink when you can get beer instead?

I went from Germany to Scotland to be with Mum, Granny, and Uncle Sandy. We didn't do all that much, just focused on enjoying each other's company. This would be the last time I would see my grandmother before her passing in September 1991. And she was in rare form! I remember her asking me, 'How did it go?'

'I did really poorly, actually.'

'Ah,' she said. 'Well, not everyone can win. You represented your country, and you did your best. Well done.'

She and Mum had always told me where you placed didn't matter, that it was all just about representing your country, but this time it had a bigger impact than ever before. I understood, because I had been there. I had represented my country.

After four wonderful days, Sandy and I took the train down to Manchester to spend two days together watching the England-versus-India test match. It was a great match, and an historic one – Sachin Tendulkar scored his very first test century. In a strange twist of fate, we ended up staying in the same hotel as the English players. Every night, Sandy would find the players and tell them off in his own little way. 'You shouldn't bowl so many no balls! Get more fours and sixes!' It wasn't at all malicious, and I think the players took it in good humour. Still, one morning when we were having breakfast, one of the players came in, took one look at Sandy, and walked straight back out!

By late August I'd found my way back to the Tax Office after a magnificent six weeks. It had been the busiest year of my life, and January seemed a lifetime ago. But I was still hungry for more.

In 1991 Thailand invited Australia to compete in the Thailand National Swimming Championships for the Disabled in August. I didn't need to be asked twice. This would be a magnificent trip, and one that would change my attitude to my home country forever. From the vantage point of Lampang Province, Thailand, my entire life would take on a different hue. My cushy home with my parents in Killara; my secure, well-paid job at the Tax Office; my regular routine of swimming and hanging out with my mates. I would never take any of it for granted again.

We arrived in Lampang Province at the Tip Chang Hotel, which we renamed the Tip Chuck Hotel. I'll never forget number 69 on the lunch menu: Shark Fin and Snake Head Soup. But even that was a safer bet than ordering off the menu. Someone ordered a toasted ham and cheese sandwich, and was served two pieces of bread. Another person asked for hot chips, and received a packet of Smith's original tipped into a bowl and heated up.

Every morning in this dismal hotel, we would go down and have some orange juice. At least, that's what they called it. And sometimes it was. But more often than not, it was actually watered down 'Tang'. Tang's bad enough when you know what you're getting into, but when you're expecting real orange juice, it's just offensive! We ended up sending messengers down to taste the 'orange juice' and report back on whether it was even worth getting out of bed!

The hotel aside, it was a very interesting area. Some places had only just been introduced to the concept of sewage. I heard nobody got the dole. People did their washing out in the streets, hanging over the road. The running water was dirty and undrinkable. I had to brush my teeth using bottled water and any time you had an open wound, you had to fastidiously clean and protect it or you'd end up with a flesh-eating infection. You really had to watch yourself.

We strived to accustom ourselves to the Thai way of life. We avoided salad; we drank bottled water; we did everything right – or so we thought. But even so, it wasn't long before our sheltered Australian guts fell prey to Thailand's terrible standards of hygiene. One bloke got gastro from a cheese pizza for goodness' sake. Everyone seemed to be getting diarrhoea at once, but for some reason that I was certainly not about to question, I didn't.

When we went to check out the athletics track, we discovered it was no more than a piece of concrete with eight white lines. The guys couldn't believe it. Paul Christani, an athlete from South Australia, said, 'Even the greyhounds get better than this.' Running on concrete, with the sun beating down, was going to be horrendous. While most of the team were there to compete in athletics, I was the sole swimmer. Thank God for that, I thought. Famous last words! As we arrived at the pool one of the guys said to me, 'I hope you weren't counting on breathing.' The 25-metre pool was fluorescent green with algae. And I thought they had it bad in athletics! There was no way in hell I was spending more time in the competition pool than I had to, so I took to training in the hotel pool, which must have been no more than 12.5 metres long. The pool was so tiny that when I did my butterfly training, the water just bounced straight off the edges and back at me. It was like one big messy whirlpool. Then I found out why: the hotel pool was supposed to be for the local primary school. This discovery only took place when I came down to train, only to find myself surrounded by sixty kids! As the events approached we did go down and train in the competition pool a couple of times to at least get a feel for it, but it wasn't a nice feel, and we didn't feel any desire to go back there until we absolutely had to!

We'd assumed they'd have a full complement of the usual events, but most of mine were missing. All they had was the 50-metres freestyle, butterfly, backstroke, and breaststroke, and the 200-metres individual medley. My coach, Ian, said, 'Well, everything's changed! But there's nothing we can do. We're here now, and we're just going to have to go with it.' Personally I wasn't particularly concerned, but I could tell he wasn't happy, and unfortunately that frustration coloured our training throughout the lead-up.

On the morning of the opening ceremony, I felt as if I was waking up inside a furnace, and somehow as the day went on the heat became more and more stifling. Normally I like the fact that Australia gets to march first because it gives you a chance to soak in the whole ceremony. Not today. I felt like we'd been sent out to dry as we stood in the middle of the track for two hours in 39 degrees and 90% humidity in our fleecy winter uniforms.

And the horror wasn't over yet. The minute the ceremony ended, the track events kicked off. I don't know how those athletes did it. One of them, Darren Collins, actually fainted after the ceremony and had to be carried off the ground. The next minute his heat was called. He probably should have put his health first, but I understand the mindset and I would have done the same thing. He got up, he ran his heat, and he got through to the final the next day. But he was in terrible condition.

We all got back in our bus, and I was relegated to the front seat as usual. I was the only one who couldn't see the wild traffic, and therefore the only one that wasn't scared stiff by it! Road rules were more of a suggestion than a law in Lampang Province, and around every corner was someone who didn't see fit to follow those suggestions. Every 5 minutes you'd find a car hurtling towards you on your side of the road.

Back at the hotel, Darren cooled down in the bath while the rest of us had the most sullen team meeting in history. We may as well have been at a funeral. Nobody could stomach the thought of another ten days of this. For that matter, most of us couldn't even stomach the thought of our next meal. But the manager, Derry, wasn't going to let us wallow in self-pity. He said, 'It was a tough day, but we got through it. We're all okay – even Darren. He's going to run tomorrow. If he can do it, you can too.' The mood rose, but only slightly.

My first swim was meant to be in the afternoon. But on the day of my event, I was sitting there having lunch when a message came through saying my events had been brought forward. 'You're on in an hour', it said casually. I nearly choked on my sandwich. I made it to the pool in time, but there was no chance of a warm-up. I went straight into the 50-metres freestyle.

I dived in and sent water rippling through the pool with my large frame, while the other three competitors plopped in with little more than a splash. A collective 'Ooh' emanated from the crowd and I felt like some sort of superhero. I had at least a foot on all of them, so I was ahead before we even hit the water. I won all my events convincingly. I like to think it was mostly because of my good grounding in swimming in Australia, but I know my size and the impact of my dive must have made a big difference.

When I was up on the dais accepting my medal, someone had to explain to me that at the end you're expected to take the second and third place-getters arms, and hold them up for a photo. Sounds pretty straightforward, right? I took the petite Thai guys by the arms – so far so good. Then, without thinking, I straightened my arms in the air, and yanked them both clean off the dais. The photographer didn't miss his opportunity, and it was a winner of a photo. I still laugh to this day at the image of me hanging these two men from my hands like ornaments.

I followed up the freestyle with the 50-metres breaststroke and 50-metres butterfly, and the next morning, I went out and did the 200-metres medley. It was the last event of the entire competition, so the whole team was watching. Again, I won fairly convincingly and had a bit of fun on the dais. Afterwards, we drove out to Chiang Mai, where we took a cable car up an incredibly steep hill to a magnificent temple that overlooked the whole of the city. And at 6 pm, we stopped everything while the national anthem rang out around us – just as we did every night. It was my favourite part of Thai culture.

We began our two-hour trek back to the hotel. We had two buses in a convoy, but all of a sudden our bus spluttered to a halt. I felt sure we'd broken down, and I wasn't wrong. The driver found a tree branch to pry open the bonnet and filled up the coolant reservoir with water. When that did nothing whatsoever, he realised he'd blown a head gasket. That was the end of the bus! So we left it on the side of the road, and all crammed into the one bus. It was seriously squishy, and the two-hour trip turned into four hours, but it was actually pretty good fun elbowing each other for room. By the time we got home it was around midnight and I was absolutely spent. I slept well!

After another couple of days relaxing in Lampang Province – the Australian consulate even treated us to haircuts! – it was on to the last leg of the trip: three days in Bangkok. It's an absolutely buzzing metropolis, and getting around on the roads is a nerve-wracking experience. The number of cars is mind-blowing, as is the haphazard way they seem to change lanes. I couldn't understand how they weren't crashing into each other. We took a boat ride on the river, which is the other major way you can get from place to place in the city. That was a far more relaxing way to travel, but it was a bizarre experience passing through the different regions. You'd go from the absolute slums to the massive shopping hubs within minutes. The contrast was striking. And saddening.

We did the compulsory bartering thing and bought a lot of junk that seemed like a good idea at the time but mostly ended up in the bin within a few months of getting home! The bartering was such a ridiculous process when you think about it. You'd stand there for 5 minutes trying to barter a postcard down from 5 baht to 3 baht – that's a saving of about 5 cents! You could have made a hundred times that amount just from 5 minutes' work in Australia! We had a good laugh about that. But of course, it wasn't about the savings; it was about experiencing the Thai way. It was an education!

It was interesting observing who coped well without the mod cons, and who lost it. For me, it was all about getting up every day, giving it a go, battling away. I was used to facing hardship. It was my specialty! No matter what the conditions, I was always ready to have a laugh. And laugh I did. Every day. I never complained, because I loved the challenge. I loved the sense of victory that comes from getting to the end of the day and knowing you've overcome adversity, no matter how small. I hated the heat and humidity, but I accepted the challenge, and I conquered it.

It had been an unforgettable journey. When I arrived back in Sydney and my parents asked me how it had gone, I summed up the experience in just one sentence: 'That's the last time I will ever complain about my country.' It was a defining moment in my life. Only upon my return to the creature comforts we take for granted did I fully comprehend just how good we really had it. I walked into my house, and drank water from the tap. I went and sat on the toilet – what a luxury – and flushed it with no fear of the water rising back up. The little things had become big things. I said to my parents, 'How good is this! Running water. Sewerage. Different seasons. The dole. Look how good we've got it. Look how fortunate we are.'

I'd always known I was lucky, but now, at the age of twenty-one, I realised just *how* lucky. It's the only way to gain that appreciation – to see firsthand what it's like for those who aren't so lucky. It's the greatest lesson I've ever learned.

## Chapter 6
## Representing Australia

In 1991 I still harboured a quiet little dream of making the 1992 Paralympic swimming team, and for most of the year that's what I was working towards. But I was dreaming, really. My times were never good enough to compete with the greats, and towards the end of the year I started to realise that. But I kept up the national events through 1992 and 1993, and in 1994 I would finally get the chance to compete internationally again.

In the Netherlands in 1990, I'd met a woman who had Stickler syndrome, a genetic disorder that affects collagen, the main structural protein in the body's connective tissues. Stickler syndrome can cause issues with bone development, vision and hearing, among other issues. But it definitely didn't affect her voice! That woman could talk the leg off a dog. When she came out to Australia in August 1993 for the Australian Blind Swimming Championships, I offered her a place to stay, but I opted not to tell my parents that detail. I can tell you, by the end of that six weeks my parents were thrilled to see her go! Dad played the 'big operation tomorrow' card almost every night!

While she was with us, she invited me to come to the British Blind National Swimming Championships in Essex in March 1994. My brother and sister were both living and working in England at the time, so I saw it as a good chance to stay with them and visit friends and family. It would be a beautiful time to be over there, on the brink of spring.

The first week I stayed with my sister Buffy and her boyfriend Bob in their flat in Shepherd's Bush, west of London. They went out of their way to show me a good time, particularly Bob, who owned a bar and was constantly trying to get me drunk! They introduced me to all their friends and took me all over London. One afternoon we decided to have a quiet beer in Richmond Park, but got lost and had to jump a creek to get out, which was quite funny. At the time I was cursing – jumping a creek isn't really a blind guy's idea of a good time! – but we had many a laugh about it afterwards and it's actually one of my most treasured memories with my sister.

Then came the week of the championships. I stayed with Jane Brown-Clayton, an old school friend of Mum's, and her family in their lovely home in Greenwich Park. It was pretty novel to be able to walk from one end of the house to the other and find yourself in a different hemisphere. Jane's daughter Claire took me everywhere she went – to the Tower of London, to the movies, ten-pin bowling. It was very kind of her to welcome me into her circle of friends like that, and we had a lot of fun.

When Jane and I arrived on the first day of the Championships, the only seats left were next to the talkative swimmer. We couldn't believe it! Not five minutes had passed before Jane had to ask: 'How did you stand her for six weeks?' She likes to get everyone's address, so she can come and stay with them, but when she asked for Jane's address at the end I caught the fleeting moment of panic on Jane's face and said, 'Sorry, we're running late!'

I competed in seven events and I really enjoyed all of them. I could tell I was swimming really well; it was just coming easily to me. I broke an Australian National Short Course record. The mood was so positive throughout the entire meet, and although it was a small event in the scheme of things, it was great to represent Australia and to see so many people doing well.

The next day I travelled to Camberwell, London to stay with my brother Tony and his girlfriend in their one-bedroom flat for Easter. They gave me their bedroom, but I got kicked out within the first hour for snoring too loudly! I ended up sleeping in the lounge, where I woke up with the stray cat they'd taken in sleeping on my back. It was a pattern that would continue throughout my stay. But I didn't mind; it was actually kind of nice. I got up and had a shower and came out to find the downstairs neighbours at the door, complaining, 'It's leaking again!' Tony had neglected to tell me that the shower I had used drained straight into the flat below. It was onwards and upwards from there though. I played a great game of golf with a mate of Tony's at Royal Berkshire. A couple of my shots were spot on, straight down the middle, and he couldn't believe it. We whiled away the afternoons drinking in the sun with Tony's mates.

On Easter Monday we decided to go to a Premier League soccer match. We had a choice: Liverpool versus Wimbledon, or Tottenham versus West Ham. We chose Liverpool versus Wimbledon and boy, did we ever go the wrong way. When we got to the gates the bloke directed us to the family enclosure since we weren't sporting any particular allegiance. A good thing, too, because the people in the supporters' boxes were going nuts! We were more than happy to be safe and sound with the families. But that's not to say we had a good time! People were somehow sitting there in T-shirts and shorts in this freezing wind, while we furtively sipped our hot chocolates with about seven layers on. The game itself was a complete bore, ending in a 1–1 draw. The half-time entertainment, cerebral palsy kids playing soccer, was far more entertaining than the actual game. Meanwhile, Tottenham were beating West Ham 4–3 in a tense match that would have made for a great afternoon. In fact, we spent half the game listening to the other game on the radio!

After the Easter long weekend, Tony, his girlfriend, a couple of their friends and I drove all the way up to Ayrshire, Scotland to stay with Uncle Sandy. Sandy took great pleasure in taking us all out to dinner each night, and we shared some beautiful moments. Mick Simpkin, Uncle Sandy and Tony had a great game of golf, though by the time they got back I think Mick and Tony were ready for some down time. When Sandy got talking about golf, there was no stopping him! I can't judge though, I think I can be the same way sometimes. We went down to the beach near Prestwick on a beautiful sunny morning when everyone was out with their dogs, playing in the freezing cold water. But probably my most treasured memory was the simplest: just playing croquet in the backyard after dinner in the home Sandy had held dear for all those years.

In July 1994 I had to go to the Blind National Swimming Championships in Darwin in order to qualify for the FESPIC (Far East and South Pacific Championships) Games for the Disabled, to be held at the end of August in Beijing. I was there only out of obligation, and it ended up being two of the worst days of my life.

Right at the beginning of the trip, I took a long walk into town. I left in good health, and I came back with one of the worst cases of flu I've ever seen. I just felt awful, and the feeling didn't let up for the whole time I was there. We were staying at St Peter's College in Darwin in horrendous school dormitories. It was disgustingly hot and humid and the pool was a half-hour bus drive away, which would have been bad enough at the best of times, but with the flu I felt as if I could expire at any moment.

I missed both the opening and the closing ceremonies. I could hardly swim and I went through the paces of my events in a daze of pain and nausea. Somehow I got through, only to find that the bus had left without me. Thank goodness one person from the team, John Murray, was still around to give me a lift back. He was amazed how well I'd swum given how crook I was and he couldn't believe they'd just forgotten about me after the amazing effort I'd just put in for the team. I was thanking my lucky stars I didn't have any more events on the second night, but in a cruel twist of fate, the manager pushed me into competing in a relay I'd never signed up for. I was battered and broken, but I did my duty.

It was a horrible trip, but at least it was done. I knew I had qualified for the FESPIC Games. Later, I found out that people had qualified for the games without going to the National Championships. I was livid. I'd taken time off work and busted my gut to get through those championships, and these guys didn't even have to compete. I wanted so much to vent my frustration at the selection committee, but what could I do? It was over now.

The FESPIC Games in Beijing would be one of the defining moments in my swimming career. They taught me that pool events just weren't for me. Before the meet started, for whatever reason I had a feeling I was going to do really well. But as time progressed and more and more things went wrong, that feeling gradually dissipated.

It started before we even got to China. We had a layover in Singapore and when we arrived, they'd put everyone in the wrong rooms. Men were with women, and some people didn't seem to have been assigned a room at all! Management eventually sorted it out, but it was absolute chaos. While all this was going on, I realised my hand luggage had been put through as checked luggage, and I felt sure I was never getting it back.

I got to Beijing with a serious headache, and to make matters worse everyone was having a go at me, for everything from not knowing the colour of my bag to not knowing the name of the 1992 Olympic swimming pool. It was open season, and I was the target. I still didn't have my hand luggage and now the team manager had taken my passport as well. I tried to argue the point, because I knew I would need it when we got to immigration. But he was in charge, and he made me hand it over. I was not impressed, because when you're overseas, your passport is everything. You lose your passport, you're done; you can't get out of the country. But we made it through the airport, and to my relief I got both my passport and my hand luggage back.

We eventually made it to the 'hotel', as they called it. Hotel? What a joke. It was nothing more than a bunch of dormitories. We'd been told we'd have great accommodation and great facilities, and that it would be nice and cool. I've never heard a bigger furphy in my life. It was 32 degrees every day, and the smog was so thick and heavy that you couldn't open a window without someone starting to cough and wheeze. There was no way they didn't know this beforehand. It was appalling.

We felt like cattle as we entered the foyer and got prodded through a metal scanner – a process we had to go through every time we entered the place. I suppose security's not a bad thing, but after a few days we started to lose it! While we were out one day, we went past a store that sold ornamental swords and someone was struck by an idea. All fifty of us bought one, and we all arrived at once to go through the scanner. The woman went ballistic, and so did the scanner. Best thirty bucks I've ever spent! You can't put a price on entertainment that good.

We had four people in our room, and we were the lucky ones. Most of the rooms slept ten. The whole floor had four showers and three toilets. Four showers for about forty people! And the dividers between the showers didn't reach all the way down to the floor, so when all four showers were occupied, you could practically go for a surf in there. The toilets were constantly blocked up. When we went to check out the pool, they were cleaning the decks with pool water. Nothing was sacred! I wasn't surprised when people got the runs, because the concept of hygiene seemed to have just gone out the window at this place. This was Beijing, 1994. They'd been in the running to host the Olympics in 2000, and this was the standard they were holding up?

The main 'restaurant' at the hotel was as bad as the rooms. The first morning all I wanted was a bowl of cereal or a couple of pieces of toast, but all that was on offer was this disgusting rice and overcooked, soggy meat and vegetables. That was literally all they served. When we discovered an alternative restaurant we thought we'd found a way out, but the second restaurant was even more disgusting than the first. There was no Western food to be seen. And we had twelve more days of this!

There were a couple of days free before the opening ceremony and we sure as hell weren't going to hang around in our accommodation, so we got a bit of sightseeing in while we could. Tiananmen Square was amazing. I couldn't believe the sheer size of it – a kilometre by a kilometre, right there in the middle of Beijing. And the topography! It was amazingly flat. I could imagine how easy it would have been for the tanks to just roll through the square back in 1989. At 6 foot 3 and with my Akubra hat on, I turned around at one point to find fifty people following me taking photos of what must have looked to them like Crocodile Dundee! The rest of my group kept saying to them, 'He's from Sydney 2000.' We'd just beaten Beijing for the Olympics, and we certainly weren't making any friends with that remark.

As for the Forbidden City, I'm sure many people would have found it very enjoyable looking at all the beautiful artefacts, but as a blind person, a day of navigating up and down stairs surrounded by crowds wasn't my idea of a good time. The Great Wall of China, on the other hand, was one of the best places I've ever been. Even though my sight was pretty minimal, just standing there and imagining it stretching for 6,400 kilometres was mind-blowing. That's all the way from Sydney to Perth, and halfway back again. It's just beyond comprehension.

For the Opening Ceremony, Beijing University closed and made its 30,000 students 'volunteer' and anglicise their names for the competition. Suffice to say it was a big event! The Chinese alphabet goes in reverse, which meant for once we came in near the end of the procession. We walked into the stadium to the roar of fifty thousand people cheering. That was loud enough. But when the six-hundred-strong Chinese team walked in last, the noise became deafening and the stadium was afire with lights. They just went mental. It was an absolute blast, a surreal experience, and one I won't soon forget.

And so the swimming began. Every time we went to the pool, we had to cross the road. Sounds easy enough, but in fact it was quite a process. For one thing, the 'road' was actually a six-lane highway. In 1994 Beijing was home to about 8 million people, and around half of them got around on bicycles. Each time we approached the kerb, the whirring avalanche of wheels would buzz wildly in our ears. It was actually really frightening. I'm not sure whether the fact I couldn't see it made it more or less so. One of the guys ended up being hit, but we were probably lucky to get away with just the one. After we braved the highway, we then had to go down a subway that seemed to flood at even the scent of rain. At least we were all good swimmers!

Before my first event, the 100-metres breaststroke, I was marshalled in a cool room where someone was smoking. I said to my guide, 'Where is this bloke? I'm going to go over and throttle him. We're in 30-odd degrees heat in a room with no escape. I can hardly breathe as it is! This is just ridiculous.' She said something to him, and he walked away, but he let us know what he thought of us with the weight of his footsteps as he huffed out of the room!

The most people I'd ever swum in front of up to this point was about a hundred. Now all of a sudden I had to get up in front of ten thousand people cheering and playing bongo drums. There was no escape from the deep vibrations coursing through my body. As much as I tried to concentrate, the impact of the sound waves on my body was completely disorientating and I swam appallingly. The 200-metres medley was a disaster as well. But with each event I got a little more used to it, and my performance picked up. The 100-metres backstroke wasn't my finest performance, but it wasn't too bad. And in the 100-metres butterfly I was a whisker away from winning bronze. As the result registered, I blinked away the warm sting of tears. Everyone else had won gold, and broken world records. But not me. My best hadn't been enough. I'd poured everything into this, and still fallen short.

The night after the swimming ended, all the blind athletes got together for a function. One of the managers got up and called a toast. 'You've done well as a team', he said, but there was something about the way his voice rose at the end that told me there was something more he wanted to say. Then he said in a loud voice, and I quote: 'We've got four blind swimmers representing Australia, and three of them are good.' There was no doubt in anyone's mind what he meant. I just sat there, beer in hand, completely stunned. I wasn't even embarrassed, I was just disgusted. It was wildly inappropriate. I had come fourth in one of my events, but apparently that meant nothing when everybody else had won gold. I gritted my teeth, took a sip of my beer, and resolved to keep quiet. But as we walked out, I vowed to my parents, 'The Australian administration will never get the chance to humiliate me again. I'll never let them come out on top. One day they'll eat their words.' I used the situation as a motivator. From that point on, every time I got in the water, it spurred me on.

Two weeks cooped up in third-world dormitories had driven a wedge through our team. At the Closing Ceremony the blind team was literally split in two, each group sitting in a separate area. We were sick of it – all of it. By the end, all any of us really wanted was to get out of there.

On our layover in Singapore on the way home, one of the athletes drank too much and ended up in hospital. When we found him lying half-conscious on the floor of the airport, we all knew how he'd gotten there. Even though it had happened through no fault of my own, I felt disgusted and ashamed. I was wearing an Australian shirt representing my country, and this was the message we were sending to the world. Nothing official was ever said or done about it. He was never held to account, which I think is a disgrace. As an Australian representing his country, giving his all, I was totally dismayed that this was the image we were portraying. I wanted to cry out, 'He doesn't act for all of us! This is not what Aussies are really like!' But instead I just slunk onto the plane, still seething. I couldn't wait to get home and be out of the company of the drunk guy, management, the bloody lot of them. It sounds childish, but I just wanted to get home to my parents! And once we were out of customs, I wasted no time in doing so. I didn't even say goodbye to the athletes, I was so annoyed.

That swimming tournament changed the course of my career. From then on, I would approach swimming differently. I didn't know exactly what that meant at the time, I just knew I didn't want to keep going as I was. I walked away from Beijing knowing I would never represent Australia in the swimming pool again. And I felt no sadness. The abysmal treatment I'd received had spurred me towards better things. Management had been right about one thing (not that it made it okay). I wasn't meant to be a sprinter. I wasn't as good as the others in that domain. But I had something they didn't – a whole lot of stamina.

## Chapter 7
## Rowing

In April 1994, North Shore Rowing Club put a call out for people to get involved in rowing. It wasn't something I'd ever considered, but for some reason it stood out to me. Maybe this was the 'something different' I was looking for. So I rang Spencer Grace, the president of the club. 'All right then,' he said brightly, 'come down for a row next Sunday.'

To look at it, North Shore was a dump of a rowing club – a run-down old shed, ancient boats, and a single pontoon on Lane Cove River. But as I would soon find out, it had something no one else had – Spencer Grace. An Olympian, Spencer had been rowing since before I was born. Rowing was his life, and North Shore was his home. He was the heart of that place and he made it something really special.

When I arrived, I asked an elderly man if he could tell me where I might find Spencer. 'You've found him', he said.

'Forgive my asking,' I said, 'but how old are you?'

'I'm 87 years young', he pronounced proudly. And he was still rowing? Who was this guy? I tried not to betray my incredulity.

'So how does this work?' I asked. 'I've never set foot in a rowboat in my life.'

'Well, let's remedy that. We'll put you in a double scull and see how we go.'

He gave me a quick rundown of the basics of rowing – 'quick' being the active word. He was going so fast I missed half of it because I was still busy trying to process the last thing he'd said. I was more than a little nervous about how this would go. Because I was blind, he decided to get a set of headsets and come and row alongside me. I'd worked out that this guy was a bit of a character – that didn't take long – but what I didn't know is that he had a bit of a reputation for riling people. I would later learn that as we got in the rowing boat that afternoon, three people were standing on the pontoon placing bets on how long it would take before I cracked it with him!

We went out and rowed in Lane Cove River. Lane Cove River is one of the entry points to Sydney Harbour and as a first-timer it's about the worst river you could be stuck in. It's filled with boats, seaplanes, ships, bridges, and any other obstacle you could think of. And if you fall in you better hope you've had your tetanus and cholera shots! Fortunately we were in Ted Hale boats, similar to single sculls but with inflatable tubes on either side, which meant they couldn't capsize. It was a good way to learn, to just get into the rhythm of rowing with no fear of falling out.

Afterwards I walked back into the clubhouse to a silent reception. Everyone was stunned that I'd survived the experience without so much as a complaint. 'See you next Sunday!' Spencer said with a cheeky grin. I was one of four potential new members that first Sunday at the club, but by the next week there was only one: me. The other three got so peeved with Spencer that they never came back.

I can see how he got under people's skin. I won't lie, Spencer was a cantankerous bloke. He loved an argument. But I got on really well with him, because that kind of character is easy to neutralise – all you have to do is deny the response they're looking for. So any time he tried to antagonise me, I'd just laugh it off. He wanted nothing more than for someone to have a go at him, and the more I laughed the more frustrated he got. Besides, I knew it came from a good place – a passion to drive people to do better. He just didn't seem to realise when it was time to ease off on the advice and give people a bit of peace and quiet to actually try to apply it!

Spencer was also a perfectionist. If a boat was out of alignment by even a sixteenth of an inch, you'd hear all about it! He was all about technique. Spencer sent us a postcard from the 1996 Olympics saying the rowers at North Shore had better technique than the Australian team! One time at a competition, one of the blokes from North Shore Rowing Club fell out right near the finish and he was trying in vain to get back in his boat. Spencer was going off his nut because the guy could have just swum over the line with his boat. All you've got to do is be *with* your boat when you're going over the line – whether or not you're *in* it doesn't matter.

I met a couple of other great characters through the rowing club. Ben Felten was an easygoing guy but with a fiercely competitive spirit. He loved the challenge of rowing and helped instil that same drive in me. He was blind as well – his sight started to decline in his early twenties, but he refused to really accept it until he crashed his motorcycle into a tree. He'd been a great motorcyclist and held high aspirations. Some might say he was stupid to keep riding, but he was young, and he wasn't ready to give up on his dream. If anyone can identify with that it's me. He wasn't injured, but for a man with such a passion for sport it was a hard blow. You'd think going blind would have put an end to it all, but Ben wasn't about to accept that, and to this day he still competes in blind motorcycling events. He aims big – he wants to be the fastest short-distance blind motorcyclist in the world. And you know, I won't be surprised if he does it. When he's competing, Ben only has one mode – power mode. He represented Australia at three World Rowing Championships, and won gold at all three.

Then there was Ben's coach, Dick Willis, a great rower who had represented New South Wales in his day. So strong was Dick's love for rowing that he used to actually *live* at Nepean Rowing Club. Dick exuded a quiet confidence and contentment – basically the antithesis of Spencer! Because I trained with Ben so often I got the benefit of Dick's coaching as well, and it helped balance Spencer's more animated approach. Although he didn't say much, he commanded respect. He loved rowing, he loved teaching, and above all, he loved helping people.

I enjoyed rowing more than I could ever have anticipated. It was a new challenge, but also a chance to continue to use the skills I already had. It's a whole-body sport, just like swimming, but also a mental sport: listening to the catch of the oar and focusing on your rhythm. And again, just like swimming, it's all about commitment and stamina, getting out there and giving it everything. I came to love the double and quad sculls the most because you got to be part of such a close-knit team. More than any other sport I can think of, in a rowing team you have to be perfectly in tune with one another to keep those strokes precisely in time. I loved being with people and I loved that sense of oneness when you got it right. I especially loved being in the stroke seat for the double sculls because I could just pound away as hard as I wanted to and the person in the bow seat had no choice but to follow! It was the perfect sport; all I had to do was learn to coordinate my movement in a new way. That and lose a bit of weight!

I knew my weight might be a bit of an issue, but one Sunday I came to learn just how much of an issue. I was in a modified single scull, and I was weighing the boat down to the point that I was very low to the water's edge. Out of nowhere, an eight came past and sent a wave careering towards me. It wasn't even that big a wave, but it was enough to swell over the edge of the boat and send it plunging towards the bottom of the river. There I was in the middle of the Nepean River, all alone with my headset ruined and no way to contact anyone on shore. I don't know what I would have done if someone hadn't come past in a speedboat and asked if I was all right. The answer was no! They went back and told Dick, and he and Ben came out and rescued me. 'Nice one,' said Dick. 'I've seen a lot of guys capsize their boats, but I've never seen one sink. Impressive work.' I'd been treading water for a while now, and my laughter quickly turned to spluttering and choking. They dragged me into their boat, and Dick somehow managed to retrieve mine from the bottom of the river.

My first event was the Nepean Rowing Championships in November 1994. The course was from the bridge down to the end of the weir, about 300 metres. Spencer watched from the shore, barking instructions through my headset. Later on I discovered that the headset was deemed assistance. Déjà vu! It didn't matter what sport you chose, you couldn't avoid the nitpicking politics and rules. Again, there were some serious inconsistencies in their logic. In an able-bodied race it was completely fine for a coach to ride a bike along the shoreline and give instructions, but forget about using a headset. But at the time we were blissfully unaware of all that. I won, and it was a great feeling to claim victory in my first rowing competition.

It was the beginning of a long love affair with rowing. I had come back from China very disillusioned with swimming, but now all that felt like a distant memory. I had a new sport and a new outlook. Rowing was my new thing, and I absolutely loved it.

Now it was time to take it to the next level. The National Rowing Championships were to be held in Wellington Dam, Western Australia in April 1995. The dam was 2,100 metres long. Fail to stop within 100 metres of the finish line in a 2,000-metre race and you were in the rocks! So the venue left a little to be desired, but the event itself was brilliant.

When we first arrived, we went to check out the dam, and there we met Roger Blake, a rower with cerebral palsy. The first words out of his mouth were a joke, and I instantly warmed to him. He's one of the nicest people you'll ever meet, and a damn good rower to boot. If this was anything to go by, it was going to be an awesome time.

One night Roger's dad Bob decided to take me out for a practice row. I was hesitant, but Bob insisted. In Perth in winter there's no twilight – it's light one minute and dark the next. And when that minute came, I was in the middle of the lake with an eight approaching. Bob just kept repeating over the headset, 'I can't see a thing!' Just what you want to hear from the one person who's meant to be guiding you! There was nothing to stop me getting creamed by this eight. I could hear it coming, but what were we supposed to do about it when we couldn't even see the thing? Somehow we got out of the way just in the nick of time. Poor old Bob almost had a coronary knowing he was the one that dragged me out there! It was funny in retrospect, but I can tell you, neither of us felt like laughing at the time.

We had arranged to share a huge A-frame house with all the interstate disabled rowers and their parents and carers. It was a great group of people. You'd think squeezing twenty-odd people into one house would be a recipe for disaster, but it just worked. The parents and helpers would make the dinner together every night, and in the morning we'd all go down to the dam together, one big happy family. It was a gorgeous house with lovely gardens and we made some beautiful memories there. During the day we'd go out and train with the Western Australians. The rowing was great, but better than that was just sitting back and chatting with all these different people with so many different disabilities – blindness, cerebral palsy, amputation, wheelchairs. Everybody had their own inspiring story to tell.

The day came for the racing, and lo and behold, for the first time in five months it rained in Perth. But we didn't let it get in the way of our fun. I got off to a poor start in my 1,000-metre event when I did a 360° on the start line and gave everyone a massive head start. But once I got going I got up some serious speed, overtook two of the guys and almost chased Ben down at the finish. I didn't quite get there, but given the circumstances, I had to be happy with second!

I really enjoyed the competition. It felt amazing to be included in the same National Championships program as able-bodied people. It was a real breakthrough, and a far cry from what I was used to in swimming. Yes, we got to swim, but we were treated as a completely different class. In the rowing, we got our own separate events, but that's where the divide started and ended. Beyond that, we were treated the same as anyone else. The sportsmanship was first class.

A few weeks later a message came in about the World Championships of Rowing in Tampere, Finland. Finland has about one hundred and eighty thousand lakes and rivers, so you couldn't ask for a more perfect venue! Ben got in automatically because he had won at the national championships, but they needed someone to fill the second spot in the double scull, so my application got accepted as well. I didn't know it at the time, but by competing in the World Championships, I would break an 87-year drought. I would become the first person since Snowy Baker in 1908 to represent Australia in both swimming and rowing at a world championship level.

Every Saturday and Sunday for eight weeks leading up to the event, no matter what, I got up at 6 in the morning and went out to the Nepean River to row with Ben and Dick. In the depths of winter, there were times you'd march out to the river to the sound of frost crunching underfoot. One time training fell on the same day as one of my seasonal swim meets at Homebush, but it didn't stop me. I got up, rowed for 3 hours, then went back to Homebush and smashed out my events. I was absolutely flattened by the end of that weekend. Another time I'd gone out until 2 am the night before, I would have been lucky if I'd had an hour's sleep, and I needed Mum's help just to get ready! I felt like death. But I still got there. I don't know that my rowing that day was particularly good, but you know what? I got out there; I did it; I showed my commitment. And from that day on, no matter how bad a day I was having, I knew it could always be worse!

August came, and with it the epic journey to Tampere. I don't use the word epic lightly. Roger and Bob Blake had flown from Hobart to Devonport then Devonport to Sydney to meet up with me for the rest of the trek. From there we flew from Sydney to Bangkok, Bangkok to Frankfurt, Frankfurt to Helsinki, and Helsinki to Tampere. I reckon we went about as far as it's physically possible to go, and it sure felt that way.

Even once we got to Tampere, our journey still wasn't over. It felt as if we were never going to get to the hotel! But by that stage we were so tired we'd lost all concept of time. It could have been an hour, or it could have been 5 minutes. I've never been more relieved to arrive anywhere than I was when we reached that hotel.

The three of us met up with Ben, Dick, another rower called Michael Briggs and his father, and Roger's coach Kerry. We had booked four rooms between the eight of us, so we filed off into pairs, and I ended up with Kerry in a pokey little room. I was Kerry's nightmare roommate. Kerry was a neat freak; I left my clothes piled haphazardly in a corner. Kerry was a light sleeper; I snored like a chainsaw. One morning I woke to hear him ranting to Bob: 'I can't live like this! I have my clothes stored neatly and I can't find them, and this bloke has crap all over the place and he finds them in 5 seconds!' I had a good chuckle.

As well as being neat, Kerry was fastidious with his cleaning. Despite the lack of space, he decided he needed a washing line, and he strung it across the room corner to corner. Bob said, 'Are you kidding? You've got a blind person sleeping in your room!' Kerry went ahead anyway, but I'd bump the line and send his clothes hurtling across the room every time I got up. In the end he had to accept defeat and take the line down.

One night at 2am the fire alarm went off in the hotel and we all crawled out of our rooms morose and bleary-eyed while everyone ran up and down the corridors like headless chooks. It turned out to be a false alarm, but it didn't stop me from ribbing Kerry about it in the morning because he was the only smoker among us. 'You were smoking, weren't you! Don't try to deny it; we all know you're the one who set it off!'

Things just kept on going wrong for poor old Kerry. One afternoon we were hanging out in the rooms when he decided to go out and buy a few beers. But he returned empty-handed. 'What happened?' I asked.

'You wouldn't believe me if I told you', Kerry said

'What do you mean?'

'It's 300 Finnish markkas for a carton of beer!'

A few seconds of mental arithmetic later, I said 'That can't be right. A hundred Australian dollars?'

'That *is* right. They're dreaming! And the bastards had the nerve to try to sell us an esky as well!'

I had a good laugh, but I think Kerry had a bit of trouble seeing the humour!

The rest of the Australian rowing team were in another hotel, but we liked the idea of staying just with our own little group. It worked out well for us because the rest of the hotel was full to the brim with Russians – over a hundred of them! In 1995, the Russians and the Finns didn't get along all that well, so we were the flavour of the month.

Every night we'd head downstairs for dinner. They had a list of twelve pizzas, but the menu was all in Finnish so it was a complete lucky dip. I was nominated to choose on the first night, and I picked number twelve. Number twelve turned out to be a steaming hot chilli pizza. The next night Roger said, 'You're relieved of your duties, James. No way I'm letting you choose another pizza!'

There were four guys from the press staying at the hotel, and they'd often come down and eat with us. They were very interesting and we had a similar sense of humour. One night I was sitting there in front of the TV and I said 'It doesn't get much more boring than this. A blind guy watching synchronised swimming.' One of the guys just couldn't stop laughing. The next night he came in he said, 'I told everyone at the rowing centre what you said!' Days later he was still cracking up about it.

Before long, everyone knew who we were. We were the group cracking jokes with anyone that would listen, always up for a laugh, never letting the smiles leave our faces. Everyone wanted to be a part of it. Every night someone new would come over to our table and join in. Even if they didn't speak English, it seemed! One night a pilot came over and started speaking to us in Finnish. We just looked at each other awkwardly, hoping against hope that he wouldn't ask a question! It was all in good fun.

Roger is always the first to crack a joke, so we knew when the jokes started to get fewer and further between that he was having a hard time. Roger puts up a strong front, but his cerebral palsy is quite severe and he gets very stiff and sore. And after the endless flights to get here, that's exactly what was happening. He desperately needed release, so Bob found him a hydrotherapy pool. I've never seen such a sudden and dramatic change in someone. He came back a different man. I nudged Ben and said, 'Whatever's in this hydrotherapy pool, sign me up!'

A couple of days in, we went down and prepared the boats we'd be rowing in and got started on our training. They were great boats, but on this particular morning things just didn't seem to be working for me. 'I just can't row this morning, Bob!' I complained. 'I don't know what it is, but the oars just aren't going in!' I couldn't understand it. The day before I'd been rowing perfectly well.

'Okay,' Bob said, 'row back to me.' When I got back to shore they all started laughing. 'Yeah, there's a slight problem!' Bob said. 'Let me fix that for you!' He'd put the oar into the oarlock the wrong way around, which totally changed the way the oar went into the water. All of a sudden, the rowing got much easier. Funny that. At least the blind guy was on the ball!

The Championships were meant to bring together countries from all around the world, but for some reason only the English turned up. It was a bit disappointing, but at least the three guys that did turn up were the cream of the crop! We got on from the word go, and started training together. We didn't care that they were the opposition; we just cared that we were having a bloody good time rowing with them.

One day while we were training we noticed the weather starting to change, but we weren't ready to go home yet, so we just ignored it. It was a decision we would live to regret! About half an hour later, the skies just opened up. All we had for shelter was a tiny hut beside the water. We all huddled under this little awning, trying in vain to keep from getting absolutely drenched. It must have been a very funny sight, twelve people all crammed under this one fragile little roof. But the rain wasn't letting up. Someone was going to have to be the one to get all our gear back to the van. Bob, Dick and Kerry all decided to take one for the team and got soaked running back and forth. It was an absolute drenchathon.

The day before the competition was to start, we learned that of the six people in my single-scull race, four hadn't turned up: it was just Ben and me. But it could have been worse. The double-scull event I'd qualified in on the back of had been cancelled, so it was lucky I was even there. Thank God I was, or Ben would have been all on his own. But I didn't see fit to mention that. In fact, there was nothing I *could* say. He was inconsolable.

That's when John Boultbee stepped in, one of the Australian rowing administrators. He said, 'Look, what's happened has happened. Nothing you can do about it but get out there and have a great row.' Simple words, but inspirational. He said the right things at the right time in the right way, and it placated Ben when I thought nothing could. Every time I hear his name now I think, *The magnificent John Boultbee. You beauty!*

The day came for the actual competition. As I sat in the starting gates in my Australian uniform, it struck me again that not only was I about to represent Australia, I was doing it in a second sport. No matter what the outcome, I would get out of that boat a very proud man.

For the vision-impaired, they'd set up receivers at the front of each boat, which transmitted real-time instructions of where to go and what to do from an umpire on a speedboat following behind. It was a beautiful system, far better than the headsets we were used to. Every word came through loud and clear. But when a German voice started booming through my receiver it was obvious something was amiss. I realised it was hooked up not with the umpire, but with the main speaker system on the course, which was reporting in four different languages. And the umpire didn't know how to fix it any more than we did! In the end he just had to use his megaphone to direct us, which worked well enough, though it was a bit of a battle blocking out the constant babble from the receiver!

Ben rowed brilliantly as he always does, and won very easily. He deserved it, and I hoped he would enjoy the victory without lamenting the circumstances. For my part, I was completely satisfied. I had gone out there and rowed to the very best of my ability. Probably the best I've ever rowed in my life. And that was worth everything. All that training, the angst of getting up at the break of dawn all through winter, had paid off. I was absolutely thrilled.

I went over and congratulated Ben and his family. His performance was amazing, and I told him so. Then I asked how Roger had gone. I waited for the answer with bated breath, because only six weeks before, Roger had been in hospital. Nobody thought he'd even make it to Finland. But he'd beaten the odds, he'd got himself here, and I wanted so much for him to come through the experience with something solid to show for it. When Ben told me he'd won, if I'd had it in me, I would have jumped for joy. Roger had travelled 36,000 kilometres across the world, fought crippling stiffness and pain, and come through with the goods. Mate, it was one of the most brilliant moments in sport. It still stirs emotion in me even now, two decades down the track. Nobody deserved the title of 'champion' more than he did, and now he had attained it. My cheeks stung from smiling so much.

When Roger got up to receive his gold medal at the presentation ceremony, the sun was beating down like fire, yet still I felt a shiver as pure emotion rippled through my body. It's a moment I'll never forget. I felt honoured to be there, to hear those words: 'The winner of the fixed seat race is Roger Blake.' You bloody beauty! I clapped until my hands hurt, and then I clapped some more. 'Here's to one of the great names in sport', I said emphatically. Ben got his gold medal for the vision-impaired sliding-seat scull, and I managed to get a silver medal for coming in last place, which is not something many people can say! I cherish that medal, of course, but I cherish the memory of seeing Roger get his so much more.

When we went back to the hotel restaurant for dinner, the owners said, 'You've eaten here every night for a week, and I know how much our guests have enjoyed your company. Tonight, drinks are on us!' It was a lovely gesture and none of us had had a drink for three weeks, so there was no way we were saying no! The Englishmen came and ate with us and we patted each other on the back. As disappointed as we'd all been with the turnout, it had, like so many things in life, come with its own silver lining. If things had gone to plan, we may never have got the chance to have such a fun, friendly meet with all those guys.

The following day, we went out and watched the Australian able-bodied team row. They didn't hesitate to invite us, which just embodied their great attitude towards us for the whole meet. The way they embraced us was phenomenal. Every time they saw us, they'd come up to have a chat, to help us out, to encourage us, to congratulate us. But not out of pity or duty. I really believe they just saw us as part of the team – no different from them, at least not in any way that mattered. Twenty years on things have changed a lot in disabled sport, and maybe this doesn't sound all that impressive. But back then, it was. It really was. They gave us a sense of inclusion like nothing we'd ever experienced.

When we got back, Bob said to me, 'You want a nightcap?' Actually, I did. After one bourbon and coke Bob got up to go, but I convinced him to have another… and another. One quickly became eight, and I woke up filled with regret! When I dragged myself out of the room and met up with the others Roger said, 'I don't think my dad's very happy with you.'

'Why?'

'The head of Rowing Australia gave him a call at 6 this morning.'

I had nothing to say in my defence, apart from a weak 'Oh.'

'He wasn't very complimentary! In fact, the first word he said about you wouldn't make too many dictionaries!'

I guess I deserved the rap for that.

The next day we were back on the bloody planes. All five of them. I arrived at Sydney Airport feeling like I'd been around the world, because I literally had. But what a magnificent, fantastic, brilliant, superb, outstanding trip I'd had. I just didn't have enough words! It was a bringing together of friends, of a wonderful group of people who just gelled. It put the previous year's debacle in Beijing into stark focus. How different it had been to get on so easily with everyone, to feel at one with the able-bodied group, and to just embrace each other and take joy in everything that makes sport great. I wish my grandmother could have been there to see it.

Later that month, I was listening to the national anthem at the start of the 1995 Rugby League Grand Final, and for whatever reason, that's when the reality suddenly hit me. I was a dual international sportsman. I mean, I knew, of course I knew, but it wasn't until that moment that I really grasped the magnitude of my achievement. I'd done something freakish. A kid from Killara who dreamed about representing his country in sport had become a man who made it happen – in both swimming and rowing. And I'd become the second Australian ever to do it.

I liked the feeling. I liked it so much that for the next three years I managed to continue competing in both open-water and rowing events, and even a few more swimming pool events here and there, though by now I knew that wasn't where my future lay. My poor parents, about all they ever seemed to do was take me to sporting events!

On a couple of occasions I did back-to-back events, something I'm not sure anyone else has actually ever done. In January 1996 I did an 8-km swim on the Nepean River in the morning then a rowing competition in the afternoon. Then in February I competed in a rowing event on Lake Barrington in Devonport on Saturday and backed it up with an 8-km open-water event in Launceston on the Sunday. But in March, I took it to the next level. In one month, I won medals at both the National Swimming Multi Disabled Championships and the National Rowing Championships. It was a crazy few years – just how I like it!

But as much as I loved pushing myself to the limit, there *is* a limit. And there was no way I was ever going to achieve my dream of swimming the English Channel unless I poured absolutely everything into it. So when Narelle lit a fire under me that day at the pool in 1997, I knew it was time to give the rowing away. I missed it, but life is always a game of give and take.

It was fitting, though, that two weeks after swimming the Channel, I had the chance to visit Henley Rowing Course on the Thames. Henley is known as the pride of rowing around the world. In fact, it's kind of like the English Channel of rowing. Mum came with me, and the minute we arrived she charged in and accosted someone with the assertion, 'My son is a great rower.'

'Mum,' I hissed, 'What are you doing? You've put the pressure on before I'm even in the water!' A guy called John came out of nowhere and announced, 'I'll row with you, son.' He asked me what I wanted to row. I didn't hesitate. 'Double scull.' On our way down to the water John asked me what had brought us to England. 'Business or pleasure?'

I wasn't sure what to answer, so I said, 'Holiday.'

'What have you been up to?'

'Well, I spent the first two weeks trying to swim the English Channel.'

He turned to me, eyes wide. 'Did you do it?'

'Yes, I did. I was lucky enough to do it.'

We arrived at the water. 'Well, I guess that answers the question of whether you can swim! If we fall out, you're the one swimming back with the boat! Let's go.'

We rowed the 2 kilometres from the clubhouse down to the start of the rowing course. As we turned back, there was mischief in his voice as he said, 'Let's do some sprints!' I said, 'In your dreams! I swam the English Channel a few weeks ago. Not going to happen!' We took our time to come back, dodging a duck and narrowly avoiding capsizing along the way. Still, I indulged myself by imagining we were competing in the Henley Rowing Regatta. It was a sensational feeling.

It was a misty evening and the rain was starting to get heavier, but I made no effort to run for cover. Something about the rain falling on my face took me back to that dream I'd had four months earlier. I'd not only dreamed that I'd swum the English Channel on the anniversary of the day man landed on the moon, I'd also dreamed that I'd rowed at Henley Rowing Course. Now here I was, nearly five months later, and every detail of the dream had come true – well, except that my channel crossing was 56 minutes quicker in real life. Everything had come together just as it was supposed to.

## Chapter 8
## Manhattan Island

I gave myself a few months off after the English Channel, but Narelle didn't let me stay in party mode for too long! After my second Rottnest swim in February 1999, Narelle was ready to throw me my next challenge. 'Right,' she said, 'do you want to have a go at the Manhattan Island Marathon in June?' The Marathon is a 48-kilometre trip around Manhattan Island in New York. Narelle and I have this amazing connection, not romantic in the least, but still very special. Sports-wise, she knows me as well as I know myself. When she decides I should do an event, I take her word for it, and I've never been disappointed. And so, of course, I said yes. After the English Channel, a swim in enclosed water around Manhattan Island seemed pretty mild. If the wind didn't get up it should be a fairly comfortable swim. But no matter what the conditions, a 48-kilometre swim was always going to be pretty full-on.

In early March, I sat down to fill out the application form – all twenty pages of it. I spent two or three weeks just filling it in! In addition to the form itself, I had to be immunised against a half-dozen diseases and write a half-page essay about why I wanted to swim it. I wrote some garbage about being the first blind person to do this and that, how fortunate I'd been to swim the English Channel, and what a challenge this would be. I said what I thought they wanted to hear and got it out of the way as quickly as possible!

These days the Manhattan Island event has quite a following, and timing is everything. You've basically got to be hovering over the computer at midnight, ready to submit your application at 12.01 am. But in 1999 the process was a little more relaxed, and I had a great deal of help from Shelley Taylor-Smith, who I'd met at the previous year's Rottnest Challenge. She had swum the event seven times, won it five times, and was involved with the committee, so she put in a good word for me that I'm sure helped immeasurably in getting accepted into the event.

Narelle asked her friend Tony Halfhide to join our team, and having him on our side was invaluable. Tony is a man of action, and when he sets his mind to something there's no stopping him. He knew a lot of people in America, and he even went over there beforehand to go around the island and work out what we were up against. He came back with hundreds of photos. He did that off his own bat, and it helped me immensely. He even set up an account for sponsorship and kept a close eye on our finances all the way up to the event.

Meanwhile, Brooke Withers (my kayaker) had asked her friend Felicity Chaseling to be my manager. It didn't go down well with Narelle, who I know would have preferred to manage me herself. But I knew better – coaching and management are very different jobs, and trying to bundle them into one role would only detract from both. Felicity got us sponsorship from Tourism New South Wales, who paid for our accommodation, and Shelley managed to get Air New Zealand to cover our airfares. The entry fee alone was 1,500 Australian dollars, so it was a relief to find out we were getting some financial help. Felicity was already proving her worth, but I knew it would take more than that to convince Narelle.

In early April, we decided a documentary film was in order. It was a family friend, Simon, who first suggested it. He saw the appeal of my story, that same appeal that drove me to write this book – I'm living proof that you can do anything you put your mind to, no matter what your disability. Simon volunteered to put it together along with three of his mates, and we got started immediately. For the next two-and-a-half years of my life, it felt like no matter where I went or what I did, Big Brother was watching. I can't tell you how many times we traipsed up and down Manly Beach answering hair-brained questions like, 'What does the colour purple mean to a blind person?' So many days of filming. So many days of swimming. So many days just doing what I was told! And all this in between (and during) training and full-time work.

It was an almighty undertaking. I'd never been involved in a documentary and had no idea what it was going to be like. You'd spend six hours filming and it would amount to one minute of footage. It gave me a whole new respect for actors. At the tax office that ratio would never stand! I made it work for the documentary, but it was demanding. *Freestyle Man* was released in November 2001. For a while afterwards I had complete strangers come up to me and tell me how much they'd enjoyed it, which finally made the constant monitoring of my life seem worth it!

I threw myself into training full-throttle. Every night I was in the pool, and every weekend I was out in the ocean with Narelle, Sticks or Brooke. At the end of April I was meant to do the National Open Water Swimming Championships in Brisbane, but I wasn't allowed to because FINA's rules prohibit use of a whistle system. I'd taken two days off work to go the swim, so I was very disappointed and frustrated. Already I felt like the lead-up to New York wasn't going particularly well.

Then in late April, I got tendonitis in my left shoulder. Straight away I knew something was wrong. I thought, well, I can either fight this for the next six weeks, or I can admit I have a problem. I went and saw Elizabeth, my physio and she worked on me every week. But I never stopped training. I pushed through the pain, and I kept the injury to myself. Not even Narelle knew. I knew she'd want me to pull out, and that was something I wasn't prepared to do. I'd paid the money; I'd made the travel arrangements; I'd started the documentary. There was no backing out now.

Early in May Narelle organised a swim at Manly Pool to fundraise and prepare for the Manhattan Marathon. Twenty-seven kilometres: five hundred and forty laps. It would take about 9 hours, similar to the Marathon. Everyone came down – Shelley, Narelle, my family. Heaps of people took turns swimming beside me, but there were just as many playing ball, having a snag, counting laps. Just having a good time. Tony Halfhide had done an amazing job, as

I'd known he would. He loves a good time, but when it comes down to business there's nobody I'd rather put my trust in.

Unsurprisingly, I was in a bit of pain. At one point, Narelle said, 'I think you need to pick up your left shoulder.' I love how in sync she is with me, but at that moment I wished she'd be just a little bit less perceptive! I nodded dutifully and just kept on swimming. It started to get darker, and I knew it must have been nearing 7 pm – closing time. I tried to pick up the pace, but my shoulder was really starting to fail me. When I reached the end and my brother leaned over and said, 'You've got 200 to go', for a fleeting moment I thought, two hundred laps?! Of course, he meant 200 metres. I just went for it. When I hit the wall the applause was almost deafening. We had a great day and raised a lot of money.

As May drew to a close, we had planned a team meeting at Brooke's place. Felicity and Narelle hadn't been getting on, as I'd known they wouldn't, and there was tension hanging in the air. But as it turned out, it wasn't Narelle I had to worry about. I had a suspicion that the meeting would ruffle a few feathers, but I couldn't have predicted just how badly Felicity and Shelley would clash. To put it bluntly, it was a bloody disaster.

Shelley has an intensely competitive spirit. Her heart is always in the right place, but when she gets worked up about something, sometimes it can come across as a bit brash. At one point, Shelley said, 'So we're going to fly over to LA, spend a night there, then fly across to New York.' As grateful as I was to have Shelley on the team, she was out of line trying to take control of the entire itinerary. I cut in. 'No, no. We've got a couple of hours' stopover in LA, but then we're going straight to New York.' Shelley was clearly not happy, but bad luck. I was the swimmer, and Narelle was the coach. This was our territory.

Felicity had a go at Shelley over it, and things quickly spiralled out of control. Felicity got so frustrated that Brooke ended up having to take her out of the room to help her calm down. I think she was about ready to give us all the flick. She'd worked her butt off to get us sponsorship and help organise the documentary, and all she wanted was to show the documentary team how united we were. Well, we were anything but, and I wasn't reserved in saying so.

The meeting had become this massive battle of egos, only the ego that should have been most important – me – seemed to have been completely overlooked. Everything was being organised without even consulting me. I'd had a really bad week at work, the tendonitis in my shoulder didn't seem to be getting any better, the pressure of doing a documentary was getting to me, and Manhattan was fast approaching. The last thing I needed was multiple arguments going on in tandem with only a couple of weeks to go before the event.

Narelle was the first to realise, and raised her voice over the commotion. 'James, what would *you* like to do?'

'I want to fly straight to New York.'

'You don't want to stay overnight in LA?'

'Why would I want to do that?'

Reluctantly Shelley agreed to go back to the travel agent and make the necessary changes. Poor old Air New Zealand were getting hammered. I went home thinking, this is mayhem. If we can't get it together in our own living room, how are we going to cope out in the ocean?

Only two days later, we arrived in America. Our apartment on East Houston Street was far from ideal. With only three bedrooms between ten people, the documentary crew had to be relegated to the living room. And after Brooke snapped a table in half just by sitting on it, we made sure to watch our step around the furniture! But it had been paid for by Tourism New South Wales, so we weren't really in a position to complain. And while our accommodation left a little to be desired, we were training like the rich and famous. Tammy van Wisse, who was also doing the Marathon, managed to get us into the prestigious New York Athletic Club, where we trained in the 25-metre pool on the fifteenth floor.

Opposite our hotel was a pub called The Library, which served as Sticks and Shelley's local for the duration of our stay. Well, until the night Shelley gave ten dimes as a tip, and got thrown out for it! Yet another quality moment caught on camera by our documentary crew. By now the documentary was in full swing, and everywhere I went I had a microphone up my shirt and someone from the documentary crew watching. It was hard to get used to.

On our third day, we met with Rick, the head of kayaking for the swim. That's when I learned that this wasn't your typical swim. Unbeknown to me, there were five checkpoints, and if you didn't make them all in time, you got pulled out. I just sat there aghast thinking, seriously? How was it that I was only now finding this out? After six months of training, suddenly everything had changed. I had to rethink my entire strategy. Do I try to swim as hard as I can to meet all the checkpoints and hope I can hold on? Or do I just work at my own pace and risk not making it in time? A hard decision at the best of times, made even harder by the question mark over how my tendonitis would affect me. Tendonitis, conflict in the team, and now this. Could things get any worse?

The day before the swim, we had a briefing. I paid close attention to the locations and deadlines of the checkpoints. The course begins at Battery Park and runs anticlockwise into the East River, then the Harlem River, and finally into the Hudson before circling back to Battery Park. At 48 kilometres it's a bloody long swim, but on the plus side, the tides are with you. As long as I stayed on track and made all the checkpoints, I could swim at around 6 kilometres per hour and get it done within about 8 hours. It was all about making those checkpoints.

One of the organisers said, 'No matter what, when you get to the top of the Hudson, don't go right. If you do, you'll wind up in a sewage plant, and that will be the end of your swim.' I l turned to Narelle and whispered, 'You mean to say I've spent all this money coming here and I could end up in a sewage plant?' But sewage aside, swimming in the waters of New York City was risky business in itself. Manhattan Island had a long history of things being found in the rivers around it. Dead bodies, severed limbs, animal remains. It was far from inspiring.

Briefings aren't renowned for being particularly thrilling, but we did have a few funny moments. I had to hold my tongue when one of the swimmers said to me, 'While you're going around the island, if you breathe to the left, you'll have a great view of Manhattan.' As a blind right-hand breather, I must say it wasn't the most useful piece of advice I've ever received. I was in the midst of coming up with a witty response when Brooke tapped me on the shoulder and said, 'Nah, best leave that one well enough alone, matey.'

That night I sat down and had a good think about my plans for the next morning. I'd had a bit of time to come to terms with the new developments of the past few days, and by the end of the night I'd worked out how I was going to approach it. I felt prepared. Maybe not as prepared as I would have liked, but prepared enough.

The next morning conditions were lovely. It was a beautiful 27 degrees air temperature, 19 degrees water temperature, and not much wind. Brooke, Narelle, Tony and Sticks left early to prepare everything, and when they wished me good luck, I knew it was sincere. I really felt as though I was going into battle.

I was allowed a 5-minute handicap, which made it much easier for Shelley to steer me out to Norlane Brook where Narelle and Brooke were waiting. It really took the pressure off knowing I wasn't battling with thirty-odd other people just to get to the kayak. Everyone had told me the East River was very choppy, and they weren't wrong. But it didn't take long to get to the kayak.

Early on in the East River, my arm hit something. I hoped it was a log. But I just couldn't shake the feeling that it was a leg! I knew it was probably just my mind playing tricks, but that did little to comfort me. Narelle said, 'It's just a log! Just keep swimming, stay calm.' It didn't feel like a log to me, but I tried to just put it out of my mind.

I could feel people speeding past but it didn't faze me. I wasn't competing against them – I was competing against the checkpoints.

I got to the first one fairly comfortably, but I knew this was no time to relax. The next part of the swim was the Harlem River, by far the worst part of the swim. It was a long, boring stretch, and you had to really concentrate hard to get through it. With such flat, calm conditions, it's easy to get in a rhythm and completely lose track of time. And that was something I just couldn't afford to do. Making the railway bridge checkpoint was going to be tight enough as it was.

You go under fourteen bridges in the Harlem River before you hit the Hudson. I could tell when we went under one by the reverberation of the whistles. I counted them as I went along, and I knew it was going to be a strain to make the next checkpoint. Indeed it was. I made it to the railway bridge with about 2 minutes to spare.

Then we came to the Hudson – the last checkpoint. I was mentally drained, and I could tell I was swimming poorly. Now it was just a question of whether my mind and my heart could overcome the intense pain in my left shoulder. There was no doubt in my mind that I was the weakest link. Narelle and Brooke were kayaking brilliantly. In fact, Narelle had a back problem at the time, but you'd never have guessed. I had the encouragement of my whole team and documentary crew behind me, but also the expectation. The pressure was immense.

With 100 minutes to go, I felt as if I had nothing left. For a moment there, I felt sure I was going to fail. But if ever there was a time to get up and push through, this was it. In twenty-two weeks' time, Australia was holding a referendum to decide whether we would become a republic. For all I knew, this may be the last chance I ever got to represent the Australian flag. The greatest prize, the greatest honour, of all. It was all the inspiration I needed. I resolved to give everything I had for the next 100 minutes, no matter what the toll on my body! I knew it wouldn't let me down. Whenever I got mentally desperate, I just thought about the flag, and it kept me going.

I put my head down and forced myself back into a rhythm as we started out along the Hudson. My mind echoed the advice from the day before: 'Don't go right!' It's remarkable I even remembered, I was so fatigued. I veered hard left and Narelle said, 'Stop! You were already on the left hand side. You're on course. Don't worry, I'm not going to let you end up in the sewage plant!'

By the time we got within a kilometre of the finish, I had lost the plot completely. When I took a breath, I yelled as hard and as loud as I could, 'Do it for the flag!' Narelle couldn't believe someone so physically beaten had enough strength to shout. At first I think she was impressed. But then when I put my head down, did two more strokes, and yelled out the same thing again, she realised I was yelling not despite how beaten I was, but because of it. I was so wrecked I was barely making sense.

I said to myself, *concentrate*. Don't get caught up in emotion. Just concentrate, swim normally, and you'll get there. With an 8-knot current, you only had one shot at hitting the ladder that signified the official end of the swim. If you missed it you were up against the current to get back, and even the thought of that was too painful to bear. I knew there were two people close behind, so the heat was on. When my right arm finally hit the ladder, I clutched it as if my life depended on it.

I heard people clapping and cheering above me. Then I heard someone say, 'James works with the tax office.' I didn't get too many claps after that! But I was blocking it out anyway. 'My Heart Will Go On' by Celine Dion was playing over and over in my mind. It wasn't something I'd planned, but the song summed up the day so beautifully that it just sort of came to me. All the trials and tribulations we'd been through – the arguments, the injuries – I'd pulled through them all. I was here, now. I looked over my left shoulder towards the Statue of Liberty and I said to myself, 'I have survived.' And I didn't know it at the time, but I'd just completed the second part of the so-called 'Triple Crown': the English Channel, the Manhattan Island Marathon and the Catalina Channel.

Shelley's voice snapped me back to reality. 'James! Let's hurry this up!' A German swimmer was fast approaching, and I didn't want to be the guy that got in the way of his grabbing the ladder. As I climbed, I hit my nose on the ladder and felt the warm trickle of blood against my lips. When I got to the top of the ladder, Shelley grabbed me excitedly and nearly knocked me back over the edge. The doctor looked me over and said, 'The blood nose isn't ideal, but you'll live. Your heart and everything else is fine. Congratulations!'

Andrew Peken, who was working as a lawyer in New York, came down to congratulate me. He'd planned to see me finish, but, thanks to my pessimism, had missed it. I'd told him it would take me at least eight and a half hours, but in the end it took 7 hours and 53 minutes.

Someone asked me, 'How do you feel?' After the pressure of the past few months, I was so emotional I couldn't even find the words. Instead, I said, 'Look, in forty-seven weeks, I've swum the English Channel, Perth to Rottnest Island and Manhattan Island and completed them all in the first attempt.' I left it to them to work out how I felt! Between my physical exhaustion and the intense emotion, I could scarcely hold in the tears. And I wasn't the only one. After kayaking 51 kilometres with a bad back, Narelle was in total agony. She could barely move. More than any other swim I can remember, we were all so relieved to get out of the water.

We had a very enjoyable finish to the day. The team got a chance to thank and congratulate each other, and we had a photo taken together. Later that night I was presented with a trophy. Spirits were high and drinks were free flowing, but when I looked at Narelle I realised we couldn't stick around no matter how many people tried to convince us otherwise. Her back was completely stuffed and she was almost in tears. We all went back to the unit together. After everything we'd been through leading up to the swim, it was a show of solidarity. Every team goes through some tough times, but we'd got through, and we were all the stronger for it.

It hadn't been easy. For the first time in my life, I had thought I was going to fail an event. And with good reason. If I'd swum like that in the English Channel, I know I would have failed. But I still had reason to be proud. When we reached the Hudson, I was down and out. My shoulder was barely working and my mind had sunk into the depths of self-doubt. But I picked myself up, and I got it done.

The next morning I was very sore, and Narelle could hardly move. But she and I ventured out with Tony, Sticks and the documentary crew to see a friend of Tony's in Long Island. We had a lovely barbecue with them, but what I'll always remember most was not the lunch, but the trip. It was 13 June, Puerto Rican day, and ironically, whistles were blowing from every direction at a time when I would happily have never heard another whistle for the rest of my life.

We went out to Long Island on the subway, and it was one the most nerve-wracking experiences I've ever had. I'd heard so much about the subway in New York, good things and bad things, but nothing can prepare you for the actual experience of trying to navigate a sea of moving people in the dark. Don't get me wrong, I love New York. But the convergence of all these people in the one place unsettled me like nothing else, and I really didn't handle it well. Things were coming at me from all directions, and with every passing moment I felt more nervous. While we waited, a Puerto Rican lady was singing on another platform. When we eventually got in the train, a heavily pregnant woman came along the carriage begging for money, and that frayed my nerves even more. I felt genuinely terrified. It was only four stops, but it felt like an eternity. Even after we got out, it was still a long walk underground to get to our exit. A couple of kids were playing basketball along the way and it rekindled my anxiety all over again. I just had to get out of there. Finally we did.

We spent the next morning hanging out in Central Park, and I just loved it. It was a melting pot of incredible personalities, only unlike the subway, there was masses of space for everyone to just enjoy the park at their own pace and in their own way. People were painting landscapes, visiting the zoo, having picnics, playing sports... just all enjoying life in their own way. At one point Sticks went off foraging for food, and a poet saw me alone and started reading me poetry. Of course, I wasn't alone – the documentary crew were nearby as always. But it was about 5 minutes by the time he finally realised he was being filmed. He took it well, but it must have been pretty disconcerting and it was the least I could do to buy some of his poetry.

But as wonderful as our time in Central Park was, Times Square was the scene of my most treasured memory of New York. An 8-foot African-American guy came out of nowhere and asked who I was. I told him the first thing that came to mind: 'I'm James; I'm from Sydney; I swam around Manhattan Island; I'm blind.' In an instant he made a 1-minute song that rhymed perfectly and included every bit of information I'd given him. Right there on the spot. Then, as quickly as he'd appeared, he was gone. I was dumbfounded. I never even got a chance to thank him. But my trusty documentary crew, who never missed a beat, immortalised it on camera. What a moment.

The time came for us all to go our separate ways. I flew down to the Green River in Utah, where I'd signed up for six days of white water rafting with a bunch of complete strangers. At first I was a bit daunted, but I quickly settled in and had a great time getting to know everyone. Each night we'd camp on the side of the river and hike around the area a bit, then each morning we'd gather our gear and get back out there on the white water. When I inevitably fell out of the raft I felt as if I should have been scared, but as I drifted down the rapids all I could do was laugh. We had so much fun. It was an outstanding trip.

I arrived back in Australia after three weeks. On reflection, things had turned out well. But Manhattan taught me that you should never be complacent. Just because you overcome one challenge doesn't automatically mean you're going to overcome the next. Just because you've swum the English Channel doesn't mean you can cruise around doing other swims as if they're nothing – even if the rest of the world seems to think you can! Every swim is a different game, a different day, a different time, a different set of conditions; and when you front up and swim you've got to be ready for anything. It changed the way I approached swimming events forever. Complacency was no longer part of my vocabulary.

In spite of plenty of evidence to the contrary, it took a long time before I stopped thinking of myself as a mediocre swimmer. The English Channel was the first step towards giving myself the credit I now realise I deserved all along. Completing the English Channel comes with a certain responsibility. From then on, anything less than 100% effort is unacceptable. Every swim, you've got to be ready not just to do it, but to do it well. You learn how to use your mind and your body to get through these swims even when it feels impossible. You learn to put everything behind you: your past, your problems, your pain. You have to.

But until the Manhattan Island Marathon, I'd never really thought about it in those terms. Manhattan was one of my greatest victories. When my body was ready to give up, my mind took up the slack. I focused, and I got through it. I showed a grit and determination I didn't even know I had in me. I finally had to accept that the underdog tag no longer applied to me, and it never would again.

## Chapter 9
## Martha's Vineyard

When I got back from the Manhattan swim in June 1999, Shelley told me about a 25-kilometre swim in Hawaii that she was keen for me to be a part of. I started training, and I found myself really looking forward to it. But I had forgotten the FINA rules of open-water swimming. The rules that had already cost me entry into the National Open Water Swimming Championships in Brisbane earlier that same year. According to FINA, using a whistle in open water swimming is deemed assistance. God knows why, but it is. You can have a coach on a kayak next to you screaming anything they like for hours on end. But if you blow a whistle, that's 'assistance'. I was never going to be able to do the swim. But that had somehow escaped my memory at the time. I don't know, maybe I'd blocked it out! Anyway, I had Felicity send my application form off in September and waited for a response.

A few weeks later Mum called me at work and asked, 'Do you know a girl called Debbie Taylor?' I racked my brain but it didn't ring a bell. 'She rang from America at 4 am and left a message.' As soon as the time zones permitted, I gave her a call back, assuming she was on the committee for the Hawaii swim. But she quickly set me straight. 'No, I'm not from the Hawaii swim,' she said. 'I live in Boston.'

'Wait on. Aren't Boston and Hawaii like 4,000 kilometres apart? Who are you? How do you know who I am?'

'I'm an open-water swimmer. I got your e-mail and I read your application. I know all about you. And I must say, I'm impressed! I know you want to do the Hawaii swim, and don't worry, I'll make sure your application gets to the right people. But I couldn't pass up the opportunity to ask – do you want to come and do a swim with me next July? It's from Martha's Vineyard to Nantucket.'

Fat chance, lady, I thought. I had no idea who she was or how she'd even got my contact details. (I would later find out that she had a huge number of contacts in the 'open water fraternity'.) But I ended up saying I'd swim with her. Chances were it wouldn't go anywhere anyway.

My Hawaii application did eventually get to FINA, not that it was of any use to me either way. Their rules were ridiculous, but they were set in stone. The Hawaii swim was off, and that was that. Suddenly we had nothing to work towards, and it wasn't a concept any of us were comfortable with. So I sat down with Ian Byrne, Brooke, Narelle, Shelley, and Sticks, and we set ourselves a new goal. On 12 December, we would break Graham Bruce's record of twenty laps swum between Manly Beach and Queenscliff Beach. At least, that was the plan! The distance between the beaches was about 1.6 kilometres and, barring any horrifically unexpected conditions, we reckoned I could do twenty-five laps pretty comfortably.

The day came, and with it the horrifically unexpected conditions we'd joked about. The sun was blazing and 30-knot southerlies howled from the south, daring me to challenge them. In one direction they would feel like no more than a soft, comforting breeze, gently pushing me forward. But in the other, they would surge against me like a demonic force of nature. For every 10 minutes spent swimming comfortably, there were 40 minutes spent bashing myself into oblivion. No sooner would I finish the hard slog than I'd be back where I started. It was a never-ending cycle of anguish and relief.

I did twenty-three laps. A lot of people got in and swam with me, and on the twenty-third lap it was my sister by my side. By this stage I was obviously getting a bit fatigued, and even the easy laps weren't easy any more. We were with the breeze for this one, and when Buffy turned and told me to 'get on with it' I could have throttled her! As I turned to start the twenty-fourth lap, I felt the harsh wind slap against my face and decided it wasn't worth it any more. I'd already broken the record; anything from here on out was just masochism! After 11 hours and 37 minutes, it was time to call it a day. I made the record. But just like all records, it's there to be broken. As good as it feels to hold it for now, I'd be sorely disappointed if I was never outdone.

I swam into North Steyne to an amazing reception. Mum, Dad, and a crowd of other people clapped me in. I got back to shore with relief plastered all over my face. That and exhaustion. It was a rewarding day and I was grateful to have had something to take my mind off the fact that I should have been in Hawaii, but by the end I was mentally and physically beaten, to say nothing of the blistering sunburn. For days the imprint of my goggles was stamped across my face. But Brooke fared even worse, even copping a comparison to a stop sign from the mayor of Manly!

Three weeks later, on New Year's Eve 1999, while we were out at Balls Head watching the fireworks to bring in the new millennium, on the other side of the city the unthinkable had happened. At the age of 72, Des Renford had suffered a fatal heart attack at Maroubra pool. The next morning was perfectly warm, but I couldn't shake the chills. My hero was dead. While everyone around me celebrated, I felt like the sky was falling in.

Then on 22 January, while I was still reeling from Des' loss, my great mate Ched Towns died of altitude sickness while trying to climb Mount Everest. He was only 50. He was the main person who got me involved in blind sports to begin with. Without him, I wouldn't be me. And now he, too, was gone. I knew he would have died a satisfied man – what better way to go than reaching for the stars – but it didn't make it any easier to accept. Within twenty-three days I lost two of the most influential people in my sporting life.

Four days after Ched's death was Australia Day, and I was to give a speech at Kogarah as an Australia Day Ambassador. It was going to be hard to get up there while my emotions were still running high, but I knew that both Des and Ched, two incredible Australians, would have been proud to see me do it. In fact, it was Des that got me into the Australia Day Ambassador program.

Des Renford gave me many things in my life. He gave me the opportunity to cross the English Channel, which at that point was the greatest moment in my life. He was a great mentor to me and gave me so much priceless advice that I have carried with me throughout my life. But I will also be forever grateful that he got me involved with the Australia Day Ambassador program – something I consider to be one of the greatest things in my life.

Des was on the Australia Day Council Board, and in late 1998 he invited me to become an Ambassador. I didn't even know what that meant, but by the time Des was done explaining, I was in. On Australia Day, Ambassadors visit communities throughout New South Wales and give a 10–20 minute Australia Day address. You speak to locals, you attend community events and you get involved with raising awareness. When John Trevillian founded the program in 1989 he garnered seven ambassadors. Since then, the organisation has grown to one hundred and seventy just in New South Wales.

Through the Ambassador program, I've experienced places I would never have dreamed of going. Places I would never even have heard of! I've met wonderful people, the salt of the earth, and been treated like a saint. I've met other ambassadors, people who share the same passions. And the experiences that come along with it are like nothing else! A bush poetry reading, a tractor festival, a horse-drawn cart ride, thermal pools, speeding a truck through a paddock… the list goes on. I love doing it, I love giving my time. It's one of my favourite times of year.

I'll never forget my first assignment in 1999 – West Wyalong. Keen to give a good impression, I turned up in a suit and tie on a 35-degree morning. Needless to say, I was the only one! But my speech was received well despite the fact that a rooster was crowing behind me through most of it, and I got to give out all the Australia Day awards. I was asked to be involved in tug-of-war, but someone vetoed that, and fair enough. When you match a 6-foot-3 blind man up against a bunch of kids, someone's bound to get hurt!

I was also called upon to judge the winners of the damper and lamington competitions. You could not have found anyone less qualified. People always say that when you lose one sense, your others are heightened. Well, that certainly doesn't apply to me. Nine dampers were lined up in front of me, and God as my witness they all tasted exactly the same. I said, 'Number five's the one.' Oh, the repercussions! An eighty-two-year-old lady, a West Wyalong institution, had lost for the first time in nineteen years. All because of me. I could only hope the lamington competition was a bit easier. It wasn't, at least in terms of distinguishing between the entrants. But at least I didn't shatter someone's reputation! It was a really memorable day, and from that point on I knew I would continue to be an Ambassador. I just love it.

Unfortunately, that year the Australia Day address I'd worked so hard on was just 5 minutes squeezed in before the citizenship ceremony. But the day wasn't over yet. I had also been nominated for Ku-ring-gai Citizen of the Year, and I had to come straight from Kogarah to Bicentennial Park for the presentation. I arrived with about 2 minutes to spare and no speech prepared. On cue, Dad said, 'I hope you've got a speech prepared, 'cause you might win this.' I said, 'A speech? I haven't even had a shower!' I brushed it off. It's not that I don't like winning, it's just that I knew the criteria and I knew there were plenty of nominees more worthy than me. But 10 minutes later, it was my name that they called out. Dad raised his eyebrows. 'I guess you'd better think of a speech pretty quick then!'

I took the stage, and Ku-ring-gai's Australia Day Ambassador, Little Patty, gave me the award. Here I was, still wearing my Kogarah Ambassador jacket, completely lost for words. I could barely process everything that had happened over the past few weeks. But somehow I managed to put something together! I ended my speech by raising my head to the sky and just saying 'Thanks guys.' Nobody in the audience knew who I was talking to, but if Des and Ched were up there somewhere, I know they heard it. Then I took my award, and I walked away. Once the shock wore off, I was absolutely stoked. It was a lovely way to finish an Australia Day.

I know some people will be reading this wondering whether I have even considered what 'Australia Day' means for the original owners of this great land. I have. Indigenous Australians deserve so much more than what this country, this government, is willing to give. We need to put more effort into commemorating and promoting significant Indigenous events, such as the 1967 Australian referendum on 27 May that recognised Australian Aborigines as part of the Australian population and permitted the Federal Parliament to legislate specifically for them. We need to get involved with events that support the ATSI population, particularly NAIDOC week, which celebrates the history, culture and achievements of Aboriginal and Torres Strait Islander peoples. But taking away Australia Day is not the answer. It's too important.

One year, a struggling farmer came from 120 kilometres away with his two-year-old daughter just to hear me speak. What a fantastic thing. It made me realise how important these kinds of programs are for people living out in the country. If I hadn't been there that day, he would have continued going about his normal day of work, all alone. Don't get me wrong, farming is a noble pursuit. But we are a social species, and we need human contact just as surely as we need food and water. Say what you want about Australia Day, it brings people together. I already had a great love and respect for the Australia Day Ambassador program, but that day cemented it like nothing else. People in rural areas need this. They need a reason to escape the daily grind, to celebrate, to come together for a common cause. For that reason if no other, I hope the program can continue to do its great work. Taking Australia Day away from white Australians does nothing to support ATSI communities and will only create conflict. Instead, we need to broaden our reach to embrace all Australians, white and Aboriginal.

The new millennium had come on strong, hitting me with one of the most bizarre months of my life. I felt almost as if my life was directing me rather than the other way around. I didn't know where I stood or what could possibly happen next. The only way I knew how to deal was just to keep on swimming.

And so, about a month later I fronted up and did the Rottnest swim for the third time. I felt utterly destroyed before I even started the swim. With the anguish of the December swim fresh in my mind and the pain of losing my two good friends still smarting, my sense of optimism was all but gone. When I got in the water to start the swim I did so without a plan, without any real aim other than just to get it done. It was a bit of a different experience, going into a swim really not having prepared. I mean, I'd done what I could, but really, Rottnest had been a minor priority what with everything going on at home.

Ironically, it was the best time I've ever done in six Rottnest swims: 7 hours and 42 minutes. The conditions were lovely and I was very lucky. But I think my free and easy attitude played a major part as well.

At the end of the swim I stood on the shore at Rottnest and looked out towards the horizon, remembering my friends. I didn't want to move. I didn't want anyone to come near me. I just wanted to be alone with my thoughts. I'd thought I was doing the swim for nothing, but now that it was over, I had a real sense of having done it for them. For Des, for Ched, and also for my parents, without whom I would have just completely fallen apart those past seven weeks. But when you finish a swim like that, you don't get to be alone. Shelley dragged me over to the food and drink tent to recharge, but it took a bit of coaxing.

In retrospect, the swim was cathartic. After everything that had happened, I really needed it. It was as if the swim had just released the misery and helplessness I'd been feeling, and I'd come out of the water renewed. I felt happy for the first time in seven weeks, and it reaffirmed my appreciation for the incredible friends I still had to be thankful for. I had a quiet, perfect night with my team.

I came back to an e-mail from Debbie, confirming after four months of no contact that the swim (Martha's Vineyard to Nantucket Island) was on. Oh, yeah.... that. I'd never really meant it when I said yes, but my work situation meant I wouldn't have had a hope anyway. In early July I'd be working in inquiries just after the introduction of GST – the biggest change to tax in living history. Asking for leave would not be received well. I explained all this to Debbie and told her I wouldn't be able to come.

A few days later I was at a party chatting to Andrew Peken, who was in town for someone's birthday. He looked at me incredulously and said, 'You said no to that?' And he wasn't alone. Nobody seemed to be able to believe it. With the power of popular opinion, I reconsidered. Maybe they were right. Was I crazy to turn this down? I'd been invited to do an open-water swim with another swimmer – something I'd never before had the opportunity to do.

You get very few major opportunities in life, and when one arises, you should take it. If you're given an opportunity and you don't take it, you've made a mistake. But if you get the same opportunity again and you still don't take it, you're a fool. Maybe it will go well and maybe it won't, but when you get to the end of your life you want to be able to say, no matter how it turned out, at least I took my opportunities. I didn't miss out on anything for not having the guts to try. You're far more likely to regret the things you didn't do than the ones you did.

In 1972 Shane Gould won three gold medals, one silver and one bronze at the Munich Olympic Games. Then, for the next six Olympics she didn't even try out. I'm sure it wasn't easy to find the money and time to make it work, but when she came back and tried out for the 2000 Olympics, I believe that, twenty-eight years later, she was trying to make up for all those missed opportunities. She didn't make the team. I often wonder how different things might have been in Australian swimming if Shane had gone to the 1976 Olympics in Montreal. If she'd won three, four, five gold medals again, how might things have changed? In 1976 Australia didn't win any gold, and our poor performance was what spurred then-Prime Minister Malcolm Fraser to set up the Australian Institute of Sport in Canberra. The AIS has since produced a great many gold medallists and world champions. If Shane had won multiple gold medals in 1976, what would it have meant for the progression of Australian sport? We'll never know.

I say you get very few opportunities, but I've had many, mainly because of my parents' support, being able to live at home as long as I did, and having a great, stable job at the tax office. I've been incredibly lucky that I can even afford to do these swims. And that's why I love giving back to the community so much – through The Fred Hollows Foundation, the Rainbow Club, the Australia Day Ambassador program, and so many other wonderful charities. I love giving to people because people have given so much to me.

It took no more than a few minutes before I changed my mind. I went in to work the next Monday, charged straight into the manager's office, and asked for two weeks off in July. I'd built it up so much in my mind that I was truly shocked when it was granted, just like that. I walked out looking like a happy idiot with a big smile across my face. I rang Debbie and the minute she picked up I blurted, 'I'm coming!'

The swim was to raise funds for the Martha's Vineyard Aquatic Center. This would be one of the greatest swims of all time – well, in my humble opinion. As far as we knew, we would be the first people ever to do this swim – 26 kilometres from Chappaquiddick Bridge on the East Island of Martha's Vineyard to the tiny island of Nantucket. It would be an adventure like no other. Yet still I had a really hard time convincing people to come with me. Tony and Felicity had left the team after Manhattan Island, and Brooke and Narelle were busy with the Olympics and the Paralympics. Eventually Sticks put his hand up, and we managed to sway Sticks' mate Bernie Burrows at the last minute. Bernie was a dedicated member of the North Steyne Surf Club, an amazing swimmer and an amazing kayaker. We were very happy to welcome him onto our little team.

About three weeks before the swim, Debbie sent me an e-mail that made my heart sink. She was having trouble getting boats to accompany us on the swim. After the turmoil of actually making the decision to come, I was irritated. She had given no indication that this was a potential problem. I'd thought convincing me was the only obstacle. Apparently the real problem was timing. We were going to have to move the swim on account of the annual shark fishing competition, of all things.

'It's not that bad,' Debbie said, 'We'll just have to do our swim the day after the shark fishing competition. There'll be heaps of boats around then; one of them's bound to help us out.' I almost died. Not only was I potentially going to have to try to rearrange the leave work had very generously agreed to, I was also basically agreeing to act as shark bait.

I said to Debbie, 'Who else knows about this?'

'You, me, and the *Boston Globe*.'

Far out. Should I tell my team? In the end I decided to keep the whole thing to myself. I'd made the decision to do the swim. I'd taken leave. I'd gotten Sticks and Bernie on board. One way or the other, I was doing this, and telling them the situation would only make them worry.

A week before we left, Mum woke me up and said, 'You're in the *Sun-Herald*! Isn't that fantastic?' But something in her voice told me there was more. 'There's three things wrong with it though. It says you've already left to go to Boston, yet here you stand. It says that you're twenty-eight years of age, yet I know for a fact you're thirty-one. And finally, it says you're swimming the day after the annual shark fishing competition. What a joke!'

'Well,' I said, 'you're right about those first two things. But the last one is correct.'

Dad, who was listening in from the kitchen, called out, 'Will you have a shark cage?'

'Nope.'

He chuckled. 'Well, good luck!'

No anger. No disappointment. No reprimand. Just 'good luck'. It wasn't the response I'd expected, and the next night I found out why. I came home from the pool, sat down at the dinner table, and at first I was so hungry I didn't even notice the sombre mood. Then Dad said he had something to tell me, and I knew straight away that something terrible had happened.

As Dad gave me the news that he had been diagnosed with a serious illness, it was as if I lost the power of speech. I had no idea what I was supposed to do with this information. I just kind of froze up. I knew the worst-case scenario, but I couldn't comprehend it. I wanted to ask questions, but I didn't know where to start. Dad didn't give me a chance anyway. He just said, 'I'd love you to continue the swim with the American lass', got up from the table, and left the room. I felt hopeless, but I couldn't afford to wallow. Not now. I had a decision to make. If I was going to pull out of this swim I had to let everyone know now. They would understand, but they needed an answer sooner rather than later. What was I going to do? Fittingly, I reminded myself of an old adage Dad had always lived by: sleep on it. Never risk a rash decision by not thinking something through. So that's what I did.

First thing in the morning I turned on the radio, and on came 'The Last Song' by Elton John. I'm a bit of a channel surfer, so I switched to another station, just to suss out my options. And on came the same song – a song about the love between father and son overcoming the odds. How unlikely. How apt. Suddenly I knew what I had to do. I touched the Australian flag on my door and said, 'Let's do this.' Ever since, the song always moves me to tears.

Training continued as usual. For the first few days after finding out about Dad my concentration was woeful, but Narelle knew what had happened and she cut me some slack. She was the only one that knew. I'm a very private person (yes, writing this book has been a massive challenge) and I didn't want anyone to know what I was going through. I didn't understand how I felt about the situation myself; the last thing I needed was a million people asking me about it. I knew my family would keep me up to date with Dad's treatment while I was away, but it was still unbelievably hard leaving the country with the situation as it was. Dad, on the other hand, was completely comfortable with my decision. He really wanted this for me. And to this day I'm so glad I could do it for him.

By the time I got to the airport I was in the right headspace. I knew I'd made the right decision going ahead with the swim. I just knew. Dad took me to the airport. Neither of us said much, but when we hugged goodbye the tears said it all. The fact that he still wanted me to do this swim even with everything that was going on with him… it's the kind of dad he's always been. His kids come first, no matter what.

We stayed at Narragansett House, a cute little B&B with beautiful original architecture. The owners were very sweet and would come down to the beach every day to watch me swim.

Even though we didn't stay with them, Debbie's parents Buck and Marianne and her sister Lauren were elated that we'd come to swim with Debbie and were just so welcoming. I've never seen anyone so delighted to play host. Every time we went somewhere they were always around, always looking for a way to help us out. They made it a very special trip.

After the turmoil of the past week, I think a week away in Martha's Vineyard was just what I needed. It was good to get away from Manly, from work, from home. Even though we were busy with training, interviews, and all the rest of it, I was feeling more relaxed with every day. Keeping busy kept my mind off what was going on at home. I just focused on being in the moment, enjoying the island and its fun-loving people. And laughing! I hadn't laughed for a week.

One day, Bernie and I had a swim together at State Beach and before we knew it we couldn't see our beach anymore. We'd swum into the next beach without even realising! How were we going to get out of this? We eventually had to stumble up the sand, clamber over a wall and walk all the way back down the road in nothing but our cossies! Sticks had worked out what had happened and about halfway between the beaches we ran back into him. 'What were you doing?' Sticks demanded. 'We swam for a bit, I looked up, and all of a sudden we were on the next beach!' Bernie explained between fits of laughter. It was a pretty meagre explanation, but it was all Sticks was getting!

Meanwhile, Debbie was constantly busy organising things for the swim. Every day she'd scheduled some sort of interview, everywhere from a hair salon to the boat. We had a lot of fun doing the interviews, and garnered a fair bit of interest in our swim but not nearly as much interest as had been generated back home! Before I left Australia I had done an interview with Sally Loane from ABC Radio, and the minute I mentioned we were doing this swim at the end of the shark fishing competition the number of listeners started growing exponentially! The ABC kept up with my story while I was overseas, and they were thrilled when I finally finished without being taken by a shark, though I wonder whether some of the listeners might have found it to be a bit of an anticlimax! Barely a day went by that there wasn't someone at home wanting to talk to me. If it wasn't the media, it was some other friend or acquaintance with some piece of advice, at best useless and at worst disparaging.

Barely a day went by that Shelley wasn't on the phone barraging us with questions. 'Does he know the tides? Does he know what he's doing? Does he know who he's swimming with?' I'm sure she was only trying to be encouraging and maybe I took some of her comments a bit out of context, but at times I ended up really exasperated. Then again, I had to cut her a bit of slack because she obviously didn't know the pressure I was going through with my dad's health. I resolved to use her words to my advantage. I turned the frustration into motivation, and in the end I think it actually did help me along.

Debbie had organised a cocktail night in Boston just before the swim to promote it and help raise a bit of extra money for the Aquatic Center. She rounded up a lot of her friends and got some members of the press to come along, and it ended up being a very successful night. It was a great idea, but unfortunately my enduring memory of the night is not quite so great! At one point the bartender made Debbie and me a gin cocktail, which seemed like a nice gesture. But as soon as the liquid hit my lips, my mind started running through all the possible ways I could dispose of it. It was absolutely disgusting and I imagined Debbie felt the same way. But what could we do? We were trapped in front of the camera, smiling and doing an interview. We had no choice but to continue drinking this terrible, terrible cocktail. The minute the cameras stopped rolling we both exploded with a combination of coughing and laughter. I don't think I'd be able to replicate the foul taste they came up with if I tried.

We always knew the swim was going to depend on the tides. We wouldn't even be able to start unless we had a south-westerly at five knots at 8.30 am. It was a pretty specific requirement, and I knew it meant there was a chance the swim might not go ahead. It would be disappointing for me, but after all the immense organisation Debbie had done – boats, press, promotion, parties, doctors, guns (as a shark contingency plan!) – it would be devastating for her. She had gone to an enormous amount of effort, and my anxiety doubled on her behalf. Between Debbie's preparation, Dad's illness and the onslaught of unsolicited advice I was getting from home, I knew the pressure was on.

When I was younger, Dad always used to prepare me for tough days by filling my belly with food. 'The prisoner ate a hearty breakfast', he would tell me confidently. And that next morning, his voice in my mind, I did just that. We left Narragansett House with bated breath. We got on the boat at the North Wharf of Edgartown and travelled around to our starting point at Chappaquiddick Bridge. We arrived at 8 am, and the conditions were just what we needed – a 5-knot south-westerly, 20 degrees water temperature, and the tide due to start at 8.32. You couldn't have asked for better conditions. And unlike in Australia, when the wind comes out of the south-west in Martha's Vineyard, it stays that way. We were just plain lucky. I'll always admit that. I walked up to the top of the beach and ran through the plan in my head. For the first time in two weeks, the training, the interviews, the pressure, and the issues at home became no more than background noise. Now it was all about swimming.

Bernie was obviously on the same wavelength. He said, 'I just want you to focus on today. Think about how you want to swim, and what you need to do to get there. Forget about everything else.' Bernie's one of the most relaxed guys I know, but when it's time for business there's no one better to have on your side. It was excellent advice, and it's exactly what I did. Anything could happen, and I knew that from the start. A 180-kilogram shark had been caught the day before (I wasn't sure whether to find that frightening or reassuring!). But I made a conscious decision to just enjoy it. I let go of the pressure I'd been feeling. And I got out there.

The boats dropped us off and we made our way to shore. Debbie and I took off together. Charlie Blair, the Edgartown Wharf harbourmaster who had organised the swim, had to calculate how and when we needed to change directions based upon the tides. Debbie and I told him we could swim at 2 miles an hour, and he worked out the plan based on that. Turns out we were dreaming! The whole way he was continually adjusting the calculations – all in his head, mind you – and changing our course. It was very impressive. At first the currents sent us well off course, which really confused Charlie, but he got us back on track pretty quickly. He had to. We had very little margin for error, because if the current came back right at the end, it could push us back to where we started.

Between Martha's Vineyard and Nantucket Island are many little islands, and when the wind gets up, the spray of the ocean can get up to 30 feet. About an hour in we came to a little island, and Debbie decided to veer left while I veered right. Debbie's a much better swimmer than me, and she'd been in front for the whole day. So I couldn't believe it when we got to the other side and I'd gone from 800 metres behind to 800 metres in front! She hit the white water and I didn't. That's all it was. Just the luck of the draw.

There were a few times throughout the swim that Bernie jumped into the water and I could feel and hear him swimming beside me. Or so I thought. But at certain points between Martha's Vineyard and Nantucket Island, it's very shallow, and I would find out later that Bernie wasn't swimming at all; the blighter was walking the whole time! Without the benefit of sight, all I had to go by was what I could feel and hear, and he put on a very convincing show. He was walking across the ocean floor flapping his arms around and feeling very satisfied with himself I'm sure! That was quite funny to find out later.

As time went on poor old Charlie was getting more and more stressed, because he could see the current starting to change, and if we didn't make it within the next hour, the tide would come back on us and we wouldn't make it. He had good reason to be concerned, because we'd never reached the purported 2 miles per hour. He was pretty aggrieved by the end, probably just exhausted from the constant mathematics going on in his brain. He told me later that he ended up with a bin full of paper with scrawled calculations by the end of the day.

I had a really good day swimming, and it was a blissful feeling when I eventually hit the sand at Nantucket Island. I could hear people clapping. Charlie was thrilled, because he could see the current was going to turn within about half an hour, and if we'd still been out there we would have never made it. And, thankfully, we hadn't encountered any sharks! As usual, I had to fend off people's advances to get above the tidal mark without being touched. But once it was official, Charlie, Bernie and Sticks came up and congratulated me. Amazingly, this 26-kilometre swim had taken me 7 hours and 53 minutes – the exact same time I'd taken to complete the 48-kilometre Manhattan swim. It just goes to show how good the current was in Manhattan.

I barely had time to get a drink and something to eat before a microphone was shoved in my face. It was pretty daunting, but I didn't know what else to do but oblige! I did a quick interview with an American TV station, and another two or three with radio stations. But the whole time all I could think about was, where's Debbie?

About 40 minutes later, Debbie finally arrived. As soon as I saw her emerge from the water, I could feel the tears starting to well up. She ran straight up to me and for about a minute we just stood there embracing, sharing six months' worth of emotion that no one else would or could understand. Tears running down our faces, we were a mess of sobs and giggles. We finally managed to compose ourselves enough to speak, and I thanked her for the invitation and the opportunity to do this incredible, rewarding swim together. We were so proud of not only our own achievement, but what we had done for Martha's Vineyard Aquatic Center – the difference we had made for generations to come.

I was glad we got that moment alone to give Debbie a chance to really let it sink in and enjoy the moment before the media swarmed her – a chance I, as the first to arrive, hadn't been given. You want time to settle, to go away and think about everything that's just happened. For me, it wasn't until we finally parted for her to go and greet her family and do some interviews that I got my chance to be alone and think about my dad.

When we got back to Edgartown Wharf, I rang Dad and told him we'd done the swim. He just said, 'You beauty!' From then on I did all the talking, because all I could get out of him was a few muffled sobs on the other end of the line. He was so delighted he could barely speak. But that meant more to me than anything he could have said. I was so happy for him. I'd done more for him here than I could ever have done at home. Dad did eventually make a full recovery, and I like to think that I played some small part in helping that happen.

Now we had to get back to Martha's Vineyard. Debbie decided she would go back on the sailing boat, but I went back on the main boat. I got back within a couple of hours, while Debbie was stuck out there for four or five. Well, I say 'stuck' – it might well have been her way of getting some time to herself! But it did mean she ended up being late to her own function. Ernie, Martha's Vineyard's very own trillionaire, had agreed to host a function at his beautiful five-storey home. The house was impressive, but I was just as blown away by the surrounds. The house was accessible via a kilometre-long Italian marbled drive – heated for the entire length, of course. Then as you got closer to the property you'd see his llamas. The place was full of surprises!

Because I'd made it back well before Debbie, I was making all the speeches, and although they were pretty well received, I could tell everyone was anxious for Debbie to arrive. One of the organisers of the event came up to Charlie and me at one point to ask how long we thought she would be, and when we said 'About another hour?' (we hadn't the faintest, really), she almost had conniptions. When Debbie did finally arrive, she was given a hero's welcome. She made a lovely speech about the whole process. I was given an award by a group of disabled people, which was the perfect recognition. It was a lovely evening.

At midnight, 19 hours after we had set out that morning, we were about ready to collapse. Unfortunate, then, that we had somehow got ourselves locked into Ernie's place! It wasn't the worst place to be stuck, but we were long since ready to escape the glitz and glamour and return to our ordinary lives. Bernie's wife Hillary wouldn't stand for it. She just took her marks, took a running leap, straddled the gate, and jumped over. I said, 'That's easy if you haven't just swum for 8 hours, matey!' Eventually, we all got around the gate, and went and had a couple of quiet drinks at the pub. The whole day had gone brilliantly.

The next day, it rained like nothing I've ever seen. A northeasterly wind was raging at 17 knots. We'd already felt lucky to get the conditions we did, but in contrast to the next day, we felt absolutely blessed. Someone upstairs had been looking after us.

On my last night in Boston, I was asked to do an interview for *Inspire America* with a blind interviewer. *Inspire America* is a TV show that features people who have overcome adversity to achieve great things. I had to get a cab in the pouring rain out to this place, 20 kilometres from Boston, and when I got there nobody even seemed to even know where I was supposed to go. Eventually a woman said to me, 'She just got in via the subway.' I had arrived before my interviewer! When I finally met her she asked, 'Do you mind if we have flowers or something?' I said, 'Well, who cares about that, you can't see them and nor can I.' Neither of us knew what to expect, and trying to conduct an interview with neither person able to see the other was indeed as difficult as it sounds! Even stranger, we were in the next room to some dog show, and for literally the entire interview, dogs were barking behind the wall. It was a very funny interview, and I think we both enjoyed it, but I was relieved when it came to a close all the same!

On the plane back to Australia they upgraded me to business class. The hostess kept giving me strange looks and eventually she said, 'You're the man I've been hearing all about on ABC radio! They've been trying to get onto you to make sure you're all right.'

'Well,' I said, 'For now they're just going to have to keep on trying!'

This swim was one of the great moments in my swimming career. There was the usual satisfaction that came from completing a challenging swim and raising money for a great cause, but this time there was something else. Something I'd never experienced before. For the very first time in my career, I had been treated as an equal. Debbie had invited me not because of my disability, but because of my ability. Not out of pity, but out of respect. And that meant an enormous amount to me. It always will.

But one of the other great things to come out of the swim was that I'd gained a lifelong friend in Debbie, and Debbie had gained an admirer in Charlie Blair. He ended up asking her out, and only seven months later, they married in an Episcopalian church in Boston. I didn't get to attend, but later that year they had their first child, Taylor, and they asked me to be his Godfather. I duly accepted.

A failed application to swim in Hawaii in October 1999 had somehow turned into one of the best and most rewarding experiences of my life. An email that went to the wrong inbox had turned into an incredible friendship that endures to this day. And a professional relationship had turned into a beautiful marriage and a gorgeous child that I am honoured to be Godfather to.

## Chapter 10
## Gibraltar

The year 2001 was just one long string of bad luck for me. Early in the year I'd been planning to swim from Scotland to Northern Ireland but it hadn't eventuated because Narelle had received an email from an elite American swimmer saying, 'He's got no hope of completing that! Way too risky.' What a nerve! She'd never even seen me swim. After the English Channel, Manhattan Island and Martha's Vineyard to Nantucket, not to mention three separate crossings of Perth to Rottnest Island, nobody could deny my experience. But she succeeded in convincing Narelle, and I never did swim Scotland to Northern Ireland. It was probably for the best. An Irish swimmer later told me nobody had ever completed the swim on their first attempt, and he had only made it halfway before giving in to the repeated jellyfish stings. I probably should have been thanking that American swimmer!

After that fell through, I planned a swim from Palm Beach to Manly Beach in July. I'd recently been named as an Ambassador for the Rainbow Club, and this would be my first contribution. My involvement with the club had only been brief, but already it was a cause I held close to my heart. So when 7-metre swells saw the event get canned the day before the swim, my heart sank.

I'd become involved with the Rainbow Club the previous year, when I was invited to their Christmas Party at Cronulla pool. It was an eye-opener, that's for sure. Even as I arrived, one of the kids was kicking and screaming by the side of the pool, just absolutely losing it. When I asked Rob what was wrong, he said, 'That's autism.' Crikey, I thought. I've got a lot to learn if I'm going to get involved with this club. Indeed, I would get quite an education. Many of the kids the Rainbow Club helps have cerebral palsy, Down's syndrome, or autism. It can take as long as six weeks just to get them in the water. For some children just putting their face in the water is a win. When you've just swum the English Channel, it takes a while to get your head around the fact that for some people, swimming a single lap is a monumental achievement. But as time went on and I spent more time with these kids, I came to realise that it *is* monumental. When a kid swims one lap after six months of fear and difficulty, that is more impressive than anything I've done. And when I hear these kids laugh and know that I helped put the smiles on their faces… well, it's a thrill like no other.

It's a real honour to represent such a worthy organisation. It's incredibly rewarding being part of a team of instructors who just love what they do, a board that gives everything they have, and ambassadors who will stop at nothing to raise the club's profile. Most people on the board don't have disabled children, yet still they work tirelessly to help those parents who do. I've said it a million times, but one of the things I love most about swimming is the inclusion. And that's what Rainbow Club is all about – making sure everybody gets a fair go. Ron Siddons, founder of the Rainbow Club, believes that in Australia, learning to swim is not a privilege, it's a right. He's spot on, and there can be no greater satisfaction than to fulfil basic human rights.

So, needless to say, I wasn't about to let the Rainbow Club suffer just because of some bad weather. I rescheduled the swim for November 2001, and before I knew it, the day arrived. It was another stormy day, but there was no backing out this time. I started at 6 am, and I figured it would take about 10 hours. I'd organised for all my friends and family to see me in at quarter to four, and even the Governor of New South Wales had agreed to do me the honour of coming down and congratulating me at the end of the swim. But I hadn't counted on a 50-knot tailwind. I swam in to find the beach practically deserted. Where was everyone? That's when I found out. 'You've stuffed the proceedings, James!' my club captain yelled. 'It's only twenty past one!' I had completed the swim in 7 hours and 25 minutes. What now? As I contemplated this, a lightning bolt made the decision for us. We were going indoors!

We went across the road to a café, but we were all pretty downcast about the way things had played out. Tony decided we should do a re-enactment, and when nobody offered any opposition to the idea it just sort of happened! Tony and I ran out from behind the café onto the beach, just as the bloke on the PA was saying, 'James is swimming strongly out there. He will be arriving at ten to four.' We were quick, but not quick enough. One of Tony's mates protested, 'But that's him there!' We made a quick getaway towards the other end of the beach, jumped in, swam from Queenscliff down to North Steyne, and arrived at ten to four right on schedule. But we weren't fooling anyone! With not a streak of sunscreen to be seen and a hint of chicken seasoning still staining the skin around my mouth, there was no way I was emerging from a 10-hour slog! But whether we fooled anyone or not, the re-enactment felt like a terribly dishonest way to round the event out and in the end we had to come clean. The combination of my early finish and the stormy day meant very few people turned up, and no media whatsoever. We raised some money for the Rainbow Club, but the whole thing felt very dissatisfying.

In February 2002 I fronted up to the Perth to Rottnest swim for the fifth time, but after a personal best in 2000 this was to be a very disappointing day. I arrived at the finish line after 9 hours and 3 minutes – 1 hour and 21 minutes longer than in 2000 – to find blood gushing from my right shoulder and pouring down my chest. I noticed a few parents covering their children's eyes, and I couldn't blame them – I looked like something from a horror movie. I knew straight away what had happened. I'd forgotten to shave. I always breathe to the right, so that shoulder was copping some serious abrasions. In the water I had no idea I was bleeding, but in retrospect I guess I'd been feeling pretty queasy from about the 6-hour mark onwards. The First Aid attendant patched it up, but it took a lot of bandaging! It's amazing the trauma that can result from simply turning your stubbled cheek against your shoulder. When I imagined how much blood I must have lost over the previous 3 hours I could hardly believe I was still standing, let alone having comfortably finished the swim.

The year 2001 had been a debacle and so far 2002 wasn't proving much better. I was due a success! I decided it was time to dream big. I would organise to swim the Strait of Gibraltar in six months' time. It would be quite an undertaking. The Strait of Gibraltar is 18 kilometres wide, and about sixty boats come down the channel every hour. From dusk to dawn you just can't be in the water. It's too dangerous. Anyway, directing a blind man around sixty boats an hour was never going to be easy even in the daytime. But the boats were the least of our worries – at least we could plan for them. The weather, that was our greatest enemy. The Strait is virtually impossible to cross unless the wind is with you. And when it isn't – when the weather decides to get up – you're stuffed. It's as simple as that. I knew from the outset how hard it was going to be, but that's partly why it appealed to me. And if I could do it, I would be the first Australian to swim between two continents.

The idea of planning the swim was all very romantic, but as always, the reality was a little less so. Trying to organise a swim with people who don't speak English is hard work at the best of times, but when you're trying to do it in the middle of the night, it's even harder. Thank goodness one of Dad's friends spoke Spanish. I'd send all my questions to him and he'd ring whoever it was I needed to speak to, ask all the questions in Spanish, write down the answers, and ring me back. We did this almost every night. It was a very long-winded way of doing things, but at least it meant we could get things done via phone rather than email. I've always preferred phone to email, because the person can't avoid you – they have no choice but to react.

We got there in the end, and in July 2002 I flew to Málaga, Spain with my team. Narelle was at the Commonwealth Games in Manchester, but I had Bernie, Brooke and Sticks by my side. From there we drove to Tarifa, where the swim would begin. On our first day there, it was the perfect weather for a swim, not a breath of wind. Fantastic! Well, that was as good as it got. For the next four days, the wind just got worse and worse. I thought I was going to end up just sitting indoors for a week then going home. It was frightening to think that everything I'd worked for might amount to nothing. But we continued training at the beach, just hoping for the best. The seas were high and the wind was ferocious, but it was either this or give up and go home. And that wasn't an option.

One evening I stayed home while the others went out for a drink, and I remember getting up in the middle of the night and hearing the wind thumping through the house so hard I was worried it would shatter the windows. That's it, I thought. No way this swim is happening. The wind will win. Every couple of days we would have a meeting with the swim organiser, Rafael, and each time he'd tell us to just keep on waiting and hoping. There was no negotiating – if the conditions weren't right, the swim would simply be too dangerous. Rafael was a great guy, but I've never known an 'organiser' to be so disorganised! We coined the term 'Spanish time' to refer to Rafael's special timeline that ran on a completely different plane to ours. He was late to every single meeting – apart from the one where we anticipated it and turned up late ourselves. That time he turned up right on the knocker. Typical.

Of course, Spanish time in general does take a lot of getting used to. Well, I say that as if I did get used to it – I didn't! The people turn in for their siesta around midday then get up at about 9 pm and party right through the night. Good luck having dinner at a reasonable time, and don't even bother trying to get a full night's sleep. I could never get it right. I enjoyed all the paellas and sangria though, and I managed to absorb a couple of Spanish phrases. Only the essentials, of course: *Estoy ciego*, 'I'm blind'. And *Cuatro cervezas por favor*, 'four beers please!' *Estoy ciego* came in handy when the locals called the police on us for using the loudhailer on a Sunday morning! After our two-word explanation they watched what we were doing for a minute – out of curiosity more than anything I think – and walked away.

The day came to swim the Strait of Gibraltar. Bernie and Sticks were on the inflatable Red Cross boat, and Brooke was sharing Rafael's little tinny with him. I felt woefully unprepared without a big main boat, but we made do with what we had. We knew in advance that the key to the swim is to get across the channel quickly. From there it's an easy swim on to Morocco. We got off to a good early start in Tarifa, but partway across the channel the tide changed. Bernie said, 'You're right in the middle of the channel and we're going nowhere fast. The tide is against you and so is the wind. If you don't get on with it we're going to have to call off the swim.' I poured every last drop of effort, but I got nowhere. In the end Rafael called it off.

Back we went to Tarifa. It was the first time I'd ever failed an open-water swim. I knew it was mostly down to the conditions, not my performance, but it was still hard to accept. At 18 kilometres, it was one of the easiest swims you can do. Maybe I'd gone in with a bit of complacency, I don't know, but I couldn't believe I'd let the current defeat me. I trudged back to the hotel and shared the fresh pain of failure with Narelle and my parents on the phone. They consoled me as best they could, but I still felt like I'd let them down. Bernie took me out for a walk around Tarifa to try to spark me up. 'Don't sweat it, James,' he said, 'that's the way it goes. You did a really good job. The currents and wind changed and there was nothing you could have done about it.' But it was never going to work. I was devastated.

The next morning I woke up and Brooke was waiting for me in the kitchen. The minute I stepped into the room I heard the legs of her chair scrape hard against the floor and I knew she was excited about something. 'If we can swap some flights around, in two days' time there's another opportunity for you to have a swim!' she told me. 'Rafael says he'll take you out again.' So two days later, again I started at Tarifa and this time the conditions were good and I got off to a great start. Our flights were now scheduled for the next day, and I knew this was my last chance. I put in 110% right from the word go, and I got across the channel.

Things continued to go well from there. The current and the wind were with me. I was dodging the boats comfortably. Everyone was having a great time. Then I heard Bernie say, 'Stop! Stop!'

'What's the matter?' I asked.

'You've made it.'

'No, I'm not at the beach.'

'You're not allowed to get to the beach, remember? If Rafael takes you to the beach, we'll be swamped with Moroccans wanting to escape from Morocco to Spain. We'd never get off the beach!'

I remembered, but I still wasn't convinced I'd finished the swim. Bernie said, 'Put out your left hand. What's that? What's that, James? It's a rock. And Rafael says that rock is in line with the headland of Morocco. He's officialised it. You've swum the Strait of Gibraltar in 4 hours and 51 minutes.'

You beauty! Bernie, Sticks and Brooke all dived in the water and we congratulated each other. This wasn't just my victory – every one of them had worked their guts out to make sure I brought this one home the second time around. Brooke was in the water about 2 seconds after it was made official. I didn't ask her why, but we all knew how badly she was busting for a wee! I was in the middle of thanking Rafael when all of a sudden Bernie said, 'Break it up everyone, we need to get back in the boats. Don't ask any questions. Just do it.' He was acting on instructions from the Red Cross boat. They'd seen another boat further out that had hit a rock and was sinking, and they wanted to get over there and save them. But they were too late, and two people drowned. When I heard the news I was plagued by guilt that our celebrations in the water might have been the difference between their being saved or not. The Red Cross guys said they probably never stood a chance anyway, but it still hit close to home.

I got back in Rafael's tinny and, as sad as I was for the families of the deceased, my overpowering emotion was of relief. Thank God, I thought. I've done what I've come to do. We slammed it back to Tarifa.

When I got back to the hotel the manager said, 'Did you do it?'

'I sure did.'

'Let's get your name on the board, then.'

I added my name to the hotel's honour board of everyone that had swum the Strait of Gibraltar during their stay. Then I rang

Mum and Dad and Narelle. What a relief to be able to tell them that my amazing and dedicated team had somehow managed to secure a second chance for me, and that time I'd finally brought it home.

We were all just so happy that the trip hadn't been for nothing, and I was forever grateful to my team for giving me another chance at this thing. We celebrated with a sumptuous meal and maybe a few too many sangrias! While we were out, we met a group of Americans who were going to do the double relay across the Strait of Gibraltar. One of their wives said, 'We're going to go watch.' Brooke laughed and said, 'You're going to sit in an open tinny with no toilet for 10 hours are you?' That wiped the smile off her face!

The next morning we all got up with a bit of a headache. We saw Rafael and got to say one final thank you. He was scouting out the conditions for the next group of swimmers, four Indians who didn't want to swim as a team but as individuals. He thought it was the world's worst idea but apparently they just wouldn't be told, so he was hoping the conditions would do the job for him.

I'd planned a few visits in quick succession before finally heading home, as I always do! First stop was England, where I stayed with my old Newington schoolmate Chris Colfer and his family for a couple of days. I then flew to Martha's Vineyard to see Debbie and Charlie. It really felt as if we'd never parted. We took up right where we'd left off and had an amazing time together. The timing was fortuitous, because I got to be there for their son Taylor's christening, which was a great honour. I'd known them both before they even got together, and to now be sharing in such a beautiful event was a real privilege. After a few days I headed to Maryland to see Debbie's parents Buck and Marianne, her sister Lauren and Lauren's husband Tom. They're such a beautiful family and I almost felt sorry to leave. But when I saw my parents at the airport all those feelings retreated. I was home.

I had spent 2002 with a personal trainer called Lucy. I got on really well with her, but everyone felt she wasn't getting the results I needed. I hadn't lost much weight, and my fitness still left a bit to be desired. Narelle insisted I needed someone different, so at the beginning of 2003 she introduced me to Matt Logan, an ex-kayaker who held the junior record for the 111-kilometre Bridge-to-Bridge event in Hawkesbury. Matt told me later that when Narelle had asked him to train me he'd been hesitant about what it would mean to train a blind person. But he took the job, and in early January 2003 we had our first training session together.

I too was hesitant about this new partnership. The decision to leave Lucy hadn't really been mine, so it was on Narelle to prove that this really had been the best thing for me. And when I fell off the assisted chin-up equipment and broke Matt's phone in our very first session, I think we both had to wonder! (Matt never brought his phone to any of our training sessions again.) We both knew we had a long road ahead of us, but from the first session – or at least from the second! – we have been the best of friends. From the very beginning, he almost never missed any of my swimming events. He's been an amazing kayaker for the team and an incredible mentor. But beyond that, he is just a great man. I was sad to see Lucy go, but changing to Matt was the right choice. We've had many great moments together, and I'm a far better swimmer for having him in my life.

Having my personal trainer be so involved not only in training but in all aspects of my career was a big change for me. He offered the complete package. It wasn't just about your weight, or your diet, or your training regime. It was about the overall picture, and nobody understood that like Matt. Matt always knew which specific exercises to prescribe to prepare me for an event. He would analyse my events for hours afterwards, working out what went right and what went wrong. At one event where I didn't swim particularly well, he apologised for not having trained me properly! I'm thinking mate, that's not your problem! It's the swimmer's job to swim well! I was astonished. But that's how intense he is about his job. That's how good a personal trainer he is.

The first event I did with Matt was the 2003 Perth to Rottnest Island swim in February. It was the most controversial swim I've done, definitely one for the record books. We went over the day before, and arrived to beautiful conditions: no wind, glassy water, and a perfect view from Perth across to Rottnest Island. I'd trained really well for this event, hadn't missed a single day in the pool.

This was my chance to break my personal record: 7 hours and 42 minutes in 2000.

On the morning of the swim I woke at 3 to the sound of footsteps. Sticks and Matt were going outside to see what the conditions were like. When they came back neither of them spoke. I knew that couldn't be good. At 4.30 I got up and was confronted by a thumping 25-knot wind and 4-foot chop at Cottesloe Beach. If the conditions were this bad already, they were going to be an absolute nightmare by the time the swim came around. The normal start time was 5.45, but at 5.30 they delayed it by half an hour.

All the boats were out there getting ready to move into position 2 kilometres off shore. A documentary crew asked me if I was going to swim. 'It's not up to me,' I said. 'It's up to my pilot. I'm not about to endanger him or any of my crew, so if the pilot says it's too dangerous I'll be back in my hotel, no questions asked.' The swim was supposed to be enjoyable and safe, and if it wasn't, I'd bow out. After doing it five years in a row, missing out wouldn't have bothered me too much. But our pilot said it was all systems go. The MC said over the loudspeaker, 'Think of the time you want to do and add 50%!' How true that would be! Normally the winner gets home in about 4 hours, but today the winner took 5 hours and 58 minutes. It was a long day.

And a controversial one. For the first time they put buoys at the 5-, 10- and 15-kilometre marks. At each point, you had to swim between two buoys about 200 metres apart. It was the first time they'd put these things out, and to this day I believe they put them out not to streamline the event, but to pull people out when they didn't make them by a certain time. It went against all my moral fibre.

But I had bigger fish to fry. With every single stroke I either missed the water altogether or got smacked in the face by a wave. Matt was struggling too, and more than a few people vomited. It was a very tough event. I just got smacked, mentally and physically. By the end I was distraught. But with Matt egging me on and Sticks doing a fantastic job with the feeds, I completed the swim in 10 hours and 3 minutes.

I didn't realise it at the time, but I was the last person to make it through the 15-kilometre checkpoint – everyone after me was pulled out. I was the sixty-sixth person to finish, from 172 starts. Normally they give you 10 hours and 15 minutes to finish the swim, so I was thrilled to have made it just in time. Or so I thought. But while the race had started half an hour late, they hadn't added that to the allowed finish time. They were claiming I was not 12 minutes shy of the allowable finishing time, but 18 minutes outside it. When I got to my feet to walk up the winning chute, I was shoulder charged out of the way by an official saying I hadn't made it in time. I hadn't officially finished the swim. He stood there resolute, refusing to let me through. In the end I had no choice but to back down.

Matt said 'James, I have seen something brilliant today. You held your form in absolutely terrible conditions. You take that extra 50% off your time you've got six and a half hours. That is an outstanding swim. You were let down by officials, but nobody can take away your achievement.' That was all very good in theory, but it wasn't much solace. I was sore, stiff, and intensely frustrated. I then found out that Narelle, who had been kayaking for another team, asked the officials on three separate occasions to be allowed through the official channel to come out and kayak with Matt to help me across the line, and every time, they refused. I suppose she could have gone around the official area, but by the time she did that we probably would have already made it across the finish line anyway. Narelle's only concern was safety, which should have been the number one priority for the officials as well. She knew Matt was giving his all, but the fact was we were starting to struggle, and all she wanted was to give us a bit of support. But the answer was no, loud and clear.

An hour later, they presented sixty-five people with a trophy. Everyone that finished – except me. After the presentation, I was having something to eat with my team, and my boat pilot came over to express his commiserations. 'That is one of the most disgraceful things I have ever seen,' he said. 'A blind man swims 10 hours and 3 minutes against 4-foot chop and gives his all, and they treat you like that. It's disgusting. For what it's worth, I feel honoured to have seen you swim today. It was a great swim.'

I took a lot of encouragement from that. Here's someone who'd never seen me swim before, and he'd really noticed me. He'd recognised the effort I'd put in. And as it turned out, he wasn't the only one. A lot of people came up to me afterwards and expressed their disappointment about what had happened. Disappointment not just about what had befallen me individually, but about what it said about the swim. It had gone from being a real community swim to being all about rules and regulations. In the past, they used to allow people to keep swimming (at their own risk) and finish as late as they wanted. You could come in at seven in the evening if you so desired. It used to be about supporting people to get out there and have a go. But not anymore.

I came back from the Rottnest swim feeling pretty defeated. But I wasn't totally ready to accept my fate just yet. I wrote letters to the President of the Rottnest Channel Swim Association and anyone else I thought might listen. In my favour was the fact that seventeen teams from the team division of the swim were going to sue the Association for not allowing them to finish as well. I kept up my tirade, and six weeks later a trophy and shirt arrived on my doorstep. I had finally been acknowledged as the sixty-sixth finisher. But I would never do the Rottnest swim again. It went from being one of the best-organised swims I'd ever been a part of in 1998 to one of the most disappointing experiences of my life in 2003. Even if someone begged me, I would never go back. The way I was treated that day was appalling. But I try not to let my experiences cloud others', and as disappointed as I was, I still admit that it's a great swim. In fact, I don't know if I would have been able to complete the English Channel without it.

When I finally got my trophy, it didn't feel as good as I hoped it would. I was glad to have been given my due, but a victory that takes six weeks to be recognised was bound to feel a bit hollow. Anyway, there was no time to dwell on events past – it was on to the next challenge.

## Chapter 11
## Monaco to Alcatraz

We had big plans for the next few months: a six-week, three-swim trip, kicking off in May 2003 with a swim from Bordighera, Italy to Monte Carlo, Monaco. I'd then go to Maryland for the Great Chesapeake Bay swim, and finish up in San Francisco with the Alcatraz swim. From there I would spend a couple of weeks holidaying in Europe and South America. Including a stopover in Kuala Lumpur, that made it five continents in six weeks.

The 22-kilometre Bordighera to Monaco swim was to raise money and awareness for the Laureus Sport for Good Foundation. It was scheduled for the day of their annual function, the forerunner for the Laureus World Sports Awards. Chris Colfer was working for Dunhill, a subsidiary of Laureus, and he arranged for them to sponsor me. Before I knew it, my airfares were paid, and they were contributing to the cost of accommodation and organising the swim as well. I couldn't believe my luck!

Sticks and I flew to Nice via Vienna. The layover was meant to be short, but we arrived in Vienna to a strike and ended up having to stay the night. Fortunately we managed to get a flight to Nice the next day, and a representative from the Sport for Good Foundation drove us all the way down to Monaco. But not a day passed before we were back at the airport again, meeting Matt and Narelle. Matt had hired a car and was going to follow our driver back to Monaco. But after a 24-hour flight, trying to get used to following a car at 100 miles an hour while driving on the wrong side of the road proved a bit of a challenge! He was in quite a state by the time we got back to the hotel, and his passengers weren't feeling so great either! We wound down at the Monaco racing track, where we had dinner at the top of a big tower that overlooked the track.

The next day, we went out to Bordighera to check out the course and get to know our pilot and boat. But when we went to check the finish line, there was oil slicked across the water as far as the eye could see and the gates into the finishing area were firmly closed. It looked like we wouldn't even have a chance to do the swim.

Fortunately, they managed to get the oil more or less cleaned up before the swim, and it was deemed safe. They opened the gates to the harbour, and we had a chance to practise the final leg of the swim. About 100 metres out from the beach was a roped-off area, and I would have to clear this rope to get to the finish. The first time I tried to swim up and over this rope was an absolute shocker. I got completely tangled in nets I didn't even know existed while the people of Monaco looked on bemused. We had a bit of a laugh thinking, God, if that's how well I can manage the thing now, how am I going to go after 6 or 7 hours? It was going to be fun and games, that's for sure. We went through the process another couple of times and calculated the number of strokes from the gates to the rope – 300 – and from the rope to the beach – another 50. And that was it. That was as much training as I was going to get!

We were back the very next morning for the real deal. We'd organised for the great Mark Spitz, nine-time Olympic gold medallist in swimming, to come down and see me finish, and I could barely contain my excitement. Chris Colfer came out in the boat with us, and even took a turn at kayaking for a little while. Having Chris involved was a real treat. I'd stayed with him for a few days the previous year, but this time we really got a chance to get to know each other again. And I was eternally grateful to him for teeing up the sponsorship deal for me.

We started at 11 am, aiming to finish by 4. I had a lovely breeze behind me and it looked as if we'd make it easily. After the first hour,

Narelle said, 'You're smashing it! Mark Spitz will have to get down there quickly if he wants to see you finish!' Thanks, Narelle. No sooner had she spoken than the wind did a full 180. Suddenly I was battling a massive headwind.

For a while, we barely moved. I swam on the spot for one and a half hours. Four pm came and went, and we were still miles from the finish. I kept swimming, but I shuddered to think how late we were going to get in. I just hoped we made it before dark. My mind fluttered from Mark Spitz to the Sport for Good Foundation dinner and back again. Who was I going to disappoint more, I wondered. Meanwhile, our fuel was running so low that Matt and Sticks had to take the inflatable boat to get more.

I was at the point of despair when suddenly I hit a current that was working for me. At that same moment, the wind let up. I travelled about a kilometre in what seemed like about 5 seconds. I was moving so fast that for a while there my team lost track of me. Next thing I knew, Narelle was telling me I was at the gates. You beauty! Three hundred strokes to go, I recalled. I counted as I went, but at number 300 I was still nowhere near the rope. That's how tired I was. But finally my fingers hit the rope. And, what do you know, I went straight over of the top of it, stroked my fifty strokes, and landed on the beach. It was the only time I got it right – but it was the only the time that mattered. I had made it to the end, and Mark Spitz would be waiting to welcome me. I was elated.

But when I arrived on the beach, the only people waiting to welcome me were a reporter and two women. Mark Spitz was nowhere to be seen. Where was he? I found out later that because we were so far behind, he'd had to leave and get ready for the Sport for Good Foundation dinner. It was disappointing, but of course I understood. He sent his regards, and that was enough for me. But as the reporter started interviewing me and the younger of the two women, for the life of me I still couldn't work out who these people were. It wasn't until two-thirds of the way through the interview that it finally dawned on me – this was the brilliant South African one-legged swimmer Natalie du Toit, and the other woman was her mother. I was so dumbfounded by the whole situation that I actually never even asked what they were doing there. I can only assume Mark Spitz had sent them down in his stead.

After the interview, Natalie's mother started fussing over me. 'All right love, let's get you some food. Let's get you warm.' I felt fine, but I let her feed me anyway! Then Sticks arrived. He congratulated me briefly, but there was no time for pleasantries. The Sport for Good Foundation dinner was starting in three-quarters of an hour.

We ran back to the hotel, got ready in record time, and made it to the dinner – just! We were literally surrounded by sports luminaries. At first it was exhilarating, but as the proceedings wore on and our stomachs remained empty, it got harder and harder to pay attention. Eight pm passed, then nine, and still no sign of dinner. We were all filling the void with wine, which also wasn't doing much for our concentration. Chris was starving, and decided it was time to do something about it. 'Is there anyone who doesn't want their bread roll?' he asked. 'Please pass them along!' He couldn't believe his luck when fifteen of the twenty bread rolls at the table were passed up. The first course finally came out at 10 pm – cold tomato soup. It wasn't the gourmet delight we'd been hoping for, but we weren't in a position to pass it up. I felt like I was going to collapse and die If I didn't get something substantial in me soon. When the next course came out, a beautiful piece of steak about an inch thick, we all breathed a sigh of relief.

About midnight, Edwin Moses, the runner who was organising the event, asked if I would get up on stage and talk about my swim and what I had done for the Sport for Good Foundation. And so I stood in front of 900 people, the cream of the sporting crop, and *they* clapped and cheered for *me*. I was absolutely chuffed.

The next night was the World Sports Awards in Monaco, a black-tie affair. I finally got a chance to chat to Mark Spitz when he came over with his son to congratulate me on my swim and apologise for not being there at the end. We ended up having quite a long chat and I could tell he was genuine in thanking me for my efforts. A minute later someone came over and said 'Mate, you don't know how impressive that is! Mark Spitz hates social functions. He rarely even talks to people. For him to come over and talk to you is the highest honour. He must have really wanted to speak to you.' Well, it wasn't lost on me. I was incredibly honoured.

Every second person I encountered left me in awe. I was stoked to see Michael Milton, Australia's most successful Winter Paralympian of all time, win the disability award. I spoke to the Prince of Monaco, Martina Navratilova, Dawn Fraser, Boris Becker, Mick Doohan, Marvelous Marvin Hagler. John McEnroe particularly impressed me; he was so down to earth and just lovely to talk to. I've heard that he comes to every event he's invited to, which shows a great humbleness that I really admire. Maybe I was a bit surprised because all I had to go by was what I'd seen on the court, but it just goes to show that a little bit of white line fever doesn't necessarily reflect what a person's really like. When I left at the end of the night I felt like I was walking on air. I couldn't believe I'd even been in the same room as these people, let alone chewing the fat with them over champagne.

The next day, as I was waiting at the airport to fly to London to stay with Chris, I saw Mark Spitz weaving his way through the crowd with his wife and his son. He was there simply to shake my hand one last time. Wow, I thought. I've done something right in this part of the world.

I spent a week with Chris, and we had a wonderful reunion dinner one night with a few guys from Newington that were now living in London. While I was there, I was invited down to do a 3-mile swim at a river in Brighton to raise money for the Lifeboats Association. Obviously, I agreed.

When I arrived at Brighton, I was surprised to see Alison Streeter. She was doing the swim as well. 'Who am I going to swim with?' I asked.

'Oh, just swim with us.'

'But who is going to guide us? Are there whistles?'

'No, we'll just guide you down the river.'

Okay. This was going to be interesting.

We got down to the water and I started swimming with a group of people, most of whom I knew from the English Channel. I found a position about 3 feet behind another swimmer, where I could feel his kick. It was a perfect guide for me. If he just kept up his speed and stayed there in front of me, I'd be able to stay in line no worries. And it worked really well... until halfway down the river, for some reason, he got out. Huh. What was I going to do now?

Thankfully, Alison's mates saw that I was struggling and came and swam with me to the end. We had a photo with the mayor and were thanked for our contribution. We then faced a trip across cow-pat-laden farmland to get back to our cars. It was never going to go down as one of my greatest achievements. But I'd helped out another charity, and it felt good. But not as good as what was to come.

I now headed across the Atlantic to America to do three days of white water rafting in the last 111 miles of the Colorado River in the Grand Canyon. My white water rafting trip in Utah four years ago had been a great experience, but it wasn't all that well organised and the group I was with didn't quite gel. But this trip was a completely different story. It would be one of the greatest experiences of my life.

I arrived at Las Vegas airport unsure how to go about finding my group. I heard a guide giving a spiel about a white water rafting trip in the Grand Canyon and thought I'd found my way, but then he mentioned that the trip was for two nights. I started to feel a bit panicked. My trip was supposed to be for three nights. Was I at the wrong place? Was I in the wrong group? Luckily, when the guide couldn't find my name one of the blokes from my actual tour must have overheard. 'I think you're listening to the wrong spiel', he said, and pointed me in the right direction. Thank God! I was also pretty relieved to know that the man I'd been listening to wasn't going to be our guide. He was a stern ex-teacher who sounded as if discipline was the only aim of the trip. If he'd turned out to be our leader I might just have walked straight out of there!

We spent the first night at a ranch near the Colorado River, which sounds all very nice, but for my poor roommate it ended up being the worst possible start to the trip. The next morning he said, 'I thought there was a freight train running through this place last night. It was you snoring, matey!' But it was nothing a couple of coffees couldn't fix. I was really looking forward to the helicopter ride out to the river, but my enthusiasm was severely misplaced. It was the first time I've ever been in a helicopter, and I hope it's the last. My body refused to adjust to the idea of going straight up and straight down through thin air. I seriously couldn't handle it! Even after we touched down, my belly took a while to accept that we were back on solid land.

We had a group of ten on one raft – three sisters, a father and his twelve-year-old son, a mother and daughter, a couple, and me. It was a great group of people. Meanwhile, the other group, which turned out to be part of the same trip, had twenty-eight people squeezed into two rafts. But overcrowding wasn't their only concern. They were all over the shop! One day we passed them as they were trying to set up camp and they clearly had no idea what they were doing. I said, 'Thank God we got away from them.' The guy next to me cracked up. He knew just what I was talking about! 'And thank God we got away from that teacher!' I said.

I positioned myself at the front of the raft, where I got smashed by every single wave. That's not a complaint! It was magnificent fun. I felt like I was getting the authentic experience, getting soaked with water good and proper! But I think I enjoyed it even more the time I leaned forward as we hit a wave, and the water missed me and hit the couple behind me! That'll teach them to pick a 'safe' spot on the raft! It was just good, honest fun.

That night, and each night thereafter, we set up camp, cooked dinner, then had a glass of wine and shared some stories around the campfire. I finished the first day relaxed yet elated at the same time. I'd just had a great day of white water rafting in a stunning setting, and a beautiful – well, acceptable! – dinner with a great group of people. How good was this. I lay down on my too-small camping bed under the evening sun that first night and just thought to myself, I'm in the depths of the Grand Canyon. All I can hear is the wild rush of water. No one can contact me. No one even knows where I am. For some people that might have been a bit of a disturbing realisation, but not for me. I felt more connected with the world than I ever had. The water seemed to have a life of its own, a perpetual energy that you couldn't help but be swept up in. Yet at night, that same exuberant water became somehow lilting and rocked me into a beautifully sound sleep.

We eventually reached Hoover Dam and got on a little boat back to Las Vegas. I got back to the hotel, put some music on, and took some time to reflect on one of the most magnificent experiences I would ever be lucky enough to have. I loved every minute of it – well, maybe not the trips to the makeshift toilets and the mosquito swarms. But almost every minute!

The next morning, I was up early to catch a plane to Maryland to compete in the Great Chesapeake Bay Swim: just over 7 kilometres under the Chesapeake Bay Bridge. I would stay with Debbie's sister, Lauren, who had kindly organised a kayak and whistles for me. The day before the swim, Lauren took me out to meet my kayaker and have a training run.

'So if I need to stop you,' the kayaker said, 'how do I do that?'

I said, 'Well, just shout at me. You should be close enough.'

'I can't do that. I just had a tonsillectomy!'

God, I thought. Here we go. This was going to be an interesting day all right. But there was nothing I could do about it now! It was him or nothing. 'All right,' I said, 'if you have to stop me, blow ten short whistles in a row.'

Normally the night before a swim I'm all about preparing, getting myself into top condition for the next day. But I wasn't really worried about the swim – it was only 7 kilometres. So I went along with Lauren to her mate's place and had a dinner and a few glasses of wine in the rain. The wine was homemade and tasted absolutely disgusting, but it was the only thing keeping me warm so I downed a few glasses anyway! It got to the end of the night and I realised that perhaps my decision making hadn't been top notch. Doing the swim the next day wasn't going to be much fun.

When I arrived the next morning, I asked the organising committee the big question: 'So how does this actually work?'

'Well, we've got 500 people swimming.'

'Do you have waves, five or six waves?'

'Oh no. We've got two waves of 250 people.'

Interesting. 'Does the fastest group go first?'

'Oh no. The slowest group goes first.'

What madness was this? It made no sense! The defending champion had to swim through 250 people to get to the front! 'So how do you finish? Do you have a timing chip?'

'Oh no. But here you go.' She gave me a piece of paper about 3 centimetres by 1 centimetre. 'You've just got to give that to the people at the other end.'

'Where am I supposed to put that?' Plenty of rude comments were running through my head, but I held them in.

'You put it on top of your head and put your cap over the top. Then when you get to the other end, you take your cap off, and there it is stuck to your head.'

I looked at this lady thinking, if you did that in an event in Sydney there would be a riot! These people were absolutely mad!

It was a tidal swim, which meant that with every minute that went by, the tide was going out further and making things harder. So when I got through 45 minutes of briefings, presentations and sponsors, I was already feeling a bit antsy. Then they sang the National Anthem and I almost shouted out, 'Get on with it!' We eventually got in the water for the first wave, all 250 of us. And so the chaos began. Barely 20 metres in I ploughed into the back of a guy who had unexpectedly stopped. The kayakers were freaking out that they'd hurt someone. But as time went on the crowd thinned out a bit.

You had to stay within a metre of the edge of the Chesapeake Bay Bridge at all times or you'd be disqualified. It was a hard ask, but at least being under the bridge made it easier to hear the whistles. I was so scared of being disqualified that I just powered through the swim, never even stopping for a drink break. I got to the end and was just glad that this ridiculous swim was over. I took my cap off and, yes, the piece of paper was there stuck to my head. The *New York Times* interviewed a few swimmers, myself included, and I had a chuckle when I saw that one of them had complained, 'What was with those bloody whistles?' She was a bit sheepish when they told her what they were for. I walked away with a smirk on my face thinking, that was just the most absurd swim I've ever done in my life. The thought of that comical paper-under-the-cap system still makes me laugh.

The next day I travelled to Martha's Vineyard to see Debbie, Charlie and Taylor. It was fantastic to see them again. We whiled away the hours swimming, yabbying, and fishing. I caught a 28-inch striped bass, and oh, the satisfaction of catching your own dinner! It was a beautiful meal.

Now I was off to stay with James Shellshear and his fiancée Anna in Medellín, Colombia, where he was teaching English and History. I couldn't wait to see him again, but I won't deny that the excitement was mingled with apprehension. In 2002, Medellín had 3,700 murders. I knew my parents wouldn't approve, so when I told them I was going to Colombia and they assumed I meant British Columbia, I didn't correct them. They weren't too impressed when they found out, but by then I was home safe.

Despite its dubious title of 'murder capital of the world', James absolutely loved his city, and he made it his personal goal to make me feel the same. It wasn't a hard task. On my first day in Medellín, James had a friend show us around his beautiful flower farm up on the hill. The flowers there are so incredible that they ship them right around America. I remember standing on the hills 1,000 metres above the city of Medellín, and even though I couldn't see, the beauty of the place was palpable.

I managed to explore the mountains with James and his family without incident, yet walking down the street to the pub to watch the soccer, I somehow fell straight off the sidewalk. I just mistimed my step, toppled over and smashed my knee so hard I felt sure I'd broken it (I hadn't). When the agony subsided, I downgraded my self-diagnosis to a torn ligament – something my physio would confirm when I returned home – but I was all right. I could walk... just. James thought the whole thing was hilarious, and for the rest of the trip, every time we walked down that street he would joke that they were building a statue to mark where I fell over. It was typical of James's humour. Even at school, I remember he was always coming up with ridiculous nicknames for all of us and even took it to the next level by using them as the basis for songs! Nothing much had changed, and I wouldn't have had it any other way.

When I took out my disposable camera to take some photos of Medellín, James said, 'Try and keep a low profile. There are already 150 people watching what you do every minute of the day. It's unusual enough for them to see a gringo wandering around, but a blind one? That breaks all the rules!' He was right. No matter where I went, I was followed by curious eyes. At one point, a bloke took James's glasses off and gave them to me thinking it would cure my eyesight. I thought it was the greatest crack-up of all time. A real classic. I just had a great time with James and his family, and forgot all about its rich history of crime! James made me feel completely safe, and I never once saw any evidence of the dangerous society I'd anticipated.

In fact, my overwhelming memory of the city of Medellín is how proud their people are. Their city has such a bad name – and with good reason I guess – but it didn't dampen their love for the place they called home. And they were just thrilled to have someone from overseas come to their country. They treated me like royalty. They loved the novelty and joy of having me around, and I think there was also an aspect of admiration – that I knew the dangers associated with Medellín and I'd come out there anyway. I'd made an effort, and to them, that was worth celebrating.

On to the last leg of my trip – San Francisco and the Alcatraz swim. But as I was about to leave Miami Airport, an electrical storm came through and delayed the plane for 5 hours. I was struggling with my sore leg and couldn't believe my bad luck, but it ended up working almost in my favour. I've always admired the way Americans treat the disabled, and this was the perfect case in point. They approached the situation very calmly, and did everything they could to help me out. One bloke bought me dinner, and the airline offered me either a room for the night, or the option to stop over in Chicago before heading to San Francisco. I wanted nothing more than to get out of Miami Airport, so I gratefully accepted the flight to Chicago. They upgraded me to first class, and paid for my hotel. It was unbelievable.

I arrived in San Francisco the next day, and when I got to the hotel I asked the guy in reception, 'How cold is it out there in the water?'

'Fifteen degrees.'

'Beauty. Thanks man.'

'Do you need any help?'

'Well, as long as you're offering... can you go and buy me a disposable camera?'

He laughed, but he did as I asked! The camera got a good workout on that afternoon's bus tour (with commentary, naturally!) of San Francisco.

The next morning, I met up with Gary Emich, who I'd got in contact with through some American swimmers I knew. He was going to swim with me, and when he got there he launched into an animated brief on how the swim around Alcatraz would work. I knew he'd done the swim before, but it was nice to see that he was as excited as I was! It was only then that the penny dropped for the bloke at the hotel: 'So that's why you asked all those questions!'

The next day was the swim to Alcatraz. We would swim from San Francisco Rowing Club out to the eastern side of Alcatraz, circle around it, then come back in via the western side. I took off with Gary and his mate, who together have amassed some 1,000 crossings of Alcatraz. I was in good company! The water was 12 degrees when we started, but by the time I got around the back of the rock it was down to 10. It took me 45 minutes to get out there, but an hour and 45 minutes to get back. The tides were horrendous! You can't tell me that those three escapees in 1962 ever made it, because here was a group of talented swimmers who could barely make it even in still, sunny conditions.

As we came back around the west side of Alcatraz, we unexpectedly joined a big group of swimmers completing an official single crossing from the island. I ended up getting entangled in their event and eventually I made it into the cove, under the bridge and to the finish line. But it didn't feel quite right. The bloke at the end thought I was part of the event and said, 'What's your problem?'

I said, 'This is not where I'm meant to turn up.'

'Yeah, yeah.' He rolled his eyes. He must have thought I had hypothermia. 'Who's the president of America?'

'George W. Bush. It's the Summer Solstice, 22nd of June.'

'Well, there's obviously nothing wrong with you. Off you go.'

It was a pretty rough appraisal, but he was right. There was nothing wrong with me. I'd completed a double crossing of Alcatraz, and I'd had a great deal of fun. The history of the place made it a particularly thrilling swim, and being out there with Gary and his mate was just fantastic.

On my final day in San Francisco, I went on a tour of Alcatraz. They asked, 'Have you been to Alcatraz before?' I said, 'Yeah. I swam there yesterday.' They just looked at me as if I was mad and waved me on. The audio tour of Alcatraz was really well done, and I delighted in learning all the history and imagining how terrible it must have been for the inmates. When they talked about the mystery of what happened to the people that escaped I said, 'Well, they didn't make it, that's for sure!'

Finally, after a whirlwind six weeks, it was time to go home. I'd raised funds for the Sport for Good Foundation and been acknowledged at the World Sports Awards. I'd met the Prince of Monaco. I'd white-water rafted in the Grand Canyon. I'd swum the Great Chesapeake Bay. I'd conquered Alcatraz. I'd been everywhere, man! And I'd had the time of my life.

## Chapter 12
## Cook Strait

After coming back from Alcatraz in July 2003, the question on everyone's lips was, 'What's next?' More than anything I wanted to set up a foundation to raise money for swimming, but I just wasn't in a position to do it. You can have all the good intentions in the world and you still won't get very far unless you've got a team of lawyers, a committee... in short, a lot of people willing to give a lot of time. Back then I just didn't have that. It was a marvellous idea, but it was never really going to get off the ground.

Instead, I vowed to dedicate myself to something even more ambitious: to do a swim in every continent except Antarctica (that would be too crazy even for me!). Australia/New Zealand, South America, North America, Asia, Europe, and Africa. I'd been thinking about it since 2002, but now the timing just seemed right. There were a few raised eyebrows, a few quiet mutterings of 'Well, that's ambitious!' But nobody seemed to doubt I could do it.

Narelle, Sticks and Matt put their hands up to be part of the team, and we commenced preparations. We worked out the scheduling and set a plan to swim 'around the world in 925 days' as we would come to refer to it. From 5 March 2004 to 15 September 2006, we had our work cut out for us.

I decided I would start with the Cook Strait, a 30-kilometre swim between the North and South Islands of New Zealand. It's a hard swim to even get a spot in, because the conditions are only appropriate from late January through to late April, and the whole thing is run by a one-man organising committee. There are only nine or ten spots available for the whole year, and to get one of them you're looking at applying two or three years in advance. But the stars aligned and I got a spot.

And so the process of training began again. Pool swims, ocean swims, tethered swims. Working out the logistics, trying to replicate the conditions. And what conditions they were! The Cook Strait turns up some of the worst conditions in the world. The winds from the Pacific Ocean and the Antarctic Ocean all converge at this one point to test you to your absolute limits. Anyone that's ever stayed in Wellington will know what I'm talking about.

On 25 February I set out for Cook Strait with Matt Logan. Unfortunately he ended up having to leave before the swim because of work commitments, but by then Sticks had arrived with Chad Schneider, a swimmer I'd met at the 2003 Rottnest Island event. Chad was a swim coach, and nothing gave him more joy than being a part of helping people reach their potential. I couldn't have asked for a better guy to welcome onto my team. Chad had attempted the swim in 2002 but had to pull out 8 kilometres from the finish because it just got way too cold at 14 degrees. If it had been warmer, I bet he would have succeeded comfortably.

We turned up at the car hire desk in Wellington, and Matt asked me to hand over my driver's licence. Of course, the bloke on the other side of the desk didn't get the joke, but the two of us got a kick out of it! We got the car, and off we went to Wadestown. American swimmer John Yudovin had hired a house there for the entire 10-week season but managed to get his swim done on the third day! So in an amazing stroke of luck, he said as long as we paid the cleaning bill, we could stay there rent-free. That was just magnificent. To come back to a warm, cosy, quiet house, to get a good night's rest, to have somewhere to dry your wet gear. That was crucial. I've never forgotten his generosity, and when he passed away a couple of years ago I sent a message to his wife with one last thank you.

The house was huge, with at least four bedrooms, an open-plan kitchen, a great barbecue area out the back, and lovely wooden floors. When we got the keys, the owners of the house took one look at my white stick and descended into a private little panic, aghast at the thought of what it could do to their floors. Of course, there was no way they could say anything!

That night we met up with Phil Rush, the organiser, and he went through the swim with us. He's done doubles and attempted triples of the Cook Strait, and holds the record for the fastest triple crossing of the English Channel – by far – so I hung on his every word. He rehashed the importance of the conditions, and assured us that he'd organise a time for us that would give us our best possible chance.

The next day Matt and I got straight back into training. The conditions weren't particularly flash, but then we knew they wouldn't be. Besides, the worse the conditions, the better the preparation. The wind lived up to expectations, and with it whipping against my ears I could hardly hear the loudhailer and ended up swimming all over the place. It was a relief when Chad arrived that afternoon and got in the water with me, relieving Matt of his duties. I don't know how much longer Matt would have managed to put up with me otherwise!

A Japanese swimmer went on the first tide but had to get pulled out with hypothermia. Now it was my turn, and I could only hope I wouldn't suffer the same fate! Every night we would call Phil, and every night he would say, 'No. Not tomorrow.' Night after night. On the fourth night things were looking good, but as soon as we got up the next morning and saw the conditions it was obvious it wasn't going to happen.

By now Matt had gone home, leaving just Chad, Sticks and me to continue the training program to the best of our ability – which turned out not to be that great. One day I went out for a swim in Wellington Harbour, with Sticks and Chad kayaking beside me. Well, I say beside me. Chad and Sticks aren't the world's best kayakers and the wind was as powerful as ever, so for the majority of the swim they were going one way and I was going the other! It was only a matter of time before something went wrong, and before long I was swimming obliviously towards the pylon of a jetty. Chad dived overboard, sprinted towards me, and caught me by the ankles with about an inch to spare. As much fun as Chad's heroics had been, we decided that Wellington Harbour wasn't necessarily the ideal location for our training going forward. Instead, Chad and I swam the beaches together. But by now I felt as if I'd trained as well as I could, and we were happy enough to relax a little on the training and allow ourselves a bit of fun.

I'll never let Chad live down the day the three of us played mini golf. It was all square coming up to the eighteenth hole, and I got a hole-in-one. Chad couldn't believe he'd been beaten by a blind person! The afternoon we decided to go and see a movie was another memorable one. Chad and Sticks had decided to let the blind guy decide what we'd see, and I chose *The Passion of the Christ* over *21 Grams*. It took a good half-hour before we realised that the whole movie was in Arabic (with subtitles, but a fat lot of good that did me!). We tried to get our money back, but apparently a complete inability to understand the movie wasn't grounds for a refund. So we spent 2 hours listening to people talking in Arabic. It was a very funny time – at least in retrospect!

We were having a great deal of fun, but I have to admit that a lot of the time my mind was elsewhere. I had met a girl, Jenny McGee, and not a night went by that we weren't on the phone. I'd met her only a month earlier, in a way I would never have thought possible – online dating. These days it seems to be about the only way anybody *does* meet, but at the time it was quite uncommon. All credit to my mate Peter Duncan, who wouldn't let up until I tried it. I was cynical – in fact, I was completely convinced it would never work – but here I was (albeit after a couple of pretty horrendous dates!).

I'll always remember the night I found her. She was into scuba diving and travelling, and I sensed a kindness in her profile. I had to know more. We got each other's email addresses, and it didn't take long before Jenny asked the question I'd been too scared to: 'Want to meet on Saturday?' I didn't bother booking anything, just figured we could choose a place on the day. Which would have been a perfectly good plan under normal circumstances. But the day before the date it finally clicked – it was Valentine's Day. It was going to be impossible to get a restaurant booking!

The least I could have done was to arrive on time, but after a morning training session I arrived 10 minutes late, and Jenny was waiting for me. She knew I was blind, but she said to me later that when she turned up she realised she hadn't asked me one question that might have helped her to identify me! She'd been glancing furtively around the main street of Manly for the whole ten minutes, eyeing up every person that so much as stumbled, wondering if they might be blind. She was so relieved when I finally turned up, she forgot all about my tardiness! Thank God she stayed. She said, 'I've taken the liberty of organising a restaurant since it's Valentine's Day.' Although technically I feel this should have been my domain, I was grateful that at least one of us was on the ball!

I find a lot of people are unsure how to act around a blind person, but Jenny wasn't bothered in the least. I was drawn to her from the outset because she was so relaxed and easygoing. Normally dates make me anxious, but within minutes her attitude rubbed off on me and I realised I felt completely at ease with her as well. It was a beautiful lunch, and by the end of the meal I felt as if I'd known her far longer than the two wonderful hours we'd spent together. Neither of us wanted the date to end – so we didn't let it. We went to the Steyne Hotel for a few more drinks, then Jenny invited me to come along with her to a mate's fortieth. As soon as I agreed, I thought to myself, wait a second. I've known this person for a few hours, and I've just said yes to meeting sixty or seventy of her friends. What have I got myself into! I was out of my mind with nerves, but Jenny's friends couldn't have been kinder.

We ended up spending the whole weekend together. What a turnaround from failing to book a restaurant on Valentine's Day and turning up ten minutes late! We kept seeing each other every weekend, and we enjoyed this incredible ease with one another that I've never had with anyone else. It was painful having to leave just when our relationship was hitting its stride, but I'd made a commitment. I was going to cross Cook Strait, no matter what.

With two days to go until the end of the tide, I was starting to worry that the entire trip had been in vain. But the night before the last day of the tide, Phil said the words I'd been waiting to hear: 'You're on tomorrow. The conditions look good.' Fingers crossed.

I was nervous when I awoke the next morning, but we got the conditions we were hoping for. Chad drove us to the 36-foot boat where my cousin Parke, who was planning to film the day, and a New Zealand reporter were waiting for us. I was shifting my weight from foot to foot, anxious to get out there and get it over with. I knew it was going to be a long, tough day.

As we boarded the boat Phil said, 'The current's running north today, so we'll head over to the South Island and start from there.' It was about a 2-hour boat ride, so we all popped some seasickness tablets. Well, all except the reporter, who felt confident the conditions were calm enough that he didn't need it. He looked quite content actually, anticipating a lovely day drinking tea, watching me swim, and writing my story.

As I swam in to the beach I was feeling great. It was 15 degrees water temperature, which wasn't too bad. A sunny day, not much wind. Really good conditions. The first few hours went brilliantly and by the six-hour mark the mood was optimistic. Chad looked off into the distance and announced, 'We'll be having a celebratory drink shortly!' Phil gave Chad a disgruntled 'mmm', and continued gazing at the horizon, a troubled look on his face. Within only a couple of minutes, it was obvious why. Sixty-five-kilometre-per-hour winds arrived, and with them four-metre swells. From that point on it was going to be an almighty battle. People said it was good that I couldn't see what was happening, because I probably would have given it away. Maybe they're right. But I just resolved to bash through the waves. I'd done it in Rottnest the previous year, and I could do it again.

The guys had to fight to keep circling around me in the inflatable boat, blowing the whistle every time they came close to me. It was pretty frightening. The boat was being catapulted up and over the angry waves. Getting a feed to me was impossible, and in the end they even had to jettison the loudhailer and a bunch of water bottles just in case they had to drag me into the boat. For the next two hours, Chad dedicated himself to lying on the nose of the boat to keep it down. Sticks' job was to blow the whistle, and Phil's was simply to get me back safe. Meanwhile, the main boat went off on its own little tangent. For possibly the first time in history, the life jackets came out. The main boat was going up and down. The inflatable boat was going up and down. I was going up and down. Helicopters were hovering. It was all happening.

After 2 hours or so – though it felt like forever – I finally got to within 600 metres of the North Island. The shore was so close, but ever so far, and the water temperature was rapidly dropping. It took me 40 minutes to get from 600 metres to 100 metres out. I heard Chad's voice beside me. 'Mate,' he said, 'Phil's called it off. We're this far from being winched out of here by helicopter. The swim is over.'

James swimming in enormous swells Cook Strait, New Zealand.

Like hell it was! There was no way I was accepting that. I'd come this far, and I wasn't going to stop until I'd touched the rocks of the North Island. Phil had already officialised the swim, but I wouldn't back down. Then at that moment, fate made the decision for us. A massive wave scooped us up and sent us both crashing into the rocks. 'Welcome to the North Island,' Chad said. 'Now let's get out of here!'

We swam the 150 metres back to the main boat. I'd been told beforehand that at the end of the swim, Phil's MO was just to pick you up and throw you onto the floor of the boat. And that's more or less what happened! But it was with good reason – Chad later told me that he'd never seen anyone as white as Phil in his life. For my part, I must have been quite a sight writhing on the bottom of the boat struggling to get my thermals on. I was shaking all over the place. I'd been through the wringer. We all had.

For a while we just sat motionless in the boat, none of us saying a word. When I finally got a bit of strength back, I realised the reporter was nowhere to be seen. When I asked after him, Parke said, 'You don't want to know.' It was then that I noticed the repeated retching sounds from the other end of the boat. Turns out those seasickness tablets might have come in handy after all. He vowed never to report on another swim ever again. The rest of my team weren't faring much better. Parke hadn't even set foot off the main boat, and he was still shaking!

By the time we got back to the car, we were all still kind of dazed. I'd swum the Cook Strait, but I'd beaten myself into oblivion. You lose a bit of objectivity over the years, but I still reckon that's the hardest swim I've ever done. The hardest, and the most fascinating. It was out of control – literally. I was glad just to survive.

What a sense of relief we all felt as we walked through the door to the house. Warm, dry, cosy. At that moment all the things we normally take for granted felt like the finest luxuries! We ordered some pizzas at the pub, but none of us lasted beyond the first drink before collapsing into bed.

It took us all a few days to get over the mental battering, but that was nothing compared to the weeks of recovery from the physical beating I had copped. But I knew how hard it could be when I signed up, and just knowing I'd swum the Cook Strait made it all worth it. What a fantastic achievement. I was the first blind person and the fourth Australian to swim the Cook Strait. And to do it in such horrendous conditions! I knew I'd done something pretty remarkable, and it felt amazing. The first leg of the six-continent world tour – check. I could only hope the next one would be easier.

But to be honest, right now, that was the last thing on my mind. All I could think about was getting back to Jenny. I got back on 7 March – three days after her birthday – and took her out for a sumptuous dinner to make up for my absence. I brought along a Verdelho thinking it was a red wine – Jenny's favourite – but as soon as I took a sip I realised it was a white. It wasn't the first time I'd betrayed my complete ignorance when it comes to wine. Fortunately, wine expertise wasn't one of the qualities Jenny was looking for in a man, and our relationship continued to bloom. We picked up right where we'd left off, not letting a week go by without seeing each other. It just felt so right.

For Easter, Jenny invited me down to her property in Jindabyne. We had a lovely weekend with a few friends, including Jenny's brother Pete. Meeting the big brother is always a bit of a hurdle in any relationship, and I went in nervous, but I needn't have. Pete had the same kind, easygoing nature as his sister and he accepted me with open arms, particularly when we realised we shared that all-important love of sport.

Before I knew it June came around, and it was time to leave for the next leg of our little world tour – Argentina. I was excited about the swim, of course, but I wasn't ready to let Jenny go again. It felt like no time at all since I'd come back from New Zealand. Everything was going well between us, but we were still riding the wave of the new relationship. We hadn't put it to the test yet. Between that and my strong reluctance to leave her again, it felt like the right time to take a leap of faith. We promised to meet each other in Boston right after the swim. From there we would spend three weeks travelling through Boston, London, Paris, and Prague.

That's right. Less than six months after meeting, we were planning to spend 24 hours per day together for three weeks running. Were we crazy? Maybe. 'Going overseas together is the true test of a relationship', my brother said to me before I left. 'Finding out whether you can stand each other 24-7! Good luck brother.'

But between now and then stood a 60-kilometre stretch of the Parana (not piranha, thankfully!) River, which is about a kilometre wide and runs for nearly 5,000 kilometres through Argentina, Paraguay, and Brazil. We scheduled the swim for 6 June, the sixtieth anniversary of D-Day. I seemed to be making a habit of coinciding my own achievements with other momentous events! In Rosario, just under 300 kilometres from Buenos Aires, the water wouldn't be all that warm, but at least being near the equator it wouldn't be terribly cold either. Sixty kilometres sounds like a long way, and it is, but we would have the advantage of an eight-knot current behind us, and that would make a world of difference.

Matt and I left first, and at the time the only viable way to get to Rosario was to go Sydney–LA, LA–Washington, Washington–Buenos Aires, then finally to Rosario via a 5-hour bus trip. I'll admit it was a damn long way of getting there and Matt wasn't particularly happy about it, but he went along with it in the end. Sticks came a couple of days later via the much more respectable Sydney–Santiago–Buenos Aires route, and Narelle finally arrived the day before the swim.

Before the swim we did get a bit of a chance to just soak up the atmosphere in Rosario. I really enjoyed Argentina. I enjoyed the people. You'd think with the language barrier communication would be a struggle, but they're so friendly it just doesn't matter. They have such a warmth about them; just being around them is enough to make you feel good. It's really quite remarkable given the poverty much of the country faces. One night we went to a restaurant and noticed a kid come in looking really hungry. It stirred mixed emotions in me. We gave him some food, and it was a wonderful feeling, helping someone in need. But my thoughts couldn't help but drift to the thousands of kids we didn't help.

Eventually our attention turned to training. The amazing thing about the Parana River is that, with a powerful 8-knot current, training is as simple as just swimming up against the current. So strong is the current that legend has it one gentleman attempted to swim from Rosario to Buenos Aires thirteen times over thirteen years, and never made it. It took him thirteen years to work out that it's physically impossible to overcome that current.

Matt would sit there in the kayak, Sticks would sit on the bank, and I'd battle my heart out just to stay in the one spot. You couldn't move. You couldn't get out. All you could do was just keep swimming. I'm sure for some the feeling of swimming and getting nowhere would feel unbearably futile, but to me it was just fantastic training, nothing more, nothing less. I even got to do a couple of sessions with the famous Argentinian marathon swimmer Claudio Plit, who to me is an absolute icon. He's been swimming open-water events for 30 years and has never failed to complete one. It's a stellar record, and unrivalled as far as I'm aware. His support was an enormous help to me.

By 10 am on the morning of the swim, we were all set. We'd known in advance that we couldn't leave the start time too late. The swim would probably take somewhere between 8 and 9 hours, and paddling in the dark among ocean-going cargo ships near 200 m in length that left a wash behind that lasted for several hundred metres after they passed, wasn't a challenge any of us were keen on facing! Claudio had organised a kayak for Matt and a boat for Narelle and Sticks. The boat was so small that Sticks and Narelle had to come to a complete halt anytime they wanted to change positions, just so they could get up and walk around each other. By the end of the day they were so stiff they could hardly move. But we graciously accepted what we were given! Claudio would also be out there on the water in a police boat.

We were ready to go, but where was the police boat? Waiting for them didn't even bother me that much in itself. It was the knowledge that now we were bound to get stuck in the dark for the last leg of the swim that really ramped up my nerves. The swim was never going to be easy, but now the delay had added an extra level of difficulty. The police finally arrived at 11.30. They were armed with guns, which made us even more uneasy. If we harboured any intentions of complaining, they were quickly put to bed!

With our less-than-ideal start, I swam very poorly to begin with. It took me a long time to get into a rhythm. We started in a little tributary off to the side of the Parana River, and it seemed to take forever to get out of it, but the minute we got into the river, there was no question where we were. I felt this enormous surge of water behind me, and with it a surge of exhilaration. Time to relax, I thought. I'm in the river. The current's behind me. It's all good from here.

But of course, the distance was always going to be a challenge, even with the benefit of the current. Sixty kilometres is a long way in itself, but to get from one end to the other you actually end up swimming a darn sight more than that. Every hour, on the hour, a 200 metre cargo ship would come upstream, and it sure as hell wasn't going to get out of my way. And so, every hour, I would swim 900 metres across the river, and 900 metres back. Making matters worse, one side of the river was home to wheat silos, which regularly pumped pollution into the river.

Between the ships and the pollution, it was a very interesting swim. Matt and I had done enough training in the river beforehand to feel like we knew it pretty well, but what we hadn't planned for was an insect leaving Matt with an eye infection. He was finding it very hard to paddle, but to his credit, he stuck with it for most of the way. Not just paddling, either. Feeding me, hydrating me, giving me updates. But what I remember most is how supportive he was, always asking how I was feeling, when really, I should have been the one asking him! I remember about three feeds from the end, a wheat silo pumped a huge load of sludge right out in front of me, and when he asked how I was feeling I didn't mince words. He pumped me with sugar at the next feed, and I was fine. But I owe a large part of my success that day to him.

Numbered buoys every kilometre along the river showed how far we'd come and how far we had to go. After all the stationary training swims, a sign of actual physical progress was a nice motivator! Despite all the disgusting muck I'd been ingesting throughout the day, I was still swimming strongly. But an hour from the end, the moment we had dreaded arrived: it got dark. We attached light sticks to my cossie, for what it was worth. Just before the finish line was a bridge that we had to get under. As we approached the bridge, Matt could see a ship coming the other way. It was going to be tight, but there was no turning back. He just had to work it out, tell me what to do. 'As soon as we get under the bridge, swim diagonally left, and into shore.' I could hear the urgency in his tone, but instead of letting it worry me, I let it drive me. I sprinted into shore in front of a restaurant where I was greeted with unexpected (but very welcome) applause. Little did I know that I had evaded the ship by no more than a minute or two.

I often think my job is almost the easiest of everyone in my team – all I have to do is swim. It's my team that carries the burden of motivating me, supporting me, keeping me safe (and paddling!). And for Matt, that day, that burden had been enormous. So much kayaking, so much back and forth across the river, so many ships to navigate. So much Spanish! When we got to the end and hauled ourselves out of the water, I think Matt was probably more relieved than I was.

It had been a long, hard slog. Don't get me wrong, the harder the slog the greater the satisfaction, but I wasn't sorry when it was over! Claudio invited us all to have dinner with his brother, who owned the restaurant, and a few of his friends. Well, we had more steak than I've ever had in my life. It just kept on coming, and we didn't stop eating for 3 or 4 hours! But what I remember even more so than the steak – and it was bloody good steak! – is how lovely it was to just sit down with Claudio and his mates, and have a good old-fashioned chinwag.

We spent another couple of days in Rosario together, just relaxing. I made the newspaper there, which was a bit of a laugh. The night after the swim Narelle and Matt felt too sore to go out, but Sticks and I went out for a few beers. Well, I had a few – I lost count of how many Sticks had! As we were walking back home, we were accosted by a group of ten or twelve Argentinian men inviting us – well, it was more of a demand than an invitation – to their party. As soon as we sat down they fed us this straight whiskey, and I'll never forget the horrendous taste! But we had no choice but to drink it. For an hour, the whiskey kept on flowing, and I think we both felt too intimidated to put a stop to it! But eventually we managed to extricate ourselves from the party and stumble home. I hope to never have to taste the stuff again, but if I'm honest, it's a happy memory, and a funny one. As forceful as their approach might have felt, I know that deep down all they wanted to do was welcome us. And it felt nice to be included. It's all just typical of what the people are like in Argentina: very, very welcoming.

After everyone had gone home, I was left to make my way to Medellín, Colombia for James Shellshear's wedding. Far out, what a stressful day. Not only was I in for an hour of flying from Rosario to Buenos Aires, 6 hours from Buenos Aires to Bogotá, and an hour from Bogotá to Medellín, but when I got to Buenos Aires domestic airport I found out that I also had to take a 1-hour bus ride to the international airport. At Bogotá there was another extended journey from international to domestic, and this time my only hope of getting there was to be guided by someone who didn't speak any English. I was about ready to throw in the towel! But I managed to get to the domestic terminal an hour before departure. I was just sitting there, keeping to myself, when out of nowhere I was offered cornflakes. I was stunned, though not so stunned I didn't accept. Of all the things, I never thought I would be eating cornflakes in an airport in Colombia!

When I arrived at Medellín, James picked me up. I was pretty darn relieved to have made it after my whirlwind day of travelling, and it felt really special to be able to stay with James and his fiancée Anna, to share a room with Pete Duncan, and even to catch up with James' parents for a bit. It was lovely to be back in the city, which now held a very special place in my heart. Medellín is a truly beautiful place. Its people know that, and now I knew that.

James had planned a bit of a surprise for Anna that night, and we were all going to be part of it. James, Pete and I went around to the flat where Anna, her mother, and the bridal party were staying. We hid behind a car while James called the band he'd hired. As soon as James got the signal, we all walked into her flat, band playing, and she was just as surprised as we'd hoped! Halfway through the song we all joined in with various instruments, though I have to say I think the band was better off without us! I can't remember what instrument I played or even what the song was, I just remember how touched she was by the effort we'd put in.

The wedding itself couldn't have been lovelier. The ceremony took place in an ornate church. Peter Duncan was both best man and MC, and did a great job, though I'm not sure everyone got the joke when he got up for his speech as best man and thanked the MC! There was barely a dry eye in the house when James's Dad talked about how happy they were to welcome Anna into their family. It was a great time.

After a few days in Miami with Peter, the time came to meet Jenny in Boston. Our first few days together were blissful. Things were going well. We were passing the test!

On our first morning, we went downstairs and were met by the manager, who seemed to have been waiting for us. He walked over briskly and said, 'I want to apologise.'

'What for?'

'We're getting our Braille menus re-done at the moment and we don't have any available.'

I don't read Braille, but something told me that wasn't the right thing to say. I looked at Jenny as if to ask, 'Do I laugh? What do I say?' But all I got in return was a knowing grin. In the end I said, 'Oh, that's nice. Thank you'. That seemed to satisfy him, and he returned to reception.

I looked to Jenny and I said, 'How crazy was that? In Australia there wouldn't even be a Braille menu to begin with, much less someone apologising for its absence!' But that's America for you. I've always believed they are far more advanced than Australia in their treatment of people with disabilities, and every time I visit they prove me right again. They strive to include the disabled in every way possible, and that's why the manager felt he had failed me. This was all very new to me. But I could definitely get used to it!

The next night we treated ourselves to dinner at a fancy restaurant. In America, the dining experience mirrors a production line: one person takes you to your table, another gives you a menu, and yet another takes your order. So after I'd put my cane under the seat, the waiter had no way of knowing I was blind. When he gave me a menu, Jenny thought it more fun to play the part of overbearing wife than to explain the situation. The waiter seemed to take exception to this demonstration of female dominance, and made repeated attempts to get me to take a menu. And every time, Jenny would hen peck it away. He ended up red in the face, deeply indignant that Jenny kept taking charge and I didn't even put up a fight. Jenny, meanwhile, was revelling in it. When he came with the dessert menus and asked me pointedly, 'Would you like dessert?' Jenny reached over, snatched the menus from his hand, and said 'Oh yes!' We played this game all night long, and it just didn't get old! But fun and games aside, I'm glad I couldn't see the menus, because the prices were extortionate. The steak wasn't even all that good. But then again, seeing this bloke squirm was worth a dozen great steaks!

After a few days in Boston, Jenny and I flew down to Martha's Vineyard to spend two magnificent days with Debbie, Charlie, Taylor, and their second son Tristram. Well, they were certainly magnificent for me, but looking back I wonder whether this was the beginning of the tension that would gradually start to build between me and Jenny. Debbie was quizzing Jenny on every possible topic. I knew she just wanted to make an effort to get to know her, but I can see how it might have come across as intimidating to Jenny.

Indeed, I would have a chance to experience it for myself only a few days later in London, where we spent a few days with Jenny's good friend Colin and some of her cousins. The whole time I felt as if they were judging me and by the end of our stay my nerves were frazzled. Finally it came time to go to Paris. Now it was back to just the two of us, which at the time came as a great relief. Little did I know that things were about to go even further downhill.

From the minute we arrived in Paris it seemed as if nothing was going to go right for us. We got there late and missed the first tour we'd booked. We nearly got run over trying to cross the road to our hotel. We were tired and grumpy. But we dragged ourselves out to the cruise we'd booked on the Seine River. I'm used to people describing things to me when I'm sightseeing, but of course this was the first time Jenny had experienced that. 'What can you see out the window?' I asked.

'Trees', she said wearily.

'What colour?'

'Green trees, James.'

About the only good thing about that cruise was the wine. The food certainly wasn't any good, but worse than that, for the first time ever Jenny and I weren't enjoying each other's company. It took me longer than it should have to cotton on to Jenny's frustration. Relationships are hard at the best of times, but when you can't see someone's facial expressions it certainly doesn't help. I knew Jenny was just tired, but it still hurt that the connection we usually felt wasn't there. The night got harder and harder to bear, and the air between us felt thick and heavy. I knew I was grating on her nerves, but I didn't know what to say to fix it. I'd never been lost for words with Jenny before. I know she was feeling pretty terrible herself, guilty that she wasn't describing things like Sticks sometimes did, but she just didn't have the energy.

After my inability to see created friction between us that night on the Seine, I was chuffed when I got to turn it around and make it actually work in our favour! On our Moulin Rouge tour, they thought my vision was just mildly impaired, so they gave us front-row seats to make it easier for me to see. I was about to say something, but Jenny elbowed me in the side and I shut up. Jenny got to enjoy the show from the best vantage point in the house (and I didn't ask her what was going on even once!). I guess there's got to be some advantages to being blind. Even though I couldn't see, I really enjoyed Moulin Rouge. There's this majestic atmosphere the moment you step through those doors, and a little bit of the magic stays with you even after you leave. But the tension from the river cruise was still hanging over us, and we could both feel it. At times I had myself completely convinced that the relationship was over.

Prague is a beautiful city and helped lift the feeling of unease between us, at least a little. We enjoyed our time there, but around every corner Jenny discovered another of the many perils of dating a blind man. One afternoon we went into a glass shop and I wanted to buy something, but Jenny said, 'Don't even think about it! Stop right there. Stand there, and do not move. Do *not* move.' I felt like a naughty child. The shop attendants were very pleased to see the back of me.

A few hiccups aside, we did have a brilliant time. From Moulin Rouge to Euro Disney, Bruges to Prague, we built some beautiful memories together. Still, when I got home, I knew things hadn't gone well. It felt to me as if Jenny had spent the whole trip feeling frustrated, and the fact that she called her parents to come and get her from the airport instead of accepting a lift from my parents only deepened my concerns. The night I got back my brother asked me to tell it to him straight – how did it go? 'The truth is,' I said, 'you were absolutely right. It was a test, that's for sure. And I'm not sure I passed.'

I had been totally out of my comfort zone from day one. In Sydney I'm independent, more or less. Even without my sight I have a sense of where everything is, I have a great support system, and everyone speaks English. But overseas, I was totally reliant on Jenny for the first time. It was something she'd never experienced before, and it put a great strain on our relationship. But looking back now, as hard as it was, it was a necessary learning process. You can't love everything about someone, all the time, and committing to someone is about taking the good with the bad.

I decided the best shot was to give Jenny some space for a couple of weeks and just see what happened. If I hadn't kept my distance, I really wonder whether the relationship would have survived. I think she had the same idea, because it wasn't until two weeks later that we finally spoke to one another again. I built up the courage to call, and invited her to a Rainbow Club function. I was terribly apprehensive about how it would go, but that night, as I held her close on the dance floor, she pulled gently away from me and put her hands on my face. We stood still for a moment and I was about to ask if something was wrong, when she whispered, 'I love you' and kissed me gently. Hearing those words sent a surge of warmth through my body. All my doubts fell away at once, and for a moment I felt a little lightheaded in the most perfect way. Finally she pulled away and I got to say the words back to her: 'I love you too.'

## Chapter 13
# Getting married

From there the relationship just kept getting better. In the last week of August, Jenny's company rewarded her for her good work with a weekend away at Rose Bay, and she asked me to come. The company paid for us to go to the spectacular Cirque du Soleil. Well, I was told it was spectacular, but circuses aren't really the most thrilling prospect for blind people, and halfway through I fell asleep on the shoulder of the Managing Director! It was pretty embarrassing, but fortunately his brother was blind, so he realised how boring it must have been for me and took it in his stride.

The next day, the company had chartered a seaplane to take everyone to Palm Beach for lunch. At first I assumed it was for employees only, but when I found out that Jenny was allowed to bring me along I decided to capitalise on the situation. It wasn't something I'd thought a whole lot about beforehand, but once the idea hit me I couldn't let it go: What could be more romantic than a proposal on a seaplane?

Initially I was going to do it on the way down, but I realised that wouldn't work because then we'd be stuck at a staff luncheon rather than being able to go and celebrate (well, assuming it went as planned!). But when we got back in the plane to return to Rose Bay, the time felt right.

Jenny snapped her seatbelt in, turned to me, and said, 'Right. Don't disturb me. I'm putting my headset on.' Perfect. For ten anxious minutes I sat there thinking, 'What now?' But I could only sulk for so long. Either I was going to do this or I wasn't. So I tapped her on the shoulder, and pulled her headsets off.

'What?!'

'I want to ask you a question.'

'Out with it then.'

'Will you marry me?'

'Shit.' She paused for the longest five seconds of my life. Then she said, 'Yes. Oh, yes.'

The rest of my life's achievements suddenly paled into insignificance. The woman of my dreams had agreed to marry me, and I was flooded with a warmth and joy like nothing I'd ever experienced. She kissed me, the most passionate kiss I could ever remember – but also the briefest. Then she promptly put her headset back on. But she squeezed my hand. I knew exactly what she was doing: she was making sure nobody else knew what had just happened. We're very private people, and neither of us wanted to share our engagement. At least for now, this was just for us. We went back to the hotel, and shared a bottle of champagne in the soft waning light. I'm no wine connoisseur, but it was the best champagne I've ever tasted in my life.

There was one more thing I had to do before we could share our happy news. Before asking Jenny to marry me, I'd run the idea past my parents. They were sitting in front of the TV watching the Olympics when I said, 'I need to ask a question.' They half-acknowledged me, but when there's sport on it's always hard to get their attention! So I just kept talking. 'I'm thinking next week, after my charity function, I'll go and see Brian and ask him whether I can marry his daughter.' Dad snatched the remote off the coffee table, turned off the TV, and said 'This is big news.' Wow, I thought. Turning off the Olympics, this is serious! We had a long chat, and Dad convinced me that asking Brian before Jenny was a big mistake. This was Jenny's decision to make, no one else's, and Jenny deserved to be the first to know about it. I'll never forget, Mum said, 'Does she know that you're disabled?' I said, 'No, Mum. We've been going out for six months, and she doesn't suspect a thing!' Classic Mum.

At the end of our chat Dad said to me, 'Good on you, mate. This is absolutely fantastic. Go for it.' When it came down to it, it wouldn't have mattered what anyone else thought – this was between me and Jenny. But it was still wonderful to know that I had his blessing and then some.

When the time finally came to ask Brian's blessing, I knew it wouldn't be quite so easy. But I certainly didn't foresee just how difficult it would turn out to be. I sort of waited for my moment – a moment that just never seemed to come – but when he started getting ready to go to Mass, I knew it was now or never. Here goes, I thought, and I just came out and said it. 'Brian, I'd like to ask you a question.' When I got no response I was intimidated as hell, but there was no turning back now. I said, 'I love your daughter more than anything in this world. I want to marry her.'

Brian said, 'What have you got to offer my daughter?'

I'm thinking, oh God, I wasn't briefed on this question. I was fumbling over my words like a raving idiot. I don't even know what I said, but thank God Jenny's mum Patricia came to the rescue and said, 'We always joke in this family.' He wasn't joking, and I knew that, but at least I was off the hook for now. Jenny was in the kitchen listening in and thinking, far out, he's getting hammered here. We laugh about it now, but in the moment I felt like a child being asked to stand up in class and answer an impossible question. That night we took Patricia and Brian out to dinner, and even though I'd never quite managed to resolve the question of what I had to offer, Brian seemed to have relaxed a bit. I think he knew we were right for one another, it was just his protective father mechanism kicking in!

Next, I told my parents, who were just as excited to hear the news the second time around, and I asked Mark Johnson to be my best man, my brother Tony to be a groomsman, and Pete Duncan to be our MC.

We set the wedding date for 9 April 2005. The next seven and a half months were a blur of wedding planning. First up was the issue of who we would invite. Brian wanted to have all of his extended family – including Jenny's thirty-four first cousins – and neither of us had the gumption to argue. We ended up with a guest list of 180! The idea was overwhelming at first, particularly for someone with only three first cousins! But I got used to it and realised that having nearly 200 people there to congratulate us on our big day could only be a good thing. To squeeze everyone in we needed a big venue, and we settled on the Manly Pacific.

Two of Jenny's uncles, Jim and John, are priests, and they were thrilled to marry us, which was very special. But we didn't want to burden them with the marriage paperwork, so we had a Catholic priest in Dee Why help us out with that. He ended up giving me an extended lecture on getting married and having children. I'm thinking, 'Matey. You've got no leg to stand on giving advice on either of those subjects! You've never been married, and you don't have children. Stop while you're ahead!'

Before the wedding we had to either go to an engagement encounter weekend, or spend one night per week with the priest over five weeks. We decided it would be easier to just get it all done in a single weekend, and so we found ourselves living in close quarters with twelve other couples. For three days, we discussed every possible issue that we needed to be prepared for in married life, from the wedding itself to children and dealing with conflict. It was an interesting weekend.

On the Saturday night, I wanted to go to a mate's buck's night, but I wasn't allowed out. I felt like a child not being allowed to choose where to spend my Saturday night, but there was no getting out of it. So, instead of bar-hopping, I sat there answering relationship questions. I'm always the first person to put my hand up in these situations, and I put in my two cents for almost every question. Until the last one: 'What would you do if you were pregnant and you knew your child was going to be disabled?' I just folded my arms and said nothing. Later, Jenny said, 'You should have seen the look on everyone's face as they turned and looked at you! And to make matters worse, it was the first time for the whole night that you actually kept your mouth shut!'

A few weeks later, Jenny helped me move out of Mum and Dad's house and into her flat. I was nervous to leave the only home I'd ever known – and the only home I knew my way around! It was going to take a lot of getting used to. But I was up to the challenge and I couldn't wait to live with the love of my life. I'd been spending every weekend at Jenny's for the past three months anyway, so I was getting pretty tired of spending half of my life living out of an overnight bag. I was ready for this new phase. I loved waking up with her every morning and going to bed with her every night. It just felt right.

In fact, now that we were engaged, it was a strange concept to me that I'd ever lived without her. Where initially I'd been hesitant to invite her to my swimming events, now it just seemed natural that she would come along with me. When January came around, I asked her to the Australia Day Luncheon with me for the first time. But the invitation itself was as far as I got. I neglected to tell her anything else about the event – like maybe that it was a lounge-suit event, or that it was the official Australia Day lunch for 1,500 people, including politicians such as Bob Carr and Gough Whitlam. I arrived in a suit, of course. She arrived dressed in a pair of trousers and a collared shirt, ready for a light lunch with a few ambassadors. To rub salt into her wounds, that year Australia Post chose fashion designers to feature in the 'Australian Legends' commemorative postage stamp series that was being promoted at the event. What are the chances! I didn't hear the end of it for a week. Actually, scratch that. I never heard the end of it at all! Every Australia Day lunch is a painful reminder, and Jenny will never let me forget it.

Nonetheless, she did come along with me to my Australia Day speech in Warialda that year, and we had a magnificent time. After my speech we visited an old people's home and ran into some real characters! A bunch of old men were preparing for their daily 'medicine' – a can of beer! One octogenarian in particular couldn't get enough of Jenny and was hugging her what seemed like every 10 minutes. A brazen old lady took one look at the chaperone and said, 'Gee, you've gotten fat.' Fortunately he took it in good humour! I love that about old people, just as I love it about kids – they say what they mean, no question about it! It was a great experience.

Meanwhile, the wedding planning continued. We booked the St Mary's Immaculate Catholic Church in Manly for the ceremony. Then there was invitations, a videographer, a photographer, the dress, the suits, the speeches, the readings… until you've actually organised a wedding, you just can't understand the incredible scope of the organisation required. We went all out on a videographer, because we wanted me to be able to listen back on the day, since I wouldn't be able to see the photos. But I didn't forget to take the time to remember why we were doing all this. Sometimes I would sit back and just marvel at the fact that a year ago, I hadn't even met this woman, and now she was the centre of my world. I couldn't imagine life without her.

But the wedding wasn't the only thing on my mind. By the time I'd proposed, plans were already underway for the next swim in the six-continent series: Africa. Our choices of location were pretty limited, as there were only so many places that would have the appropriate accessibility craft, swimming organisations, and facilities. We ended up going for South Africa. The plan was to do a 25-kilometre swim out in the ocean in and around a place called Simon's Town. But a simple newspaper story would change everything. In early December an article appeared in the *Manly Daily* about a woman who swam every morning in Simon's Town until, one morning, all that came back was her swimming cap. She'd been taken by a great white shark. When Jenny read this, she looked me in the eye and said, 'Sorry matey. You're not doing this swim. I want more than a swimming cap to come back for our wedding.'

Back to the drawing board. We settled on the Vaal River, which originates near Johannesburg and runs for 1,120 kilometres down to the Northern Cape west of Kimberley. Jenny felt more at ease knowing there were no great whites, and we made an unspoken agreement to put the possibility of hippos and rhinos charging us out of our minds. I would swim 13 kilometres down the river and 13 kilometres back, starting from the dam wall. I probably should have put more thought into the fact that it would be my first long-distance swim in a freshwater river with no current, but for whatever reason it didn't really cross my mind.

The swim was set for Saturday 26 March 2005. A lot of women wouldn't take well to their fiancé taking off to another country just weeks before their wedding, but Jenny was more than understanding. All the wedding details were taken care of, and she knew how much the swim meant to me. Narelle, Matt and I arrived the week before. It was the usual team, but it certainly wasn't the usual situation. Narelle's mother had passed away only a couple of weeks earlier, and for a while it looked as if Narelle might not come at all. Could we have done it without her? Sure, probably. But she'd been with me all along, and doing one of these swims without her just seemed unthinkable. When she decided to come I breathed a big sigh of relief. I was glad for her, as well. This swim might be just what she needed to get her mind off the grief.

We stayed with the generous Colin Sinclair, a man Narelle knew through her swimming contacts, and his wife and son in their beautiful home in an affluent area of Johannesburg. I came to Johannesburg with a few preconceptions, for sure – what the people would be like, what society would be like. But I really had no idea until I got there. The whole way back from the airport, Colin's eyes were darting back and forth from the rear-vision mirror, checking that no one was following us. When we arrived, we had to pass through a 30-metre-high security fence and close it securely behind us, only to be met with a pair of wide-eyed, salivating Dobermans. The house itself was rigged with masses of alarms, all linked to the local police station. And it wasn't just Colin that was so security conscious. The house across the road had two 24-hour security guards.

Coming from such a free, open, friendly country, it was a real eye-opener. Growing up in Killara, we didn't even bother to lock the doors! Life in Johannesburg would never have been for me. Even just being there for a week, there was always this base level of fear. You can build your fences as high as you like, but if you want to truly feel safe, you need to live in a safe country. But everyone's different, and at the time I think Colin felt that he was doing enough to keep his family safe. That said, three or four years later the family moved to Durban, and I'm sure it was because they were sick of feeling so unsafe. By then Colin had three kids, and it must have been exhausting having to worry about their safety all day, every day.

Colin's a great kayaker, and I guess that's why he chose to live opposite a manmade lake where he ran kayaking races every Friday night. For us it was incredibly handy, and in the lead-up to the swim we did a lot of training in that lake. Even more conveniently, Colin ran a kayaking shop, which meant Matt had his pick of over a hundred kayaks. Of course, we didn't just train in the one lake. We spent a bit of time in and around the area in different lakes, just acclimatising to the local conditions, and made the hour trek out to the Vaal River the day before to work out the logistics and meet the pilot.

On the day of the swim we set out around 7 am to make sure we had enough daylight. Narelle was in the inflatable boat with the pilot and a friend of Colin's who had volunteered to be timekeeper. Matt started in the kayak, but Narelle switched places with him now and then.

I hopped in thinking, yes, 26 kilometres is a long way, but at least it would be a relatively easy swim. I'm not sure where I got that idea, but it ended up being one of the hardest swims I've ever done. With no current and no salt, I had no buoyancy and my legs felt as if they were constantly sinking. Scratch that – they *were* sinking!

It was Easter Saturday and heaps of people were out on their boats having a good time (and wondering what the hell I was doing swimming down the Vaal River!). Logistically it probably wasn't the best, and at times Matt and Narelle got quite frustrated trying to see where I was and steer us around the boats, but from my point of view it was great. Having all that energy surrounding me really spurred me on, and the first part of the swim went well. As in the Parana River swim, I had the advantage of markers every kilometre to let us know how far we'd come.

But in the fresh water, it was harder work than I could ever have imagined. After what seemed like an eternity, we reached the 13-kilometre mark and turned around. We were halfway. Only halfway! This was going to be an almighty struggle. From there it just got harder and harder. By the end it felt more like cycling than swimming as my legs dropped further and further down. Then the cramps set in. I flailed around in the water, switching from freestyle to breaststroke to backstroke and back again, anything to ease the pain and just keep moving forwards.

And of course, the light was starting to dim as dusk approached. The inflatable boat had no lights, so once night set in there was no way we could realistically continue. I was sore, tired, and beaten, but I simply had to pick up the pace. With 3 or 4 kilometres to go, I felt a shooting pain surge up my leg. I knew the feeling well, knew it was 'just' cramps. But the pain was enough to make me doubt whether I could actually finish this thing. Then I thought of Jenny. Jenny, the most understanding woman in the world. She'd been willing to let me come on this swim just two weeks before the wedding, and not only that, but actually encourage me and support me the whole way. Was I really going to come home only to tell her I'd failed to complete it? No way. I put my head down and plugged away as if my life depended on it. I pictured Jenny, the wedding, the buck's day. My focus was slipping away, but I just kept kicking and stroking. Suddenly, the dark, angry clouds of an approaching thunderstorm appeared in the distance. Great. If the fatigue and cramps didn't get me, perhaps lightning would.

Then I hit something. It was the sand at the bank of the dam wall. I'd made it to the end. And I could hardly get up! As Narelle hauled me into the inflatable boat, my muscles were crying out for reprieve. Now that I'd stopped, the aches somehow felt even sharper. But I didn't care. I was just happy I'd finished. In the distance the lightning was crackling, and Narelle said quietly, 'My mother's come to say well done.' I heard a few sniffs, but I could tell her tears were borne of joy. I was almost in tears myself. She'd made the right decision coming with us, and I think at that moment she finally made peace with her mother's loss. 'We did it, matey', I said to her, and she rested her head on my shoulder.

'James,' the pilot said to me, 'I've done a lot of distance events, and not just swims either. Athletics, triathlons. We know what's involved. We know how much it hurts, how hard it is to keep up the mental game. And we've just watched you do that for 10 hours and

47 minutes. God, it hurt just watching you towards the end there! But we're freaking delighted. That was a brilliant swim, mate. A brilliant effort. Don't you ever think otherwise.' I needed to hear that. I'd given everything; I felt spent and empty. But now I was reminded that I felt like this for a reason. I felt like this because I had achieved something amazing today.

We made our way back to land, where Colin's friends had gotten a fire going. I sat down beside it to try to warm up, and a bloke came up and asked, 'Would you like some rum?' I'm sure he had the best of intentions, but really? That was the last thing I wanted! I took some Coke instead, and had a little bit to eat. Then I promptly vomited it all back up. You take in that much water, eventually it has to escape somehow!

One of Colin's mates offered to drive me back to Colin's place. I assumed we would just go back the way we came, but when I asked him he looked horrified. 'God, no! No way we'd do that. Too many red lights.'

I asked the obvious question. 'What happens at a red light?'

'Well, if you do see one, you go straight through it. You stop for a red light, you'll just get mugged.'

Once again I was reminded what a sheltered little life I'd led.

We only had a couple of days left in Johannesburg before going home, but we made the most of them. The day after the swim we went to the local zoo, and it was really good fun just walking around and seeing all the animals. We bought some beautiful hand-carved giraffe statues, which I still have to this day. That night I took everyone out for dinner. As we walked in – I'll never forget it – we passed a big sign: 'Please leave your guns here.' Everywhere I turned, I was reminded of how frightening South Africa really is. It didn't stop us having a really great night though.

As we were waiting to get on the plane to go home, Narelle realised she'd lost the precious gemstone she'd bought only a couple of days earlier. Well, lost is probably the wrong word. It had been taken out of her bag. For the next hour, I sat there waiting as she ran around the entire airport retracing every step. Quietly, I knew she wasn't going to find it, but of course she had to try. Then, wonder of wonders, just when she was about to give up, she found it at the bottom of a bin (she was pretty committed to the search!). The stone had been so well packed, the would-be thief couldn't get it open, and just chucked it in the bin! What are the chances! As the final call was being announced over the PA, she ran back red-faced and grinning, package in hand. We flopped down into our chairs and grinned at each other. 'Think we need a double Scotch after that one!' I said.

The South African swim made it three legs down and three to go in the continental swims. I'd heard a lot about South Africa, but I'd never been, and I'm so thankful I got the opportunity. I left the country with a much better understanding of what it's like, a heightened sense of the fear and insecurity that go with living there. I had a great time, of course, and I met some wonderful people, but I would never consider living there.

After the Cook Strait, I didn't think any of the other swims would even come close in terms of difficulty. But the Vaal River gave it a run for its money. It was a unique swim in terms of the conditions, and despite the trials and tribulations it was a great experience. But, as always, I was pleased when it was over! Not least of all because I got back knowing that in nine days, I would be marrying the love of my life. And in only two days, I would be enjoying my last night out as a bachelor.

Mark had organised for my buck's party to start at the Waitara Bowls Club, where we would play barefoot bowls all afternoon. I dressed in chinos and a shirt, but when I arrived I was presented with a cap, goggles, and a pair of red Speedos, which I was forced to wear outside of my chinos all day and all night. That looked ridiculous enough, but with my white cane as well I really looked a treat – just ask the guy who put his foot in it joking about the cane being part of my outfit!

All my mates were there, including Dean Reeves. It meant the world to me that he was there. He would've been in my bridal party too, but he was in the Navy at the time, helping the recovery effort in Indonesia after the terrible tsunami in 2004. So for him to fly home especially to be there for my buck's party and wedding was something special. I always knew he was one of those friends who would do anything for me, and here he was proving it.

We had a lovely dinner at the Belgian Beer café in the rocks, and from there it was bar-hopping for the rest of the night. Mark had one stipulation: no wine or spirits before midnight. (Once the clock ticked over into the new day, I could get as plastered as I liked!) He was keen to avoid a repeat of his brother's buck's, where the night ended way too early because the groom was so drunk he could barely move. His plan worked, though I was far from sober! It must have been quite a sight for Jenny seeing me drunkenly trying to get my Speedos off over my trousers when I got home.

The big day arrived, and it was a stunner – sunny and 25 degrees. A beautiful day for a swim, I remember thinking – force of habit – but an even better day for a wedding! I spent the morning at my parents' place getting ready with Mark and Tony. The wedding was to start at 3 pm, so around 2 pm Dad drove us down to the church. On the second try, that is – he was so excited he went the wrong way and had to do a U-turn! This from the man who was so afraid of being late that as kids we used to imitate him: 'You can never be too careful. What if there's a crash on the Harbour Bridge?' I was touched to know he was as rattled as I was.

We arrived at the church and stood at the altar in nervous anticipation until, after what seemed like an eternity, I heard Pachelbel's Canon start to float down from the organ. The hairs on the back of my neck stood up. The moment I'd been waiting for had finally arrived. I anxiously waited as the flower girl, the pageboy, and Jenny's bridesmaids walked down the aisle.

Then Mark touched me on the shoulder and said the words I'd been waiting to hear: 'Here she comes.' With Brian by her side, Jenny walked down the aisle towards me. At the altar, Brian shook my hand and I knew once and for all that he really did want to accept me into his family. It was a moment I'll never forget.

Having Jenny's uncles marry us was very special; I know it meant a lot to Jenny and her family. I stumbled for a good few moments putting the ring on Jenny's finger, but I got there in the end. As we walked out of the church everyone was congratulating us and I could hear from the nasal tone to a few people's voices that we'd prompted a few tears! We had some photos with family and friends at the church, then we and the bridal party went down to Shelly Beach. One of the best beaches in the world.

Shelly Beach faces west so we still had a lot of light. We took pictures up on the top of the beach, down on the sand, looking back onto Manly. It was just a beautiful afternoon. We had time for a few drinks, just the bridal party, before heading back to the reception, and that was one of the most special parts of the day. Having a chance to just slow down for a minute and enjoy.

Then it was on to the reception at the Manly Pacific, which was just a phenomenal evening. Pete Duncan MCed brilliantly (and then promptly hopped in his car, drove to Canberra, and ran a marathon! There's nobody quite like Pete.). The speeches were great, thanks in part to Jenny's good management: She had enforced a 9-minute limit per speech. It's not something I would have even considered, but at my brother's wedding speeches went on for a total of 2 hours, and by the end of it half the room was asleep. She said, 'No way I'm letting that happen at our wedding. Forty-five minutes max, then it's time to party!' She was spot on.

The 9-minute limit forced everyone to really put a lot of thought into how they wanted to use those 9 minutes. To make them count. I had that in mind when I made my speech. I shared my memory of making a wish at the Wishing Statue on the Charles IV Bridge in Prague the previous year. Today, that wish had come true. 'There are 500,000 words in the English dictionary,' I said, 'but 499,997 don't mean much. "I love you" are the only three words that truly count.' My cousin, who is high up in the public services, said he thought my speech was as good as any he'd ever heard.

Everything went just as planned, though even if the day had fallen apart at the seams it wouldn't have stemmed our joy. Surrounded by our closest (and our most distant, let's be honest!) friends and family, we had made a commitment to stand by each other forever. It was the best decision I'd ever made.

For ten days, we honeymooned on Tokoriki Island, Fiji. It was a beautiful time, full of joy and cocktails. But finally, on 27 April, it was time to return to the real world. We'd bought a home in February and negotiated an extended settlement until May, so we came back and moved straight into our new home, a lovely place in Daisy Street in North Balgowlah. Built in 1912, it was a beautiful single-storey cottage with three big bedrooms, lounge, dining, kitchen, and a verandah out the back. At the time it was absolutely perfect for us, and we would live there for six years. It was the beginning of our happily ever after.

## Chapter 14
## Turkey and Thailand

The fourth leg of the continental swim series – Europe – would be 25 kilometres across the Aegean Sea from Gökçeada to Anzac Cove. I'm a bit of a history buff; ever since high school I've been fascinated by Australian history. I'd studied the Gallipoli Campaign at school and it just enthralled me, the thought of arriving at this windswept place and fighting for it in World War I. I often thought of the 8,709 Australian soldiers and 2,779 New Zealand soldiers that died.

So from that point of view, this was one of my most iconic swims. It's a swim that I'd always wanted to do. I tried in 2001, but the guy I was emailing made me work very hard for very little. It wasn't just the struggles of English-to-Turkish translation, it was a general feeling that all he wanted was to find a way to take my money. In the end, I was sure he was just having a lend of me, and I bailed. It would have been sensational to have had the chance to do it, and I was very disappointed, but I accepted that it just wasn't going to come together. Now, four years on, the time was right.

But I wasn't only doing it for me. The swim would raise money and awareness for the Eye Foundation, which gives grants to ophthalmologists. It's always been one of the most thrilling parts of swimming for me, having that opportunity to really make a difference in people's lives. The Eye Foundation funds research into the full spectrum of eye diseases that can cause blindness, with the ambitious aim of eliminating blindness worldwide. It's a cause that's very close to my heart, and I felt honoured to be able to help them in some small way.

I knew organising this swim was going to be a long process, and I'd actually gotten the ball rolling about a year earlier. It was an intimidating thought that to even have a chance at doing this swim, I'd need to send hundreds of emails and be prepared for many lengthy phone calls in the middle of the night. I knew I was going to be up against it, but I also knew I could make it work. I *would* make it work.

I started by emailing the Australian Prime Minister, the New Zealand Prime minister and the Turkish Prime Minister. I wanted to let them know not just what I was doing, but why I was doing it. I knew how important Gallipoli was to these countries, and I didn't want them to think I was desecrating it, or disrespecting the soldiers in any way. I didn't want to make it a media stunt. I did it because I love the history of World War I and what it meant for the relationships between Australia, New Zealand, and Turkey. That was always the emphasis for me.

Surprisingly, the New Zealand Prime Minister was the only one who responded to my emails. I was disappointed, but I wasn't deterred. I continued contacting people, and so many people ended up getting involved. I had people from the Department of Defence, the Department of Foreign Affairs and Trade, the Commonwealth War Graves Commission, the Australian Embassy in Turkey. By October 2004 almost everything was in place. The Turks were happy, the Aussies were happy, the Kiwis were happy. We were all set for September 2005.

Then in late October, I found out that my main contact in Turkey had been sacked, and I had to organise the entire swim all over again. God, I can't even tell you how disappointed I was! And not just disappointed, alarmed. Alarmed at the magnitude of the task ahead of us. We had the same hard slog to look forward to, but a hell of a lot less time to do it. Of course, the fact that we had the South African swim thrown in the middle there didn't help. And then there was the small matter of our wedding! But we made it work. The emails resumed, and they would continue right up to the week before we left for Turkey.

Paul Given from the Department of Foreign Affairs and Trade was a godsend. He always kept me in the loop, but all he wanted from my end was for me to just keep plugging away. 'Don't worry about the paperwork,' he told me. 'That's my job. Trust me, they always make you sweat before they give you an answer. Just get yourself organised. Get yourself over here. That's your only job!'

Well, if that was my only job, I was going to make sure I did it well! Sticks, Matt and I went as hard as we ever had at the training, in the ocean, in Manly Dam, in the pool. The swimming was easy, knowing I was working towards such an important and exciting goal. But the ongoing email trail was frustrating, time-consuming, and most of the time pretty damn fruitless. Was the swim even going to happen?

Before we knew it, it was the week before the swim was scheduled to happen and we still didn't know where we stood. But we'd put in so much preparation that the thought of not doing it just wasn't something we were even prepared to consider. So I got on the plane to Istanbul, and I hoped for the best! It was tough, not knowing, but the alternative was even tougher. In the end, thank goodness, we were allowed to do the swim.

When we got to Istanbul, we went out for a lavish seven-course Turkish meal with Hakan, a good friend of my sister's. We had such a lovely night sitting and reminiscing, and I fell instantly in love with Istanbul. What a cool city. Unfortunately our time there was all too brief. I'd thought Istanbul and Gallipoli were pretty close, but they're really not. It was a 5-hour drive between the cities – in a cramped hire car along some of the crappiest roads I've ever seen at that – but it was all part of the authentic Turkish experience!

On the way, we stopped off at a restaurant in the outskirts of Istanbul to go to the toilet. If I'd known what it was going to be like, I probably would have just held on! It was literally just a hole in the ground. I wasn't expecting all the creature comforts of Australia, but this was a restaurant in Turkey, not a third-world country! Crikey,

I thought, what's a public toilet like? At any rate, it was another 'authentic' experience to add to the list! We made our way to our hotel in Çanakkale, near Gallipoli, and took a well-earned rest.

Sticks joined us not long after, and we had a little window of time before we had to get across to the island of Gökçeada to do the swim. And during that window, we did one of the best things I've ever done. We went to the sights in Gallipoli, just the three of us. It sounds so simple, but to me it was heaven, fulfilling my lifelong dream to go to Gallipoli and getting to experience it with two of my best mates in the world. I soaked up every detail as Matt and Sticks read me the names and stories of the soldiers, and described the sights.

On the way up to Lone Pine, it was so windy we couldn't hear each other speak. Yet somehow when we got to the top everything fell silent. Even the birds stopped tweeting. Everything stopped but the soft lap of the waves against the shore below. It was such an eerie sensation, and I think for me without the sense of sight the silence was even more all-encompassing. I just stood there gaping. Wow, I thought. What a place. What a story.

Then just when I thought it couldn't get any better, we went to the Nek. I'd read a lot about the Battle of the Nek, in which 570 people fought for a 200 square-metre piece of land, and only 40 lived to tell the tale. When we covered it in history class I remember everyone saying, what a waste of time, what a waste of life. And I always agreed… until I actually went there. Standing on that little, seemingly insignificant piece of land, I realised that if Australia had won the Battle of the Nek, and New Zealand the Battle of Chunuk Bair, it would have got them to Çanakkale and potentially changed the entire course of the war. I walked away thinking, every soldier died for a reason. And I'll always believe that. It made me realise there's only so much you can learn from history books, and you can't necessarily believe everything you read. Going there and seeing for myself how important that piece of land was, how worthwhile the battle, opened my mind to a whole new way of thinking. Yes, we lost a lot of people. But it was worth it.

I was also awestruck to learn that while 8,709 Australians died, 80,000 Turks died. The Australian history books never tell you that part. It's a shame, really, because I think it really goes to show how well Australia did in the overall context of the battle.

We would come back for one last visit to Çanakkale after the swim, and while we were there a Turkish man came up to us and asked whether we were American or Australian. When we said Australian, he bowed to us in the middle of the street. To me, that was one of the most outstanding moments of the entire trip. It epitomises the respect and camaraderie between Turkey and Australia, in spite of everything that's happened.

Every morning when I woke I was humbled by that same feeling of awe. I walked on this sacred land day after day, yet the impact never diminished. Here I was, ninety years after the Battle of the Nek, knowing that deep beneath the soil I was treading were the bones of the fallen. Every day I had to pinch myself. I was really here, in the place where all these important battles took place. It was just magnificent.

That evening we had to take a boat across the Aegean Sea to get to the island of Gökçeada, where the swim would start. It turned into a bit of a rush in the end and by the time we got on the boat I was hungry and had a headache, so finding ourselves on a crappy, cramped little boat immediately put me in a bad mood. The seas were choppy, and I could barely keep my bum on my tiny, uncomfortable seat. I could only hope things would get better from here on out.

We arrived at Gökçeada in the middle of the night, weighed down by masses of luggage, with no bloody idea where we were meant to be going. We eventually found out that we were supposed to be staying on top of a hill. Just when it seemed like things couldn't get any more difficult. In 24 hours, I'd gone from one of the best days in my life to one of the worst.

Eventually we managed to get in contact with someone from the place we were staying, and they took us up to the top of the hill. Wouldn't you know it, none of them spoke English. I'm thinking, can this get any worse? I was in one room, and Sticks and Matt were in another, so at least I had my own room. At least I would get a good night's sleep. Yeah, right. The windows had been left open, and a swarm of mosquitoes were buzzing around my head. Between that, intermittent police sirens and shouting neighbours, I didn't get a wink of sleep. At one point I went and lay down in the toilet just to try to evade the mosquito army, but even there I wasn't safe from their buzzing and biting. It was a horrendous night.

We now had to try and get in contact with our pilot and crew. Although the people we were staying with couldn't really speak English, we managed to have a few stilted conversations, and they told us the boat wouldn't leave until it was light. I hoped they were wrong. Or maybe something had been lost in translation. I'd been counting on starting this thing really early, because everyone knows the best time to swim is in the early morning when there's virtually no wind. But they insisted we'd have to wait for daylight. That would add another hour and a half to the day! My anxiety just kept on rising. When we eventually got in contact with the boat pilot, he confirmed what we'd been told. We wouldn't start until it was light.

On the morning of the swim, 25 September 2005, we awoke to the ominous sound of thumping wind and rattling windows. I'm thinking, here we go. I've spent eighteen months organising this swim, and now it's not even going to happen. All the trials and tribulations, all the effort and time, all the anticipation and excitement. All for nothing.

Matt went down to see the pilot, and came back with the news I'd been dreading. 'Sorry James. There's a 30-knot head wind in a direct line from here to Anzac Cove. It's too dangerous. They won't do it.' I could feel my heart beating hard in my chest. I couldn't accept it.

'Well?' I said. 'What are we going to do now?'

'We'll see what happens. Maybe the wind will drop. Maybe we'll be able to do the swim after all. You know if it was just me on a kayak we'd be out there in a heartbeat. But we can't do this without the boat. We're playing by their rules now.'

While Sticks and I sat up in the house on the hill squirming, Matt kept up communication with the pilot, and eventually we had to concede that, no, we couldn't do the swim from Gökçeada to Anzac Cove. But we came to a compromise. We would punt from Gökçeada across to the other side, then swim 12 kilometres down the side of the Aegean Sea, where the shoreline would shield us from the wind and we'd be close to safety if things got hairy.

We all piled into the boat. As I was mulling over where we were going and what we were going to do from here, and trying to deal with the anxiety and disappointment of having to change our plans at the last minute, I was asked to convert 12 kilometres to nautical miles. My brain was already in overload, what was one more task? So I set about dividing 12 by 1.852 in my head. Eventually we got to our starting point, and I hopped in, thinking, thank God. I was just thrilled to be in the water at all.

Most people breathe to both sides, but I've always found it more comfortable to breathe exclusively to the right. Today, that preference was my saviour, because the wind was coming from my left. The wind actually helped me in that the lap of the waves against my chest acted as a good indicator of the direction I was facing. As long as the waves were hitting me from the same direction, I knew I was swimming in a fairly straight line. I could hear the whistles pretty well, too. Of course I was still disappointed that I wouldn't get to do what I'd planned. But I was still swimming into Anzac Cove. And if I let a few missteps get in the way of my excitement, I'd regret it forever. So I got in and I did what I had come to do – I swam. I swam really, really well.

And everyone on the boat was having a grand old time. To look at them all, you'd never guess anything had gone amiss. And, really, in the scheme of things, it hadn't. Any minute now I would be swimming into Anzac Cove. They say every cloud has a silver lining, and a few minutes later I got mine. By swimming down the side of the Aegean Sea instead of across it, I was able to swim to shore 400 metres short of Anzac Cove at the Anzac Memorial.

The head of the Commonwealth War Graves Commission met Matt and I at the bottom of the steps and we walked up together.

He shook my hand and said some kind words, and I felt such a sense of pride and accomplishment. I'd made it to the Anzac Memorial. I stood in front of the 'zed', and I observed a minute's silence. As I reflected on what it meant to be here – more than that, what it meant to be Australian – the thrill of the moment overcame me and I felt the tingle of warm tears running down my face. This was why I was here.

We got back in the water and swam the last 400 metres into Anzac Cove, and this time it was Sticks that was with me. Another silver lining – in a way, I got to finish this historic swim twice. Once with each of my team. It was very special. I got up on the beach and observed another minute's silence. The unfettered emotion rose up again and the tears resumed as I cast my mind back ninety years to the moment they arrived at this beach in the dark, with leagues of Turkish soldiers against them. And here I was arriving in beautiful sunlight after 4 hours of swimming free in the ocean, standing with my mates and the best Turkish crew I could have asked for. I walked along the beach enjoying the feeling of sand between my toes and let myself imagine how very different this place must have been ninety years ago. Not for the first time, I realised how incredibly lucky I was.

The boat pilot asked me what I was thinking. I said, 'I've got the Mustafa Kemal statue in front of me, Lone Pine and Nek behind me, and fields full of incredible history all around. I'm thrilled. I'm overwhelmed. I'm proud, and I'm grateful to the ANZACs who fought here with such strength and passion.' To me, Gallipoli is the greatest place in the world. And after eighteen months and more than a few curve balls, here I was, at the end of an amazing swim. Few moments are as dear to me. Even though the swim didn't work out exactly as I wanted it to, in the end the thrill was just as great. And to top it all off, we generated some great press for the Eye Foundation.

After I came back from Gallipoli, we were going to appear on Channel 7's *Weekend Sunrise* on a Sunday morning in November to promote the Eye Foundation and Gallipoli. But in a cruel twist of fate, the week before the interview part of the Lane Cove Tunnel collapsed, causing massive damage to a nearby apartment block. One of the biggest stories to come out of it was about a little bird called Tweety, who ended up holed up in amongst the rubble for two days before finally being rescued. On the Friday before the show, I was ready and waiting for my appearance when I got an email saying, 'Sorry mate, we're going to interview Tweety Bird instead of you.' I'd been bumped off by a bird, and one thing's for sure, my mates weren't going to let me forget it. 'Can't wait to hear the bird's answers to the questions!' They still bring it up from time to time, cheeky buggers.

Next up was the Asian leg – a 22-kilometre swim from Mai Khao Beach to Patong Beach in Phuket, Thailand, in February 2006. This swim was totally different from any other swim I'd done before. On paper, it looked like it would be a cinch compared with Cook Strait. Twenty-two kilometres in calm water seems pretty harmless. But I knew better. The water temperature was going to be 28 degrees. As someone who loves it around 15 degrees and whose body falls apart when humidity gets even slightly high in Sydney, this swim would test me enormously. How did we train for this? Well, hanging around in Manly wasn't going to be much use. Instead, we sought out the hottest places we could. It was my worst nightmare, but it was the only way. Swimming in the heat was a totally different ball game to swimming in the cold. In the cold, you're thinking about getting fluids and water down you as quickly as you can so you don't lose heat. This was the polar opposite. If you stopped, it was because you *wanted* to lose heat!

One sweltering Friday night in the middle of January, we went to the pool at the footy stadium. The middle lane is always the warmest, and on this particular night it was hovering around 28 degrees. I swam for hours in the baking heat. Every time I stopped for a feed I'd make sure I drank an entire bottle of water, and tipped another over my head. I must admit, I had a hard time adjusting. I spent a lot of time just trying to get my head around how best to swim in these conditions. I'm a bit of a free spirit in the water; I try to listen to my team's instructions but it's not uncommon for me to drift off a little! But for this swim I knew that wasn't an option. If I didn't watch myself and follow my team's instructions to a T, I could easily end up overheating. And if that happened, I'd be in hot water... so to speak!

My team was Matt, Jenny, Brooke, and her partner Grant Robinson – that same Grant Robinson who had won my first 15-kilometre event way back in 1997. He had been an excellent open-water swimmer in his day and I'm sure he could have gone on to swim the English Channel if a shoulder injury hadn't put an end to his career. But, to his credit, rather than letting it get him down, it spurred him on to help others reach their goals – just as he was doing for me on this trip. It was the first time Jenny had come along for one of my swims, and it meant the world to have her there with me.

Luckily, Brooke had friends who were members of a hotel chain in Phuket and we managed to get free accommodation in a beautiful resort. The place was amazing. It had four or five restaurants just within the resort, with both Thai and western food. At the end of the day we'd kick back and have a drink looking over the ocean and the pools. And never a day went by that we didn't take advantage of the cheap massages! There was even a little boat connecting all the resorts around an artificial lake which gave us access to a few different shopping options. Having such beautiful accommodation made an enormous difference. But it stood in stark contrast to the lifestyles of the Thai people surrounding us.

We were in Phuket just over a year after the 2004 tsunami that destroyed so many businesses along Patong Beach. Our hotel had been fortunate enough to avoid the brunt of the tsunami, and all the main infrastructure survived. But even then, regaining lost tourism was still an epic challenge. It was heartbreaking yet fascinating to watch the people rebuilding infrastructure, rebuilding tourism, rebuilding their lives. And even after everything they'd been through, they were all so incredibly friendly and welcoming. Experiencing their kindness and hospitality was really special.

The beach in front of the hotel had a mapped-out area for people to swim away from water sports, and every morning that's where we'd train. We'd have breakfast, then walk straight out into the ocean. It was just so easy! And it was a good chance for us to get some practice swimming in the hot conditions before the big day.

The day came for the swim: Saturday 18 February 2006. I was facing one of my biggest challenges. I knew we'd done all the right things in training, but still, the pressure was on and I wasn't sure how I'd perform. It's easy enough to go out and train for half an hour early in the morning, close to shore where it's not all that warm. But to do it out there in the open for 7.5 hours… that was something else entirely. Still, today the current would be with me and there was barely a whisper of wind. If I didn't perform today, I'd have no one to blame but myself. We wanted to start just before daybreak. Time wasn't against us by any means, but I knew that the sooner we got out there the cooler the water would be, and for me, that was everything!

Just as I was getting off the kayak into the main boat, I fell and hit my arm. I'm thinking, that's just what I need. Ten seconds in, and I've already hurt myself. I'd been nervous about the swim anyway, and even this small misstep sent me into a bit of a spiral. If there was ever a time for Jenny to have been there for me, this was it. She just spoke to me quietly, kept me calm, and reassured me in that angelic voice of hers until I was ready to let it go and get in the water. That's why when I found her I knew she was the only 'other half' for me. She always knows exactly what to say. No one else gets me like she does. By the time she was done with me, my attitude had done a full 180. Today was going to be a great day.

For the first 3 or 4 hours I was swimming really well – unusually well! It was hard work, but by the same token, I think I'd really built it up in my mind and maybe the anticipation was worse than the actual experience. Every half-hour I would have a drink of water and a feed, and douse myself with an ice-cream tub full of water. Drinking water, carb syrup, dousing water. I had to keep repeating the sequence in my mind, because if I mixed up the drinking water and the rinsing water, I'd be paying for it the next day with gastro! The change in routine had me a little bit confused for a while, but eventually we got that into sync. Meanwhile the sun was rising higher and higher, and the water was getting warmer and warmer. At about the 4-hour mark the wind, which had been behind us at the start, changed into a headwind.

This was where I sort of lost it a bit. I was hot and bothered, and really not dealing well with the knowledge that all my good swimming so far had only gotten me halfway. And it was only going to get hotter from here. Again Jenny came to my rescue, hopping in the water beside me to do what she could to lift my spirits. Thinking maybe all I needed was a bit of an energy boost, she also gave me some honey. Bad move. My very next stroke it all came straight back up. But Jenny's words did settle me a bit, and kept me going for the next couple of hours. When we eventually reached the headland of Patong Beach, relief washed over me. I always get stronger when I know I'm in the finishing stretch. Finally, we were up to the easy part.

Wrong! Turns out it's actually 3 kilometres from the headland to the shore of Patong Beach. It was only when Matt said we had another hour to go that the realisation hit me. But it didn't completely damp my enthusiasm, and with the help of my little cheer squad I managed to maintain my speed. I still remember the massive change I felt when we got to about 400 metres out from shore. In an instant, the water depth seemed to go from almost inconceivably deep to very shallow. At that moment, my stomach turned a little. It might have been the masses of salt water I'd ingested, but more likely it was the realisation that this may very well be the point where the tsunami just swamped everything.

At Patong Beach, there's only about 200 metres of sand before you hit a six-lane highway, the other side of which is a bustling hub of businesses. I've never seen anything else like it. I thought back to the point where the water suddenly got shallow, and I couldn't help imagining how suddenly the water must have lurched towards the shore at that point. Towards the beach, the highway, the businesses, the hotels, and everything else in its path. The fear those poor people must have felt. I remember hearing it on the news when it happened – I think we probably all do. It was absolute carnage. Even now, over a year later, they still hadn't finished fixing all the buildings and electricity lines.

When we got to within 300 metres of shore Matt said, 'All right, guys. We started this together, and we're going to finish it together. Grant, Brooke, Jenny. Jump in the water. Let's bring this home together!' By this stage I was so ready to feel solid ground under my feet that I wasn't even listening. I was just swimming as hard as I could, which unfortunately didn't work out all that well for Jenny. The poor thing spent the whole 300 metres just struggling to keep up. Eventually, she ended up just grabbing hold of the kayak and coasting in that way. But I know she was glad to be there with us as we walked up the shore of Patong Beach. What a great feeling, finishing this swim with the team that got me there. With my beautiful wife. What a day. What an achievement. Every swim on this six-continent series was throwing up its own little challenges, and as testing as they'd been, I was feeling more proud of myself with every swim.

I collapsed on the sand, and within 30 seconds a Thai bloke came over to try to sell me a shirt. I'm sure he knew what 'no' means, but he certainly didn't let it deter him! He asked me where I was from, and I said, 'Out there', pointing to the ocean. Fortunately Brooke speaks Thai, and at this point she came over to fend him off. Whatever she was saying, it didn't seem to be having much effect. But when I vomited in front of him, he took his leave! There were plenty more peddlers of useless goods wandering the beach waiting to intercept, so we didn't stick around much longer.

You know, you do a lot of planning for these swims, and it's always a strange mix of emotions when all of a sudden, just like that, it's over. For me, completing a swim in 28-degree water meant a lot, because it proved something to me. It proved I could swim in the heat, yes, but in doing so it proved I could swim in *any* conditions. It proved I was a bona fide marathon swimmer. I'd done swims in everything from 11 degrees to 28 degrees, in whipping winds and angry waves. I learned a lot about myself, I'd done myself proud, and I felt deeply satisfied.

Just being able to sit at the dinner table with my favourite people at the end of one of my most accomplished swims was a real treat. Matt's girlfriend Jeannette arrived just as we were all about to retire to our rooms, having flown in earlier that day. She walked in bursting with energy and said, 'Let's go out!' Grant had already fallen asleep at the table, my eyelids were threatening to give up at any moment, and the rest of us didn't look much better. So all she got from us was a few raised eyebrows, headshakes and mutters of 'In your dreams!' Five minutes later, we were all in bed. I still chuckle when I think about Jeannette's face when she got such a dismal response to her enthusiasm!

Now that the swim was over, we all took advantage of where we were and had a heap of fun in and around Phuket. Brooke, Grant, Matt, and Jeannette went to Phi Phi Island while Jenny and I stayed and had a relaxing spa day together, followed by several rounds of happy hour cocktails. We had a great time together, and it was all the more special because it was the first time I'd really been able to share that post-swim euphoria with her. It was a pretty full-on week! And I wouldn't change it for anything. Five down, one to go.

## Chapter 15
## Catalina Channel

Now it was back into the planning, back into the training. The sixth and final swim in the series would be the Catalina Channel, USA. We planned to do it in September 2006, which gave us six months to train. The 33-kilometre Catalina Channel swim is known as one of the greats, and it can throw out some pretty crazy conditions. The greatest difficulty comes near the end when the wind picks up. If you're not swimming really hard, it can easily get the better of you. I knew getting up to speed would be a huge challenge.

I also knew I wasn't getting any younger. By now I was 37 years old, I'd been swimming for almost ten years straight, and my body was starting to tell me it had had enough. It wasn't unexpected; plenty of other marathon swimmers had told me that by the time you get to your late thirties things start getting tough. Who knew how much longer my body would be able to hack it? For all I knew this could be my swan song, and I had to give it everything I had. But there was another driver as well.

By this stage in my career, charity was becoming more and more important for me. Throughout my career I'd been so lucky in so many ways, and I desperately wanted to give something back. My dad, an ophthalmologist, had gone to university with Fred Hollows, so I decided I would call The Fred Hollows Foundation. By chance, the usual Head of Partnerships at the Foundation had just gone on maternity leave, and a woman named Penny Tribe had replaced her. And what a magnificent woman she was – and is. That day marked the beginning of a long and rewarding association with Fred Hollows, and with Penny herself.

In many ways, it's been life changing. The Fred Hollows Foundation changed my entire attitude, not to fundraising, but to the Indigenous people of Australia. I'm forever grateful to have been brought up as I was, in a well-off family in a beautiful part of Sydney, but what you don't get in that situation is any kind of education about Indigenous people. I'm the first to admit I was very ignorant in this regard, and The Fred Hollows Foundation changed that. I am now a big advocate for Indigenous people.

If you'd told me in my teens that in 2008 I would be writing to my local federal member, who happened to be Shadow Indigenous Minister Tony Abbott, to ask him why the government was spending so little on Indigenous health, I would have laughed! At the time only 82 cents in every $1,000 of the surplus budget went to Indigenous children's health. The financial equivalent of three chocolate Fantales, as I believe I worded it. And we're talking a $22 billion surplus. I never thought I'd be doing that, but that's the effect The Fred Hollows Foundation had on me. That, and it gave me the immense satisfaction of contributing to curing people's eyesight in developing nations. I couldn't believe it when I first found out that a person's sight can be restored with a mere 25 dollars. How incredible.

I was in the pool every day and in the gym with Matt at least twice a week. For our big weekend swims, we swam in any body of water we could find, and we found ways to do tethered swims outside the confines of my parents' pool. We attached the rope to Narelle's surf ski in the shallows at Shelly Beach, or to a kayak at Forty Baskets. From March to September, I trained harder than I ever had.

Then, as always, there was the paperwork. Five horrendous forms, and myriad fees and medical checks. It was a bother I could have done without, but you do what you have to. I secured one of the three available pilots without any ado about me being blind. At least this time, unlike the English Channel, the application forms were accepted without having to meet with the committee or jump through any hoops. It was done and dusted.

We had two big swims in the lead-up to Catalina. The first was from Shelly Beach to Collaroy. Matt would kayak with me, and Jenny would pick us up. It's about a 4-hour swim, and it can be pretty tough depending on the conditions. I awoke that morning to a thumping 20-knot southerly wind, and sure enough, when we got down to Shelly Beach we were greeted by 15-foot waves. Yep, it was going to be tough.

While I was waiting for Matt to pick me up, my mate Rob King walked past and asked what I was doing.

'I'm going for a training swim from Shelly Beach to Collaroy.'

'Are you kidding?' He'd been planning to go for a surf himself but hadn't even got into the water.

'We'll be fine,' I assured him. 'We're just going to swim along the beach with the wind. We'll be fine.' Famous last words.

We started with the wind behind us as expected, and I swam really well. But as we got to Collaroy Point, all Matt could see was 200 metres of white water. 'You'd never forgive me if I took you in there', he said. Here was a bloke who held the junior record for kayaking in the 111-kilometre Bridge-to-Bridge, and *he* wasn't willing to go in there? What did that mean for me?

'What are we going to do then?' I asked. 'Turn around and swim back against the wind? That'd take forever. It's taken me over 3 hours to get to here *with* the wind. It'll take 6 to get back.' Not only that, but it would be getting dark, and we hadn't taken provisions for that. Now it started to rain and I thought I heard the distant rumble of thunder. For the first time in my life, I felt truly scared. I realised that from Collaroy Beach all the way back to Manly, the conditions were the same. You couldn't get in to shore. There was no out.

Contingency time. We had no choice, we had to swim back against the raging wind. We had the kayak, the paddles, my carb gels, and my water bottles. That was it. We didn't even have a phone. 'Well,' said Matt, 'here goes.' It was just the two of us against the elements. And the sharks. I tried not to think about that. I tried not to think about how long it was going to take. How tired I was going to be. Whether we had enough water and energy gel.

About 15 minutes in Matt said, 'This next bit looks pretty gnarly. You hold on to the back of my kayak and I'll get us through it.' Things were seriously out of control. What if there really was no way out? Suddenly Matt yelled, 'James! Stop!' He'd seen a fisherman. The fisherman, whose name was Costa, agreed to give us a lift back to Manly, helped us lug all our gear onto the boat, and let us give Jenny a call to let her know the situation. He was happy to help, but I could tell he was wondering what the hell we were doing out there. Fair enough! Costa handed me an Up-and-Go drink, which I promptly brought back up. Crikey, I thought. What an adventure. When we got back to Manly Surf Club there was Jenny waiting for us, worry plastered all over her face. We came in with a bit of a smirk thinking, we dodged a bullet there! But on a more serious note, we did learn an important lesson that day. We're not invincible. We shouldn't have taken on the conditions that day.

When we got home all I wanted to do was curl up under a blanket, but it was only 3 hours before we had to be at a birthday function. God almighty! Well, there was no time to lose. I got straight into bed to steal as long a nap as I could and asked Jenny to wake me when it was time to get ready.

'Costa's called to see if you're all right,' she said as I opened my eyes.

'That's nice of him,' I murmured.

'Guess what he did after he dropped you at Manly?'

'What's that?' I asked, still half asleep.

'He went and helped another swimmer who was in trouble. Poor guy, all he did all day was pick swimmers up!'

The next morning we went and had breakfast with Rob King. I think he already half-knew the answer when he asked how the swim went. 'We had to get rescued', we admitted sheepishly. He grinned. 'I told you so!' I gave him a bit of a smile back, but it was more to cover my embarrassment than anything else. We can laugh about it now, but the truth is we made a huge mistake that day.

The next big swim was to kick off the fundraising for The Fred Hollows Foundation. On 29 July, six weeks before Catalina, I would swim 30 kilometres from Manly Wharf to the Harbour Bridge and back. At about 8 hours, this would act as a sort of qualifying swim.

On the day, we were meant to have a 30-foot boat as well as an inflatable boat. The start time came around and we were all set with the long boat, but the bloke from Manly Wharf who was meant to be providing the inflatable boat hadn't turned up. We waited a while, but it soon became clear he wasn't going to show.

I tried not to let it bring me down. Everything else was going swimmingly. When we took off from Manly Wharf the water was about 19 degrees, it was a beautiful sunny day, and all my mates had come in to see me off. And a lot of people had already come past and donated on a whim. I love seeing that kind of thing. Inflatable boat or no inflatable boat, this was going to be a great day.

Jenny was the designated person to deal with any concerns, which would have been fine if she hadn't been out of town on her way back from her uncle's funeral in Albury. Every 5 minutes someone would call her and ask, 'Where's James? What are his bearings?' She'd ring Brooke, Brooke would give her the low-down, then she'd ring them back. The whole way back from Albury she was in the car saying, 'Yes, he's there. No, he's over there... He's somewhere. Yes, there he is. He's near that.' All the while having no idea what she was really even talking about! A boat show was going on at the time, and at one point a man called to tell Jenny the Tasmanian boat was coming into the harbour and to make sure I didn't go near it. Jenny called Brooke and passed on the message. 'You mean that freaking ginormous thing over there?' Brooke joked. 'Well, all right then.'

All these things were happening around me, but of course I had no idea. I was just having a good time. Things were on track.

Then, I turned at the Harbour Bridge and realised there were ships and tankers coming towards me. I was most of the way back when the Maritime Services Board came up to the boat and said, 'You're going to have to get out of the water.'

'Why?'

'Because you haven't got an inflatable boat or a jet ski with you.'

I couldn't believe it. There were a lot of things I would have liked to have said to that bloke from Manly who'd promised us his inflatable boat. There was no way around this. I had to pick myself up, get into the main boat and relinquish the remaining 2 hours of the swim. The whole exercise felt like a waste. It's all very good swimming well for the first half of a course, but it's the second half where you find out what you're really made of. When you're tired, annoyed, bored, sore... that's when you really find out how good your team is. And that's what we'd missed out on.

I swam back into Manly Wharf and all my mates clapped me in as if nothing had happened. But it didn't matter how many people said what a great swim it had been, I didn't believe it. I was just devastated. My qualifying swim, our last chance to all come together as a team, had been destroyed. And although I'm sure it didn't affect the amount we raised, it really hurt that I wasn't able to finish it properly for The Fred Hollows Foundation as well. Penny Tribe had been waiting for me down at the Harbour Bridge, and I hadn't even shown up. I was almost in tears. I'd poured my heart and soul into organising this training swim. It really meant something to me.

Three months later, I was at the pub and I saw the bloke who'd promised us his boat. I couldn't even bring myself to talk to him. You shouldn't hold a grudge for that long, I suppose, but the wound still felt fresh. It still stung. He would never have any idea what he'd taken away from me.

We'd planned to have the next weekend off, but after what had happened I didn't want to. I still felt like I had something to prove before we set off for Catalina. Maybe that was what pushed me over the edge, I don't know. But two days later, I got one of the worst bouts of diarrhoea of my life. I spent six days on the toilet and lost seven kilograms. It took a lot out of me, and at the time I thought it spelled the end for my Catalina swim. But in hindsight, maybe being forced to have that week off was a good thing. And it was a testament to how hard I'd worked, how well I'd prepared, that I could still get back into it a week later and give it a red hot crack. And, as I told myself, better to get the runs four weeks out than on the day.

In the second week of September, Sticks and I left for Catalina. Matt and Narelle would follow two days later. We stayed in LA with a friend of Narelle's, and we managed to squeeze in a few theme park visits and lavish dinners before knuckling down to really prepare for this swim.

The physical training was one thing, but trying to prepare mentally was the hardest. The Catalina swim starts at midnight, which meant I had to start training to stay awake through the night and sleep through the day. It was the only way I could acclimatise to the task. I found it extraordinarily difficult, but I pushed through and managed okay. Thankfully a lot of American sports coverage continues right through the night, so that was at least one thing to keep me going!

We did countless interviews for Fred Hollows, but I'll always remember one above all others: with a bloke from Radio RPH in Adelaide who rang me at 2 am. He was shocked that I answered the phone, which made me wonder why he was calling at this hour in the first place. But I was glad for the distraction. 'I'm trying to acclimatise', I said, as if that explained everything. 'I can do an interview with you right now if you want.' He fumbled over his questions a bit to begin with, as he hadn't quite been prepared for me to oblige!

We'd scheduled one last interview for the day before the swim, with Robert Penfold, a foreign correspondent for Channel 9 News. Most of the questions were pretty standard, about training, timing, feeding, dealing with the pain. So I couldn't even tell you how it came up, but I managed to let it slip that Jenny was pregnant!

Jenny and I had been trying for a while, and had finally turned to a fertility specialist. On 10 July, after many rounds of

IVF, Jenny took me out for dinner and told me the great news. I was absolutely thrilled when I found out, and the joy was all the richer for the fact that we'd had to try so hard to get there. When we went to that first ultrasound and Jenny described what she was seeing inside of her – the curled up little figure with its tiny arms and legs – I could barely speak. I couldn't believe that we had made a real human being together. Fortunately, Jenny was having a really great pregnancy – no morning sickness or back pain at all so far – so as usual, she was behind me 100% for Catalina. But there was no way she was coming with me. No way we were risking the baby in any way.

We would cross to Catalina Island on the *Bottom Scratcher*, a charter dive boat. Catalina forces you to commit two cardinal sins of marathon swimming. One, swimming at night, and two, going the entire distance of the swim on the boat. It's always hard having to travel by boat to your starting point, because you get to see just how easy and quick it is to get across the stretch of water. Then you're expected to get in and put every ounce of energy you've got into achieving that same paltry outcome six times more slowly! Experiencing the sheer distance of the channel before even starting was mentally destroying. I was trying to sleep, trying to stay warm, but all I could think about was the enormity of the challenge.

But on the flipside, the great advantage of Catalina is that unless you get hit with absolutely filthy wind, you always get to do the swim on the day that you want to do it. With a starting time of midnight, the stillest time of the day, it's rare for the wind to pose any real problem. If anything, the waves usually roll with you. It's not until around 1 pm that you really start to notice the desert winds coming across the coast. So you really have to play your cards right. You have to swim hard for the first 6 hours while it's still, and ideally get 22 or 23 kilometres done in that first bracket. Then it's just a matter of holding on. For a slow swimmer like me, that was a hard pill to swallow. But I swallowed it. I knew what I had to do. If I could just get the swim done within 12 hours, I would defeat the wind. If I didn't, I would have a momentous challenge ahead of me.

It was time to begin. I made my way to shore, took a deep breath, and took off on the final swim of the six-continent series. Narelle kayaked first, but she would take turns with Matt: 90 minutes on, 90 minutes off. Even 90 minutes was a huge ask concentration-wise, because the first 6 hours were pitch black but for the moon, one big light on the boat and a few meagre light sticks on the back of my cossie. I knew I had to swim quickly for this first part but I also knew there was no point sprinting the first 20 kilometres and having nothing left in me for the next 10. It was a real mental game.

Ninety minutes went by, and it was time for Matt and Narelle to switch places. But nobody had really fully thought through how that was going to happen. 'I can't see a bloody thing!' Narelle complained. I felt like saying, 'You're guiding! You're freaking guiding! I'm the blind one. Don't tell me you can't see a thing!' But I kept my mouth shut. There were a few clashes of limbs, giggles and curses, but somehow they got it done.

For the first 6 hours I had the swell going with me. Everything was going to plan. What's great about the Catalina Channel is that the swimmer has right of way, unlike the English Channel, or most other swims for that matter. You know, it makes you feel kind of all-powerful when you approach a boat and it miraculously just gets out of your way! But delusions of grandeur aside, it makes an enormous difference not having to swerve. Every time it happened, I remembered the Parana River, where I had to make an almost 2-kilometre detour every hour, and I revelled in the simplicity of just swimming in a straight line.

Daylight started to creep over the horizon, and the team was relieved to regain the pleasure of sight. Around the 8-hour mark I hit the wall a bit. It always happens at some point on these long swims. Your mind runs out of places to go, and you just kind of lose it mentally. My team can always tell when it happens, because I start swerving all over the place, ignoring the whistle, or worse still, going left instead of right. When I'm on the mark I follow the whistles well, so it's generally pretty obvious. All it means is you have to make a concerted effort to think about something different.

One of the things I kept coming back to was something Jenny had said before I left. 'Imagine,' she'd said with a cheeky smile, 'you swim all the way to Catalina, hit the rocks, and a shark appears. Wouldn't that be some great publicity for Fred Hollows!' She did that sometimes, let her mind run off on crazy little tangents! It's one of the many things I love about her. When things got desperate, remembering these little remarks helped me keep my sense of humour about it all.

James receiving a feed from his kayaker, Narelle Simpson. Catalina Channel

But on this occasion it was Matt who took on the role of keeping me sane. 'All I want you to do is to think about two things,' he said. 'One, what you're going to call your child. I want a boy's name and a girl's name.' That one fell a bit flat, but then he wasn't to know that we already knew what we were going to call our child, and what sex it was. But the second one kept me going for hours. 'Two,' he said, 'where you're going to take your wife out the week before the baby's due. Where you're going to go, how you're going to get there, what you're going to do, what you're going to order, how she's going to react. Don't tell me now, but at the next drink break I expect to hear all about it.' For an hour and a half, that's all I thought about. It was a magnificent little trick.

I had an elaborate story for Matt at the drink break. I can't remember exactly what I said, but I do know that none of it ever happened! We did the sensible thing in the end and stayed near Jenny's parents at a hotel in Windsor. We had a nice brunch. We went shopping. Standard kind of stuff. We didn't do any of the things I said we were going to do, but that was never the point. The point was to keep my mind off the swim, and by God it worked! Anyway, it wouldn't have mattered what I imagined for that weekend. As long as it involved Jenny, it was always going to be a beautiful imagining.

The next break Matt said to me, 'You won't believe this. Robert Penfold is in his own little boat.' Robert had told me beforehand that he wanted to get a boat to come out and see us, but I never thought it would actually happen! Robert paddled his way over to us and set up a one-man cheer squad. 'Keep it up James, keep it up!'

We were nearing the end of the swim. For it to be official, I had to get above the tidal mark on the rocks on my own, without being touched. Matt kept telling me to take my time as I scrambled up the rocks, but I just wanted to get up there as fast as I could. I was slipping, and I could see how much Matt wanted to help me out, but we knew the rules – no touching. Finally I reached the top, and managed to stand up… then I promptly fell on my backside and bruised my coccyx. It wasn't the most graceful way to end the swim, but it did the job. I'd swum Catalina in 11 hours and 33 minutes. I had a 500-metre swim back to the boat, and with Jenny's comment about a shark fresh in my mind, my beaten body got up one last time. Once I was back on the boat, it finally sank in. Nine hundred and twenty-five days after I'd started, I'd completed the series of six continental swims. I'd say I was ecstatic, but even that word just doesn't seem to come close.

I didn't know this, but Robert Penfold was already on the boat when I got back, waiting to congratulate me (and ask me a bunch more questions!). He said, 'I hear you might be having a bit of time off from training now that your wife's pregnant.' Thanks, Robert.

Now instead of basking in victory, all I could think was, God, what's Jenny going to think when that appears on Channel 9 news tonight? And I knew it would. A blind swimmer swimming Catalina? Yeah, that's pretty interesting news. But his wife being pregnant? Now that's a headline. She was not going to be impressed.

I was still pretty greased up and sunburnt, and my bum was killing me! But when I got back to the house, there was one task that had to take precedence. It was time to break the news to Jenny. 'Which do you want first,' I asked, 'the good news or the bad?' She chose the good, and I proudly told her I'd swum Catalina... and then I told her the news of her pregnancy was probably going to be on that night's news. And it was. Practically the first thing that came out of Robert's mouth! But at least I'd warned Jenny in advance. She took it pretty well in the end.

What I didn't know at the time, or for a few years after for that matter, was that I had done something no other Australian had ever done in the history of marathon swimming. I was the first Australian of any sex or ability to complete the Triple Crown: the English Channel, the Manhattan Island Marathon, and the Catalina Channel. And I'd done all three on the first attempt. I was the twentieth person in history to do it, though another ninety have completed it since. But I like to think I'm the first person ever to complete it without realising! Until Murph Renford mentioned it to me years later, I hadn't even heard of the Triple Crown.

Every swimmer has their idols. The people they look up to as the real greats of the sport. For me, the people that come to mind are Des Renford of course, John Koorey, Susie Maroney, Shelley Taylor-Smith, Grant Robertson, Linda McGill (and a whole lot more besides!). To realise that my achievements were in the same league as these people, that I had achieved something even they hadn't... well, it was bloody amazing. I could barely even get my head around it.

As I sat on the boat, I remember clearly what I was thinking about. I was thinking about that night in Beijing twelve years ago, almost to the day: 9 September 1994. The night of that fateful comment: 'We have four blind swimmers representing Australia, and three of them are good.' So blunt. So thoughtless. As we'd left that night, I had vowed to myself and to my parents that one day I would make them eat their words. And today, that's exactly what I'd done. Wherever those Western Australian disabled administrators were, whether they knew it or not, they had egg on their face. The man they called ordinary had finally come back to haunt them.

I'd completed a swim in every continent in the world and I'd become the first Australian to do the Triple Crown. It had taken a whole lot of time, money, and effort, but today it was all worth it. I said to myself, 'Mum and Dad, this one's for you.' I walked away sore, tired, but deeply content. Because I had stayed true to the vow I had made to my parents. I'd done them proud. No one else knew it, but no one else had to. I never even told my parents. It was something that was just for me.

When I went to the airport the next day, our observer, John York, was waiting for me. He stopped part way through the airport, and gave me my medal for Catalina. It was a special moment. I hung it around my neck and just let the pride wash over me. And when I saw Jenny that night, I experienced it all over again. The pride, the excitement, the delight. As any happily married person will attest, nothing you do truly feels complete until you get to experience it with that one special person.

But more than that, Jenny had given up so much of her time to accommodate my training schedule. For six months I'd been in the water every morning plus two or three nights a week, and Sunday was a write-off, because by that stage it was impossible to even get me out of bed. The sacrifice she made for me was unimaginable. I don't know how she did it. So the swim was as much for her as it was for me. I was so proud to get home and say, 'I did it for you, my love.'

We'd swum Cook Strait in Australasia. We'd swum Parana River in South America. We'd swum Vaal River in Africa. We'd swum Anzac Cove in Europe. We'd swum from Mai Khao to Patong Beach in Asia. And now, we'd swum Catalina Channel in North America. All completed on the first attempt. All in 925 days. Just brilliant.

## Chapter 16
# Islands and piers

By the time I got home, Jenny was a few months pregnant and starting to show. It was about time I put my swimming career on the backburner and focused on what was now the most important and rewarding part of my life: my family.

The hospital had asked us to arrive at 6 am on 22 March 2007 for Jenny to be induced. Brooke Withers, my kayaker, drove us to the hospital and stayed on to help me out (and keep me out of the way!). But as the day wore on, not much happened, and when Annica still hadn't arrived by the following afternoon, the doctor decided Jenny needed a Caesarean. Brooke had come in to help because I couldn't see, and she kept me up to date with what was going on every step of the way.

Finally, at 2 pm on 23 March 2007, Annica was born. She came out in fine form, screaming her little head off. It was a magnificent moment, but an uneasy one. Annica was 4.95 kilograms and 55 centimetres long. Even the obstetrician was impressed. 'There's no way she was coming out without surgery!' he said. Large babies are often born with low blood glucose, so he swept her up to take her for a test, and I went with the doctor while Jenny went back to the ward. As we were wheeling Annica out, I heard her little laugh for the first time. It was the most beautiful sound I'd ever heard, and it still is. My daughter had come into the world happy. She had to stay in the special needs unit for a couple of days, but she was fine. Once the doctor had done the necessary tests, we took Annica back to see

Jenny. Patricia and Brian visited as soon as they were allowed. The whole experience was everything I'd hoped for and more.

About 8 pm I decided to go home and let Jenny get some rest. I felt like the luckiest man in the world. I had a beautiful wife and a beautiful new baby, both safe and well, fast asleep in a state-of-the-art hospital. I couldn't ask for more. But at the same time, fear and anxiety were starting to bubble to the surface. For the next couple of decades, I was going to have a 50% share in shaping an actual human being. I'm sure every new father feels these pangs of trepidation, but being blind would add in its own little challenges and I only hoped I could rise to meet them.

Sometimes I wonder how my life might have turned out if Pete Duncan had never convinced me to try internet dating. And he almost didn't. The two greatest moments in my life – marrying Jenny and having Annica – would never have happened. Yet here I stood, as close to perfection as I could imagine.

Of course, it wasn't long before that sense of perfection felt like a distant memory! Any parent will know exactly what I mean. Lucky for me, I had married the world's best mother. As much as I doubted my own abilities, Jenny never doubted mine for a second. She always said I would be a great father. And with her help, I became one. Just as she had shown me how to cook and clean when we first got together, now she was showing me how to parent with that same eternal patience. She insisted that not only could I do these things, but I was bloody well going to! She condensed it to a single sentence: 'If I can do it with my eyes closed, you can do it.' And thanks to her, I can. I never thought I'd be able to say it, but I can successfully hold, wrap, and even bath a baby. Though I've got to say, I'm not sure I ever fully mastered the art of changing a nappy.

I loved being a father, but it wasn't long before I was itching to get back in the water. I'd completed so many swims and achieved so much already, but I still didn't feel ready to stop. So it was fortuitous when only a few months after Annica's birth, Chris Colfer called me with some amazing news. Completely off his own bat, he had convinced his company, Richemont, to sponsor me for $20,000 to do any swim I wanted. I couldn't thank him enough. What an opportunity. My head was spinning with all the options. But my thoughts kept spiralling back to the same two locations: Ireland and Alaska. In the end we decided that I would swim Capitola Pier to Santa Cruz in San Francisco on 4 August, the Pennock Island Challenge in Alaska on 12 August, and Cleggan Pier to Inishbofin in Ireland on 18 August.

I'd never been to Alaska so I didn't know what to expect, but I felt pretty sure of one thing: it would be cold. I decided to buy a wetsuit, but I knew it would change the game. Swimming in a wetsuit is worlds away from swimming without one, and I'd have to spend a lot of time training in it before I'd be used to it. The problem was, I had no idea how to even go about buying a wetsuit. I should have just asked for help, but instead I ended up getting a cheap one. It fitted well around my legs, but the top part was just useless.

I'd signed up for the 11-kilometre Bondi to Watsons Bay swim in Sydney in May, and this was my first chance to try out the new wetsuit. Wearing one would disqualify me from winning the event, but I wouldn't win anyhow, and besides, that's not what I was there for. I was there to learn what it was like to swim in a wetsuit, and boy, did I ever learn a lesson. The wetsuit flooded with water around my chest and arms the minute I hit the water, and the entire swim felt like I was being pulled downhill. It was a joke. When I got out of the bay, water came cascading from my body and Narelle said, 'I'm pretty sure that's not meant to happen.' I said, 'Oh, is that right?'

The swim had been a bit of a laugh, but it wasn't something I wanted to repeat. It was time to buy a proper wetsuit. I went down to Taren Point near Cronulla and got fitted out with a very expensive wetsuit, and this time it fitted me perfectly. I'd found the wetsuit that would go with me to Alaska.

But first up was my 10-kilometre swim from Capitola Pier to Santa Cruz in America. Capitola Pier to Santa Cruz is run as an official event every two years, but 2007 was a year off. They agreed to let me do it on my own, though, as long as I organised everything myself. So I spent a lot of time doing just that, communicating with the usual organisers, taking out the appropriate insurance. Bernie was keen to come along and kayak with me because his wife Hillary is from San Francisco. It was exciting to have him along and I knew he'd give 100% – he always does – but it also felt kind of weird: it would be my first time competing in a big event without any of my usual team.

On 1 August, I flew to San Francisco. We stayed at Hillary's parents' place, which was lovely. They were very accommodating and showed me a great time. Bernie took me on an emotional tour of his marriage to Hillary – where he wrote his speech, where the ceremony was. It was great to get to spend some time with Bernie, though it was a shame that Hillary was, ironically, in Australia at the time. I trained at the local pool, which was the first I had seen of its kind: the lanes went across the pool instead of lengthways, to fit more in. We had a couple of swims down at Santa Cruz pier as well, all in readiness.

On the day, we got down to Capitola Pier at 7 am and found ourselves shrouded in fog. Bernie told me that in San Francisco in summer, sometimes the morning fog is so thick you can hardly see 10 feet in front of you. Amazing. Apparently it happens when the warm air from California's Central Valley rises, leaving room for cold ocean air to move inland, but that was something I found out later. Even though I couldn't see it, the moisture was heavy on my skin. It felt almost otherworldly.

We sat in the car for hours before the fog started to lift. Bernie was getting out every half-hour to check things out, but each time he'd come back with the same report: 'Nope, we can't start.' Finally at about 10 am he said, 'Yep, we *can* start!' We passed the fishermen, got in the water, and took off.

Along the way I was constantly ploughing through masses of kelp, which definitely slowed me down. But the fog had lifted, the water temperature was nice, and overall I swam really well. I paddled through the headlands and across the beaches, past the amusement park, and arrived at Santa Cruz pier. I had knocked out the 10 kilometres in just over 3 hours, which was an outstanding time for me. When I arrived at the beach, one of the usual organisers was there to see us finish, which was a lovely touch. It was a fantastic day, and one of my favourite swims.

The next morning, we went down to Santa Cruz beach and found an actual official event going on. It was a 2-kilometre swim. Bernie was keen for us both to enter, and the organisers offered no resistance. 'Yeah, come have a swim!' So we did. We swam well, and I absolutely loved it. It was the antithesis of the 2003 Rottnest swim, which had been all about rules and results. This swim was purely for the fun of it. They didn't hesitate to include us even for a second. It was a great swim run by great people.

The next day Hillary's parents took us all around Santa Cruz and the Redwoods State Park. The redwoods were as tall as skyscrapers, and you were lucky if you managed to wrap your arms even halfway around the trunks. We were surrounded as far as the eye could see (or so I was told!), and it felt absolutely magical. It had been a short trip, but a very sweet one, and I was sorry to say goodbye. But filled with nervous excitement for what was to come. The next day, I left for Alaska.

The Pennock Island Challenge is a 13-kilometre course around Pennock Island in Ketchikan, Alaska. I flew to Ketchikan alone, and Matt would join me the next day. On the plane, I was surrounded by a group of fishermen. When they asked me what I was doing and I told them I was coming for a 13-kilometre swim, they all looked at me as if I was mad!

I arrived at Ketchikan Airport knowing that Willy Schultz, one of the organisers for the event, was sending someone out to meet me, but that was as far as our discussion had gone. So when I arrived at the airport, I gave Willy a call. 'I've arrived!' I said. 'What now?'

'My wife should be there waiting for you.'

'Oh, okay.'

'I've got one question, though.'

'What's that?'

'You said when you applied that you were a blind marathon swimmer, but I don't remember you saying anything more about it since. Is it true?'

'Yes, it's true.'

'Oh, let me call my wife, then, and tell her to put down the sign with your name!'

Despite the initial confusion, I didn't have too much trouble finding Willy's wife. She took me to the hotel and made sure I got an easily accessible room on the ground floor. 'They'll pick you up at 7 am tomorrow for a swim', she said. In less than 12 hours, I would be swimming in Alaskan waters. It was an exciting prospect. The next day, Willy picked me up along with a couple of other swimmers and we headed down to the beach. I didn't bring my wetsuit, because I wanted to start by getting a proper sense of what the water was like. Willy followed me around the course tapping me on the foot. We swam for an hour or so and it felt for all the world like a normal day swimming. It wasn't nearly as cold as I'd thought – maybe 15 degrees or so. When we got out a couple of the others were shivering, but as far as I was concerned it was warm. The difference between my expectations and the reality was amazing. I almost couldn't believe I was okay! Maybe I wouldn't need a wetsuit after all.

Alaska was just one long good time. There were about thirty-odd swimmers and we spent all our downtime hanging out together – going out to dinner and bars, taking a horse and carriage ride through Ketchikan, seeing a show about the history of Alaska, taking a boat trip through the surrounding waterways. And of course we trained, both in the pool and in the ocean. I knew they drove on the other side of the road here, but it was a shock to me when I went to a pool and found I had to swim on the other side of the lane as well!

The swim was to raise money for the American Diabetes Association, and Willy had organised for me and one of the other swimmers to do a couple of radio interviews to promote it. After the interview, we wandered around for a bit looking for somewhere serving breakfast that wasn't battered and fried to within an inch of its life. We were walking along, possibly looking a bit aimless, when a man came out of his house and asked us what we were doing. I said, 'We're looking for some breakfast.'

'Ah,' he said, 'well, why don't you come in and I'll make you breakfast.' We followed him in and he made us a delicious omelette and some tea, and told us the story of his origins, his family, and his life. We insisted on paying for it, and he graciously accepted. It's one of the most memorable and beautiful mornings of my life. A complete stranger just inviting us into his home out of nowhere and feeding us. When he first asked us we just looked at each other incredulously, not sure what to think. But there was no catch. He was just a wonderful man, the salt of the earth.

The night before the swim we had a briefing, which proved to me just how well the swim was organised. Willy said, 'Here's how this thing's going to run. We'll meet on the beach at 9 am and get on the boat to the start line, where the boat will stay all day as the finishing marker. At the end of the swim, that same boat will take you back. Kayakers, you'll kayak to the start line from the shop.' We would start at 10 am and swim anticlockwise to take advantage of the tides, because after 3 hours they would change. I knew it would take me more than 3 hours to do 13 kilometres even with the current, so I resolved to put in my absolute best effort for those first 3 hours and get as far as I could while the tide was still with me.

The planning and execution of the swim were almost faultless. I can tell you, if a swim is well organised and all I have to worry about is my own performance, it makes an enormous difference. Not only because I'm not dealing with obstacles and issues and question marks, but because I can narrow my focus and keep my mind on the job at all times. It gives my speed and rhythm a big boost.

The day arrived, and I decided to swim without a wetsuit. I was pretty confident I'd survive. It was just a gorgeous day, 23 degrees and sunny, and the water temperature was 16. Here we were, in a country that had 4 metres of rain a year, and we'd scored the best day anyone had seen for months. There was a wind coming from the top of the island, which meant we'd be facing a headwind in the second quadrant, but it was worth it for the fact that we'd have the wind behind us for the whole rest of the swim.

The boat got to the start line, and I said to myself, 'I'm going to attack this.' Matt was there in the kayak, waiting to see how I'd go diving into the water. Back home we'd done a lot of training in getting off a boat safely. Well, that morning I executed the perfect pencil dive, then coolly put on my goggles as if it was nothing. Matt said later, 'I knew you were in form because that pencil dive was brilliant. You got straight in there and nothing was going to stop you.' And nothing did.

We had the current with us for the first quadrant, which was a nice, easy way to start. Everyone was getting into a nice rhythm with each other. Then we reached the second quadrant, and everyone separated in a matter of minutes. This is what I'd been building myself up for. I'd geed myself up to swim as hard as I could into the wind, because I knew that once I got to the top of the island it was smooth sailing from there. And I actually enjoyed the second quadrant the most, because it was the challenging one, and my concentration was on point. I was focusing on Matt's instructions, powering through my drink breaks, and swimming as straight as I could ever remember. Just as I got to the north point of the island a massive fish swam past, as if offering its congratulations. You beauty! From here on out it was nothing but a good time.

People on the island were shouting and clapping us on. As I turned the corner I felt the change as the wind and current started pushing from behind. As I got to the three-quarter mark, I could feel the change in the tide without a shadow of a doubt. It was unbelievable, I've never felt such a strong and obvious change in the water. I knew exactly where I was. 'That's the 3 hours', I said. Matt hadn't given me any time updates the whole time I'd been in the water, and he was amazed.

One quadrant to go. The change in tide didn't worry me. I was home. Really, I'd been home the minute I'd entered the third quadrant, but now the end felt really close. And I still wasn't one bit cold. I headed for the finishing line, and before I knew it I was tapping the boat. Matt said, 'Well done, mate. Great swim.' I did it in 3 hours and 39 minutes and finished seventh of nineteen swimmers in the non-wetsuit category, which was an incredible result. I felt like I'd swum as well as I ever had in my life. I made a plan, I followed it, and nothing got in the way. From go to whoa, everything went right, and it was one of the most pleasurable, enjoyable swimming experiences I could remember.

James swimming Pennock Island Challenge. Alaska, USA.

As soon as I got up on the boat, someone came straight up to offer me a hot drink and some food. For a second I was speechless. After every other swim I'd ever done, it was all about finding your gear, and getting out of there. But this... this was the royal treatment! Finally I found my voice and accepted. Actually, I was so effusive with my thanks she eventually just had to leave the room! I sat there just shaking my head in awe for a good few minutes afterwards. I couldn't believe how well done this event had been. When Matt came back from returning the kayak, he echoed my sentiments. 'This is what I signed up for!' he said. 'A brilliantly organised swim. 23 degrees. Everyone swimming well and getting along. This is why I kayak for you mate.'

When we got back to the wharf, Matt said, 'How you going, mate? You hungry?' I said, 'Not even close! I've been drinking cocoa and eating food for the last hour and a half!' He thought I was joking. This sort of thing *never* happened!

That night we gathered for a presentation dinner where a representative for the American Diabetes Association spoke and we all received a medal. Everyone, it seemed, had enjoyed the swim as much as I had, and we had a wonderful time reminiscing about the day together. It was a great evening that stretched into the early hours of the next morning. None of us was ready for the day to end. It was a day filled with joy and delight, and it will remain etched in my memory until the day I die.

A couple of days later Matt and I flew to Ireland for the Cleggan Pier to Inishbofin swim. We drove up to Galway Bay, where we stayed for the first couple of days. On the way up we stopped and had a Guinness, because it seemed like the thing to do. Everyone says the Guinness in Ireland is the best-tasting Guinness in the world, but that sure as hell wasn't my experience. Maybe it's because I'd built it up in my mind, but as far as I was concerned it tasted worse than it did in Australia! It was the first and the last Guinness I would drink in Ireland.

On the first day, I went out to do a training swim to get used to the conditions. I'd been told that if I could swim in Alaska, Ireland would be a breeze. Well, someone was having me on because it was freezing. Matt couldn't come out because we didn't have a kayak yet, but he said, 'Have a go at swimming with no whistles. But pay attention to the wind and the waves and stay close to the shore.' I didn't. I swam all over the place, but I didn't realise how far out I'd got until I heard Matt's panicked voice yelling from shore. I eventually made it back in, but I was out there for a long time and I was starting to get a bit anxious myself. Matt was there putting in everything to get me prepared for this swim, and my getting lost out at sea was definitely not part of the plan. He was furious, and fair enough, too.

We did a few touristy things but ended up spending a fair chunk of time on the phone with Ned Denison, one of the organisers, working out how we would get down to Cleggan and where we would stay the night before the swim. He found us some accommodation, and we arrived late in the afternoon. That night there was a 21st next door, and my sleep was punctuated by terrible songs and the sound of breaking glass. When I woke, tired and grumpy, I looked outside to see a 40-knot wind tearing through the trees. We were on the edge of a cyclone.

We huddled together at the pier with all the other swimmers to work out how we could make this work. The original aim was to swim from Cleggan Pier out to Inishbofin, a little island 13 kilometres away, stay the night, and come back the next day. But with the howling wind coming straight towards us, that was clearly not going to happen. Someone suggested that we go over to Inishbofin and swim from Inishbofin to Inishlyon and back, which was a similar distance.

'Are you mad?' I wanted to say. 'Are you even listening to yourselves?' Instead, I said, 'We just need to do the course in the opposite direction – go over to Inishbofin on the ferry and swim back to Cleggan Pier. If we start at 12.30 in the afternoon, with the wind, the tide, and the waves with us the whole way, even the weakest swimmers will get the 13 kilometres done within a few hours. That's our best option for sure.'

The idea got canned because we'd already organised accommodation at Inishbofin. But if we started at 12.30 we'd easily be finished by 4, which still left us with an hour before the last ferry back to Inishbofin at 5. I tried to explain that, but nobody seemed to want to see reason. It would have been so easy! We would have body surfed 90 percent of the way. After travelling all the way from Alaska, I was very disappointed.

The boat ride was turbulent; the wind and the waves were throwing us around like flotsam. It didn't bode well. When we got to Inishbofin, reality set in. 'We can't swim to Inishlyon,' someone said. 'It's too difficult.' Surprise, surprise. A decision was made to do four laps around an area near Inishbofin. Each lap would be about 3.2 kilometres, giving a total of nearly 13 kilometres. I wasn't happy about it, but I wasn't leaving without doing some kind of swim. We started the first lap, and initially it didn't seem too bad. Maybe I'd been too quick to judge, though whoever tried to tell me the water was 15 degrees was dreaming. We were lucky if it was 10. But as soon as we got around to the other side of the island it blew an absolute gale. I felt a bit vindicated, but it wasn't much consolation. It was even harder for Matt in the kayak than it was for me, rowing with six or seven layers of clothing, blowing the whistle with all his might for me to even have a chance of hearing it.

Every lap was the same. At the end of the second lap Matt said, 'Right, end of the next lap we're going home. We're gone. I'm not staying out here any longer, this is just ridiculous. It's too dangerous.' I was just glad he'd saved me having to make the decision. Sending people out in these conditions was madness. If only they'd listened to me in the first place! At the end of the third lap we made a beeline for the showers.

I tried not to let my bad mood persist, and by the evening I'd more or less let go of my frustration. We were all presented with a clock at dinner, and the night marched on with Irish music and dancing, which was marvellous fun.

The next day we got the boat back to Cleggan Pier, and drove to Dublin Airport to fly home. I'll never forget getting on the plane thinking, I'm going to be home with my wife and baby daughter in less than 24 hours. Sure enough, I arrived back in the morning and there was Annica, smiling her beautiful little smile at me. Nothing makes me melt like that smile.

I thought surely that would be my swan song, but in 2008 I agreed to do the Harbour Bridge to Manly Wharf swim to raise money and awareness for the Paralympic team. The day of the swim was an absolute stunner, and the swim went really well. Brooke kayaked from Harbour Bridge to Manly and then Narelle and Sticks used the inflatable boat for the second part. I finished the course in 3 hours and 15 minutes.

I arrived at Manly Wharf to see Matthew Levy, a disabled athlete, and his mother. That was it. No one from the Paralympic Committee, not one of the people I had spoken to. I gave a lot of my time over the few weeks before the swim, organising it, promoting it, speaking to the media, and nobody from the Australian Paralympic Committee was even there to see me finish. I was very pleased that Matthew and his mother had made the effort to come out. But there was no one else in sight. The whole thing had fallen flat, at least that's how it felt to me. I was bitterly disappointed.

We'd planned to extend the swim a little, to swim from the wharf around past Shelly Beach to North Steyne. When I arrived,

I think it's the flattest I've ever seen North Steyne Beach. Not a breath of a wave. I could have walked the last 50 metres. Jenny and Annica were dutifully waiting for me, and seeing their faces made me forget all about the disappointment of my reception – or lack thereof – back at Manly Wharf. It wasn't part of the plan, but when we arrived a surf program was doing some filming on the beach, and they said, 'Go back! Do a re-enactment for us!' So I went back and swam into the shoreline, gave Jenny a hug, picked Annica up and had a little photo shoot. Finally, some actual recognition! The day had been salvaged!

In hindsight, maybe I should have called it quits on the marathon swim side of things that day. It would have been nice to have ended it on such a positive note. Beautiful conditions, beautiful swim, and beautiful finish in front of my family. It would have been a great way to bow out. But that's not how things would turn out.

## Chapter 17
## Molokai Channel

On Australia Day 2010, I came back from Ambassador duties to an email entitled 'Congratulations'. It was from Penny Palfrey's husband, congratulating her on being inducted to the International Marathon Swimming Hall of Fame. He also mentioned Chris Guesdon, a Tasmanian who had been instrumental in getting the 10-kilometre marathon event accepted into the Olympics, and had done many marathon swims in Papua New Guinea and around the world in the 70s. Then at the bottom of the email, he congratulated me as well. I'm thinking, that's a bit strange. He's obviously got something wrong. But then I considered the alternative. What if I was being inducted into the International Marathon Swimming Hall of Fame as well? I went home and rang Penny Palfrey to congratulate her. 'Congratulations to you, too', she said.

'What are you talking about?'

'You've been inducted as well.'

I still couldn't quite believe it. I tried to confirm it on the Internet, but text-to-speech software has its limitations, and I didn't get very far. I said to Jenny, 'I think I've been inducted into the International Marathon Swimming Hall of Fame, but I'm not sure.' She laughed. 'It's true. Congratulations, my love.' The function was scheduled for May in Fort Lauderdale, Florida. I decided not to go because it was going to be too expensive for us all to get there, and I wanted to save for a swim later in the year. But I had Andrew Peken and his partner go down from New York on my behalf. I felt honoured to have him represent me – a man that had been with me from under-sevens soccer, right through high school, and into adulthood. He took so many photos I almost felt like I was there. It was a great thrill to be the ninth Australian and the first blind person to be inducted into the International Marathon Swimming Hall of Fame, to know that people truly admired what I had done. It's something I will cherish all my life.

International Marathon Swimming Hall of Fame medal.

While all this was going on, I had turned my attention to yet another open-water swimming feat. Near the end of 2009, I had received an email about the 'Oceans Seven' swims – a series of seven swims around the world, in the same vein as the Seven Summits, which is a series of climbs of the world's highest peaks. The seven swims included the English Channel, the Strait of Gibraltar, the Catalina Channel, Cook Strait, the Molokai Channel in Hawaii, Tsugaru Strait in Japan, and the North Sea between Scotland and Northern Ireland. I'd already completed the first four, so it was certainly tempting to go for the whole series. Jenny and Annica were happy for me to do it, but it was going to take a lot of money, a lot of time, and a lot of training if it was ever going to happen. I spent a lot of time emailing people around the world to try to get sponsorship, but it never happened, and I guess I never really expected it to.

At first, I wanted to attempt the 22-kilometre Tsugaru Strait in Japan between Honshu and Hokkaido – a similar distance to Perth to Rottnest Island. A friend of Chad's, Kasia, spoke fluent Japanese, and she agreed to help me out. I would send her all my questions, and she would ring up the boat pilot, get the answers, and email them back to me. This went on for a long time, but it was a lot of work for very little return. When May came around, it was crunch time. I had to decide either way whether this trip to Japan was going to happen, and in the end I had to accept that it just wasn't. All the information I was getting was so confusing, and I hate going into a swim not knowing what to expect. Narelle and Matt weren't confident either, and they were starting to suggest that maybe I should go a different route.

And so I turned my attention to the Molokai Channel in Hawaii instead. Just like that, I went from training for a 19-degree, 22-kilometre swim, to training for a 27-degree, 42-kilometre swim. Talk about going from one end of the scale to the other. From early June right through to mid-September, it was back to the hard slog of training all weekend, every weekend, and most weeknights as well. Warringah Aquatic Centre set aside a lane especially for me. Matt was pushing me to my limits with every drill you can imagine. It was full on, but if I couldn't handle this, how was I going to handle the Molokai Channel?

When we trained in the ocean I would put a wetsuit on to try to replicate the warmth I would experience; I downed litres of fluids at a time on every drink break, because that's what I'd need to be able to do in Hawaii. I started taking a bunch of different supplements to make sure my body was well fuelled for such a hot swim. We rehearsed hourly blood-glucose tests over a 10-hour swim one day at Manly pool. The last time I'd done a 10-hour swim at Manly pool was way back in 1999, and I'd got out feeling fresh as a daisy. Eleven years on, my body was definitely showing signs of wear. It was a tough day, but not as tough as the one I was training for. In Molokai I'd be looking at another 5 hours on top of that, and in much more trying conditions. But it was a good effort nonetheless, and I was happy with the way our training was going.

I'd decided to dedicate this swim to The Fred Hollows Foundation, so while all this training was going on we were also trying to raise funds for the Foundation. Fortunately, it's one of the world's easiest charities to raise money for, because it's just so well known. In fact, you're hard pressed to find anyone that doesn't know it. I've long since lost count of the number of people I've talked to about The Fred Hollows Foundation, the world over, and never once have I had to explain who Fred Hollows is or what the Foundation does. Not many charities have that kind of reach, and it's testament to the value of their work. But it also enhances the work I can do for them. When I do interviews, I don't have to explain what the charity is about, which gives me a lot of time to talk more specifically about what they do and why they're so important.

The Fred Hollows Foundation mission statement reads thus: 'We see a world in which no person is needlessly blind and Indigenous Australians exercise their right to good health.' Just twenty simple words, but they mean so much. Since its conception in 1992, the Foundation has restored vision to more than 2 million people. It is one of the greatest performances in history.

I love raising money for The Fred Hollows Foundation. I love knowing that simply by swimming, I'm helping someone on the other side of the world – in Vietnam, Nepal, Pakistan, Eritrea, Ethiopia, or wherever it may be – to regain their vision. How miraculous that someone with cataracts can have an operation in a makeshift tent in a third-world country for 25 Australian dollars and go from complete blindness to perfect vision in a matter of days. Knowing that just by swimming I am giving people all around the world a chance to see... well, it's just outstanding.

The swim was set down for 1 October 2010. I left for Hawaii with Matt and Narelle at the end of September. The flight hadn't even landed before problems started to set in. For some reason, I spent the whole flight feeling uncomfortable. Sleep wasn't an option, and by the time we touched down my back was killing me. It was a harbinger of things to come.

We stayed on the mainland of Hawaii at a lovely hotel for the first couple of days, and whiled away the time shopping and training, trying to get used to the conditions. We met the pilot in our hotel and organised how the swim would work. To take advantage of the tides and avoid the intense sun, we would set off around 11 pm. So that's when we trained. It wasn't as bad as it sounds. The water was warm, and there was just enough moonlight to see what was going on.

As we flew across to Molokai from the mainland, I tried not to think too hard about what we were doing. The swim would be 42 kilometres from Molokai Island back to the mainland, and I can tell you, if it's disheartening to take a boat across the length of a course before swimming it, it's even worse to fly across it! Within half an hour we had traversed the entire length of the course and then some!

The day before the swim, Narelle and I did one last training session, and I was finding it really hard to get into it. My back was still sore, and nerves were starting to set in. We were trying to work out how we were going to swim the event. Don't kick too much early on, we decided, because it's a long swim; concentrate on listening for the whistles; focus on trying to stay in a straight line.

On the day of the swim, we spent the whole day relaxing – a rare treat! Narelle and Matt tried to take my mind off the swim with impossible questions like 'How many kilometres do you think you've swum in your life?' But it wasn't very effective. Early in the afternoon I got up from the toilet, and as I went to hit the flush button I felt a big crack in my back. Uh oh. I hoped against hope that I hadn't done a serious injury. I wasn't ready for this swim to be over before it had even begun. I got myself back to bed for a bit of a rest and convinced myself I wasn't feeling that bad.

We left for the beach around 9 pm. Narelle, Matt, and Matt's mate Tom, who had put his hand up to be our third kayaker, started taking all the gear down to the beach while I stayed in the car. When they came back from their first run, Narelle said, 'The waves are pretty big out there. It'll be bouncy to get out. We've got our work cut out for us.' If I was skittish before, I was overwrought now. I got out of the car and sat on a wall at the top of the beach. There were a few Hawaiians up there playing guitar, but the crash of the waves against the rocks all but drowned them out. We thought of calling off the swim and trying again the next day, but it was never an option – the weather was only getting worse as the days wore on. It was now or never.

Around 10.30 pm I went down to the beach to see how the guys were going, and there was this group of Hawaiians down there singing and dancing, and talking excitedly about my swim. 'How good is that!' I heard them squealing, seemingly oblivious to the dangers we were facing! Matt said, 'Look. We've already spent an hour and a half trying to get the kayaks out to the boat. We're up against 10-foot dumpers, mate. We'll get you out there, but it's going to be hard work.' True to his word, Matt just kept on plugging away when anyone else would have accepted defeat. And Narelle and Tom showed the same steely resolve, trying time and time again. They were kayaking blind; they couldn't even see the waves coming. Matt got thrown off at least three times, leaving the kayak to come crashing all the way back to the beach on its own. And each time, drenched and demoralised, he would drag himself back to shore and start again. Even when the cramps set in, there was no stopping him.

After 2 hours they finally conquered the dumpers and made it out to the boat. All this just to start the swim! It was absolutely horrendous. They came back to collect me, and I started swimming with Narelle next to me in the water and Matt beside me in a kayak. I had to hang on to the kayak for dear life because we were just getting smashed, and smashed, and smashed. When we eventually got out to the boat just after midnight, we were already beaten to the point of submission. We felt like we'd swum 20 kilometres, and we hadn't even started. My back was battered, and Matt was cramping like crazy. Only 42 kilometres to go!

Finally, around midnight, I started the actual swim, but within the first few hundred metres I could already feel my back getting worse with the relentless crunching of the waves. I swam 13 kilometres in 5 hours, well below the 16 or 17 I was aiming for. The waves had started to let up a bit, but my swimming just kept on getting worse. By now I'd told Narelle everything that had been happening with my back and she knew I had to have been in pain, but if I didn't pick up my pace we were never going to finish this swim. 'Come on,' she said, 'pick it up. Get on with it. How's your back going?' I said, 'Terrible.' She gave me a painkiller and said, 'Just keep going!'

Not long after, we stopped for a drink break, and as I turned towards the boat I felt an excruciating bolt of pain run down my back and pierce both my legs. I turned to Narelle and said, 'Sorry mate, but that's it. I'm giving it away. I can't do another 10 hours of this. I'm in agony.' I got back on the boat, and as the adrenaline wore off I felt like I couldn't breathe. I was that bad. But there was nowhere to go. I had to stay on this bouncing boat for another 37 kilometres to the mainland. Every breath was an effort, but as long as I just kept on breathing, we'd get there eventually.

When we got back, I went straight to a chiropractor and got rushed through. 'Nice job,' the chiro said. 'You've gone and locked out your pelvis. You've done this muscle. You've done that muscle. How the hell did you swim 13 kilometres like this?' He got out a skeleton and pointed out about four or five separate injuries I'd managed to inflict on myself. 'No wonder you've got it shooting down your legs, mate.' I tried to keep up, but my main focus was still on just making it through each breath. Finally he did some adjustment that restored my ability to walk, not that it didn't still hurt like hell. But it didn't hurt as much as the disappointment of letting everyone down.

I remember calling home and telling my sorry story. Annica, wise beyond her age of three, said, 'Look. You had a go.' Jenny said, 'You made the right decision.' Logically I knew they were right, but emotionally I couldn't let go of the feeling I'd let them down. And not just Jenny and Annica, every single person that had put in the time to get me here. I was absolutely devastated.

I give 100% in everything I do, whether that's sports, work, family, or anything else in life. I learned very early in life that if you put 100% into something, you'll get 100% out of it, and I've always believed that to be true. When I had to pull out of the Hawaii swim, I was terribly disappointed, but I still walked away knowing I had put in the right training and pushed myself until I genuinely couldn't push any more. If I hadn't, it would have been much harder to take.

We spent the rest of the day recovering. We went back and saw the pilot, who said, 'Never mind. Maybe next year you can come back and have another crack.' I didn't say anything, just shook his hand and thanked him for his time. I knew I wouldn't be back. This was the end of the Oceans Seven for me. I'd spent a long time working towards it, but I just couldn't keep going like this. Japan and Hawaii had both fallen through now, and, as supportive as they were, I knew the toll the constant training was taking on my family. I couldn't do it anymore.

We spent another three or four days in Hawaii. We went to a pineapple plantation, to a few beaches, and to a bunch of great bars and restaurants, including my first teppanyaki experience. But Pearl Harbor was the absolute standout for me. I loved standing at the lookout, and visiting the memorial of the USS Arizona, the boat that was destroyed by the Japanese back in 1941. Some seventy years on, I learned that the wreckage is still leaking oil into the water every single day. It was a fascinating history lesson.

When I came back home, I knew I would never again get involved in any more overseas swims. I'd missed most of my daughter's third year of life in training, and I never wanted to do that again. Besides, I wasn't getting any younger and the swims were starting to really take it out of me. When it came down to it, I just couldn't be bothered. I wanted to have time with my family, and I wanted them to have time with me. I'd achieved great things in my swimming career, and I had a lot to be proud of. Hawaii wasn't a success, but that's the way it goes.

But swimming was too much a part of me to let it go completely. And so I turned my attention to charity. Throughout 2011 and 2012 I dedicated myself to regular fundraising swims for The Fred Hollows Foundation, the Rainbow Club, and other charities at home in Sydney. Rather than taking away from my time with my family, they were a great way to involve my family and friends in something I was truly passionate about.

Being blind, I suppose it's hardly surprising that I ended up forming an association with The Fred Hollows Foundation. My own blindness, though incurable, gives me a unique insight into what it means to restore vision. The amazing impact that can have on not only the person themselves, but their parents, their children, and their entire community. It's something that I know meant a lot to Australia's former Minister for Foreign Affairs, Bob Carr. Early in 2013, Carr dedicated $1 million to tackling avoidable blindness in Laos after visiting the country. He spoke at a Fred Hollows event and explained that part of his motivation was seeing the effect of blindness on not only the person suffering from it, but also those who care for them. 'Girls and women are most often called on to sacrifice education, employment and mobility to care for a blind relative', he explained. 'When vision is restored in instances like this, then the enrolment of girls in schools goes up.' And he hit on an incredibly important point.

When we prevent blindness, we are investing in the education and wellbeing of future generations. I'm always banging on about how important it is to take the opportunities you're given in life, but that's easy for me to say – I've had plenty of them. It's painful to think that so many people in this world spend their entire lives never getting one opportunity to escape the poverty cycle. That's why The Fred Hollows Foundation is so close to my heart. It gives people, and young girls in particular, that opportunity to get out there and build some sort of life for themselves. To do better than the generation that preceded them.

So in 2011 I organised the first 'Swim for Sight' along Sydney's coast to raise money and awareness for the Foundation. The swim would go from Malabar Beach to Bondi Beach. It seemed like the perfect swim: Malabar Beach was so safe to get out from, and Bondi Beach is a worldwide icon. We'd scheduled it for the last weekend of the annual Sculpture by the Sea festival at Bondi Beach, in early November, so we were expecting a bit of a crowd.

We managed to drum up some media support, too. They wanted to film a segment at our home, but at the time we had just moved into a unit, and it wasn't even fit for visitors let alone a camera crew. So we ended up going to Annica's childcare centre. Neither Channel 7 nor the childcare centre were particularly impressed with this arrangement, but it was better than trying to squeeze everyone into our pokey little flat. Jenny and I had to balance on these tiny seats with Annica on our lap. When they asked Annica a question, she responded with a single disinterested burp. But they managed to get her on tape reading a book to me right at the end. I was really happy with the final cut of the interview that aired. I saw the power of media, because within 5 minutes of it airing, $1,200 appeared in The Fred Hollows Foundation's account.

The day came for the swim and it was just beautiful. Everything was in place. Except for one slight problem. The currents. After two decades of swimming, somehow I hadn't even thought about the currents. So from Malabar Beach to Bondi Beach, I was up against the current the whole way. About an hour in, a baby whale came past making an awful lot of noise. All I heard was, 'You're going the wrong way!' Maroubra Beach seemed to take a lifetime to get past, and even then I was barely a quarter of the way through. Dad said to me later, 'You took about an hour getting past Maroubra, then all of a sudden you were flying!' I knew exactly the moment he was talking about, where I finally escaped the current. From there things got a bit easier.

At the top of Tamarama Beach, I was met by Chad and his mate John, who swam the last leg with me. When we reached the southern end of Bondi Beach, Murray Rose joined us as we swam into shore. What I didn't know at the time was that

Murray Rose was suffering from terminal cancer that would take his life only six months later. I'm glad he kept it private, because knowing would have taken away from the joy of the swim. I'm glad, because it took the pressure off. Off him, off me, off his family. We could all just enjoy the last months of his life with the same zest we always had, untainted by the knowledge we were on borrowed time.

We rounded the corner at Tamarama Beach and there was Murray waiting for us, along with Fred Hollows' daughter Rosa on a surf ski. Murray said, 'You're swimming well, James, keep it up.' I heard him say to Chad, 'We'll take him to the middle of the beach.' Chad said to me later, 'I wanted you to keep going towards Watsons Bay.'

I said, 'Why?'

'Do you really have to ask? I had Murray Rose on my left, and Fred Hollows' daughter on my right. It doesn't get much better than that.'

It was a great honour to have Murray swim with me. An honour that was magnified when I later learned how much pain he must have endured to be there. And I am in no doubt as to why he did it. He did it because he believes in what I do, and who I am. One of the greatest pool swimmers in history overcame all the odds, just to come out and swim with me.

We made it to the beach, and Channel 7 was waiting for us yet again. The Malabar to Bondi swim had been a success, though I was still a little disappointed that after the initial burst of interest following the article on Channel 7 news, I'd only reached a total of $3,500 for The Fred Hollows Foundation. But when I said that to Penny Tribe, she chided me for not giving myself enough credit. 'Listen,' she said, 'We got seven free advertisements on Channel 7 on a Sunday, leading up to the news. Do you know what that would have cost? Try $50,000. And you don't know how many direct donations we've received as a result of those ads, and your article on the news. I wouldn't be surprised if that raised us another twenty or thirty thousand dollars. Don't let me ever hear you say this wasn't a good effort. You raised an enormous amount of both awareness and money.' That was the first time I'd really thought about it. Yeah, I had raised awareness. And I would continue to do so. From 2012 onwards we ran the event in the Northern Beaches. In 2012 we raised around $15,000, and in 2013 that figure rose again to around $24,000.

The Fred Hollows Foundation has put my life into perspective. I was brought up in an affluent part of Sydney, with affluent parents, and I went to affluent, predominantly white schools. Until Fred Hollows, I had no idea of the shocking contrast between my own life and those of Indigenous Australians. And now that I've been enlightened, I will never be the same.

I'll never forget the first time I heard that the gap in mortality rate between Indigenous and non-Indigenous Australians is seventeen years. If you're not shocked and disgusted by that figure, something's wrong. Hundreds of thousands of Australians are dying early because we don't care enough to give them proper health care. Yes, we have the 'Close the Gap' day each year in March. We plan all these extravagant events to *talk* about the problem. But we don't *do* anything. We need to take action. We need to be the voice for those who don't have one. It was The Fred Hollows Foundation that showed me that, and I will always be grateful. I've gone from having not a single ounce of knowledge about Indigenous people to being very much at the forefront of the push for better Indigenous health systems, especially for children.

But it's something that had been eating at me even before I partnered with The Fred Hollows Foundation. In 1998 I was on my way to a mate's housewarming party when the cab driver recognised me. 'You've swum the English Channel', he said.

'Yeah, that's right.'

'I work for the Royal Far West School at Manly Beach. Would you come along and do a speech for us?'

The Royal Far West is a non-government organisation that provides health services to children in rural and remote areas of New South Wales. They take a holistic approach to advocating for children's health, and that includes their education. As part of that approach, the Royal Far West School aims 'to give every child, wherever they live, the opportunity to achieve their potential'. Each year, the school works with over 1,500 students from country New South Wales, many of whom have developmental, learning and behavioural difficulties.

I went and spoke, and had such a good time. It was the first small step in a six-year association with the school. I love spending time with kids; they have this unique, fresh perspective that we adults have lost. A kid with cerebral palsy said to me, 'Where did you go to the toilet in the English Channel?' I couldn't stop laughing. Afterwards I stuck around and spent some time with the kids in the classroom. The teacher said, 'James can help you with your composite nouns.' I stiffened. Oh God, I thought. What the hell is a composite noun? Thankfully the teacher gave me access to the answers, and I managed to fumble through.

The experience was a real eye-opener, and again I was reminded of just how fortunate I am. It's hard, seeing people who don't have it as good as you do, but it's important. The more I know about disadvantage, the more I can do to help. And that's what I wanted to do for these kids. Many had come from a background of abuse and neglect, and the Royal Far West School was their first chance to be valued, to get a proper education, and to start to have their health looked after. Others had come to the school with all the intelligence and motivation in the world, yet they couldn't even read. Why? Because they couldn't see. They had never even had their eyesight tested. Even just getting a pair of glasses could change the entire course of a short-sighted child's life.

With an ophthalmologist as a father, an orthoptist as a mother, and an untreatable eye condition, obviously I know a bit about eyes. I'd heard of trachoma; I'd heard of cataracts. But I always thought of them as conditions affecting third-world countries. Ethiopia. Nepal. Countries without the resources to treat them. I was wrong. Trachoma and cataracts are rampant among Indigenous Australians, and it's a disgrace. Here we are, one of the most affluent countries in the world, and we can't even provide basic health care to the traditional owners of the land.

Fred Hollows has done an incredible job raising money and awareness to help Indigenous Australians get the health care they deserve, but we've still got so very far to go. I hope I live to see the day Indigenous people receive the same health standards to which white Australians are automatically entitled. I'm not talking about specialist surgery here. I'm talking about the right to go to a GP and have your sight, your hearing, your blood glucose tested. Is it really so much to ask?

In May 2013, Penny Tribe asked me to come along to the Fred Hollows AGM. But those kind of events aren't really my cup of tea. Actually, the whole idea bores me to tears, and I told her so. I didn't think she'd be too bothered either way, but two days later I heard from Oliver, another guy from the Foundation, telling me, 'You've got to go along to this AGM.' What did it matter to them? I couldn't work it out. But they wore me down eventually.

The whole time I didn't twig. They were trying to get me along because I was being presented with the Helping Hand award, given each year by The Fred Hollows Foundation to someone who's done a lot for the organisation. Even after I arrived, I was still blissfully unaware. The first hour and a half was standard – numbers, reports, fragments of information. To my surprise, I was actually kind of enjoying it. I loved hearing how much they had raised throughout the year, especially knowing that I had personally contributed.

When the time came for the Helping Hand award, a video started playing, and even as I heard myself on the screen I still didn't quite believe it. The CEO, Brian, was walking towards me and I thought, I've been had. Left, right and centre. I turned to Jenny and she said, 'That's right, mate.' I was honoured, of course, but the first thing that popped into my mind was, oh God! I have to do a speech on the spot? Though it was a small burden for a very big award.

I was thrilled and humbled to receive that award. Of course I was. Awards are nice. Recognition is nice. But it's not why I swim. I do it because I love swimming. I love training, I love organising events, I love being part of a team, and I love that it allows me to make a difference in people's lives, whether that be directly or through charity. I don't want to downplay the significance of the Helping Hand, but it's not about the award itself. It's what you do to deserve it. And that night in May 2013, I knew I deserved it. I'd poured my soul into the Foundation, and to know that they saw that made my heart swell.

## Chapter 18
## Bering Strait

In June 2013, I came home one evening to an email from my friend Claudia Rose, who I'd swum with in Alaska in 2007. Claudia was a vibrant, quirky personality, always up for anything. But the greatest thing about her was her obvious kindness and love for people. When she told me she was going to be part of an attempt at the first-ever relay across Bering Strait without wetsuits in August I wasn't surprised – Claudia was at her best when she was part of a team. They wanted to include at least one person from each continent, she said, and they were yet to secure an Australian. Did I know of anyone?

The Bering Strait crossing spans over 80 kilometres of near-freezing water from Provideniya in Russia to Cape Wells in Alaska. I sat at my desk thinking, what kind of fool would want to do that? Who'd be able to hack that kind of cold? Who's got the time? The only person that sprung to mind was Murph Renford. I made a mental note to call him. Murph had completed the Triple Crown less than a year earlier and had more than proven himself in cold conditions. For most people, that probably doesn't seem all that surprising. After all, his dad was one of the greats. But funnily enough, Murph never really saw himself getting into marathon swimming. It wasn't until six years after Des' death he finally decided that actually, he did want to follow in his father's footsteps. And not just on the swimming side of things – he carried on the legacy of Des' beautiful generous spirit as well, helping many young swimmers achieve their goal of swimming the Channel. Des would have been so proud.

That night I was drying the dishes at home when Jenny said to me, 'Did you see that email?'

'What, the one about Bering Strait? Yeah.'

'Are you going to do it?'

I was so shocked I almost dropped the plate. I hadn't even contemplated doing it myself.

'Annica and I will back you if you want to do it.'

I stood there agape. 'Really?'

'Really! If you want to do it, go and do it! What a magnificent experience it would be.'

She was right, of course, but it was a huge deal to even contemplate this. I'd thought my days of international swimming were over. I considered it for a good few minutes and finally said, 'Well, yeah, maybe.' I was still in shock, but by the end of the night Jenny had me convinced. It would be an amazing experience, and I had my family's backing. Why wouldn't I do it?

The next day I applied for three weeks' leave, and my manager asked why I needed it. 'I'm going to swim in a relay across the Bering Strait without wetsuits', I told her. Silence reigned, and the look on her face must have said, 'You idiot!' But she agreed to submit my application to the powers that be.

In the meantime I started the long process of preparation, which would drag on for over a month. Forms, visas, medicals, research, emails. So very many emails! At least the organiser I was in contact with, Irina Makarova, was based in Yakutsk, which was the same time zone as Sydney, so the two of us got things done pretty quickly. But I was still fielding emails from around the world at all hours of the day and night. Some mornings I'd arrive at work to five different emails from five different countries and five different time zones and think, what have I got myself into! Applying for a Russian visa was even worse: I had to fill in a form stating everywhere I had been from 2003 to 2013 – dates, times, reasons, everything. It ended up taking half the day!

At times it seemed as if the swim wasn't going to go ahead. The biggest question mark was over whether we'd get approval to enter American waters. In the end that uncertainty meant Claudia had to pull out, because she works for the American Government and stood to lose her entire career if we entered the water without proper permission. But she didn't break off contact – in characteristic style, she poured her energy into helping me achieve what she couldn't.

When I first got involved in the swim back in June, we planned to fly to Lake Baikal in Russia via Seattle for a practice swim, and go to Yakutsk from there. But at the last minute, the man who was organising it from Seattle went bankrupt and was facing deportation, and I ended up having to change my entire flight schedule. Would the nightmare never end! My poor travel agent had to deal with a new drama every day. In the end though I was kind of glad it fell through. Lake Baikal is the biggest lake in the world – 680 kilometres long, 80 kilometres wide, and 1.6 kilometres deep – and it would be bloody cold even in summer.

Now I had to work out how I was going to approach training. I had to acclimatise to swimming with just a normal swimming costume, cap and goggles, in 5-degree water. Unfortunately, winter 2013 was the warmest winter ever recorded in Sydney, so it sure wasn't going to be easy. I ended up doing tethered swims in the salted pool in our backyard at 5.30 am right through July, and at one stage the water did get down to 6 degrees. Yes, it was cold.

We were going to swim the Bering Strait in a relay, 10 minutes at a time. Narelle gave me a few pointers on how to train for it. She said, 'Doing 10 minutes having a break then doing another 10 minutes isn't doing you any good, because your body's not getting used to the shock of getting into cold water, getting out, then doing it again 10 hours later. You're much better off getting warm in between, *then* doing another 10 minutes. That way you get to experience the shock of going from cold to warm to cold, which is what you're going to be doing in Bering Strait.' So that's what I'd do. I'd swim for 10 minutes, get dressed and warm back up, wait 40 minutes, and go again. One morning our next-door neighbour came out to go to work, and heard a noise over his back fence. He peered over and did a double take. 'Oh my God', he said. When he went out to his car and saw it was 8 degrees air temperature he yelled back at me again. 'James, what do you think you're doing?'

I did two 20-minute training sessions every night with the kickboard, too, because I didn't want to do too much shoulder work with the tethered rope. But for once, I gave myself weekends off. It just wasn't worth it. The good thing about doing a relay is that you don't have to have the best endurance or stamina. You need to be able to hack the cold, and that's about it.

The lead-up to the swim was hectic. Between the training and the emails, I barely got a moment to myself. That's not to mention juggling work and family, and preparing all my gear. And to think there was still a chance it might all be for nothing. But at least I didn't have to worry about money. The only thing we had to pay for was getting there and back, and accommodation after the swim was over. The rest of it was paid for by the Russian government – all 2 million US dollars of it. They paid for all the accommodation in Irkutsk, the military plane, the massive boat, and all the staff. Unbelievable.

A week before departure, I found out that the airport I was flying into was an hour's drive from the airport we then needed to depart from to get to Yakutsk, where we would be staying. How was I supposed to get from one airport to another when I didn't speak a word of Russian? Fortunately, one of the other swimmers, Jackie Cobell from England, was flying into the same airport as me at roughly the same time. So I organised to meet up with her and we exchanged awkward descriptions of ourselves to try to find each other when the time came.

On 27 July, Jenny and Annica saw me off from Sydney Airport. It was hard leaving them behind, and even harder knowing I was completely and totally on my own – I was about to be stuck on a boat with a bunch of international swimmers I'd never even met. I knew no one. Had I made the right decision coming on the trip? I was wracked with nerves, but I needn't have been. The next twenty days would be one of the greatest adventures of my life.

I arrived at Moscow Airport and met up with Jackie, and we took a taxi to the other airport. I liked her right away, there was this inimitable confidence about her, a 'don't mess with me' attitude that I loved. She never took a backward step her whole life. I wasn't surprised when I learned that she had done the longest-ever English Channel crossing in her fifties, at 28 hours and 44 minutes.

When we got to the other airport an hour later, I was relieved to say the least. Now to find our gate. I couldn't see, I'd just learned that Jackie could barely hear, and neither of us spoke Russian! What a team! But we somehow managed to get to the gate about an hour prior to departure. 'Oh God, I hope we've come to the right place', I said. 'Well,' said Jackie, 'there's no way to know for sure! Either way, we're in for an adventure.' But before long Jackie recognised some swimmers she knew. I was feeling pretty intimidated. There were sixty-five swimmers in all, and not only did I not know anyone, but it seemed that everybody else already did.

I would later learn that these guys had attempted to do a relay of the Bering Strait together for the past two years running. In 2011, they never really got beyond the planning stage, but in 2012, they got to within a foot of the boat at Kamchatka, the most easterly point of Russia, only to be told they didn't have a permit to enter America. They were thanked for coming – for what it was worth – and sent packing. Devastating. I was glad I didn't know that in advance. I was nervous enough as it was.

There were representatives from sixteen different countries: Argentina, Australia, Chile, China, Czech Republic, England, Ecuador, Finland, Ireland, Italy, Latvia, Poland, Russia, South Africa, Ukraine, and the United States of America. This was going to be an absolute adventure. Not only the swimming, but just the challenge of communicating with so many people from so many different cultures speaking so many different languages!

We arrived in Irkutsk and met Irina at 7.30 the next morning. Everyone was struggling big time with jetlag – except me. I'd gone full circle in time zones, and was back to the same time zone as Sydney. I was all alone on the other side of the world, but at least I still had time on my side! We stayed at a sports academy for the next two days, where I roomed with a lovely Italian named Paolo. 'Not a true Italian though,' he told me, 'I don't drink alcohol, I don't like soccer, and I don't like opera!' As the only representatives of our respective nationalities, we shared a bit of a bond from the outset. He was a kind soul and an absolute Godsend for me trying to get around this massive building.

At dinner, the Russians decided to show Paolo and me a bit of 'respect'. That is, what they call respect. If you ask me, trying to force someone to drink vodka straight is about as far as you can get from respect. I'd already decided I wasn't going anywhere near alcohol, and Paolo wasn't a drinker either. But the word 'no' just didn't seem to register with them. No matter how many times we refused, they just kept pushing it in our faces and saying 'Respect!' The word became a bit of a running joke between Paolo and me. Respect didn't mean respect, it meant, 'Drink the vodka, stat!'

Things didn't really get going until 30 July, the official 'opening' day for the swim. We were swimming to commemorate the twenty-fifth anniversary of the first Friendship Flight between Alaska and Russia in 1988. The flight went ahead thanks in large part to a middle-aged Alaskan real estate agent who made the suggestion as part of a push to pry open the Soviet Union's back door after the Cold War. It was the first step in improving relations between the two countries, and paved the way for collaboration on scientific, educational and cultural ventures. Suffice to say it was a big deal, and people were champing at the bit to be a part of our commemorative effort.

We spent the morning at a ceremony in the home of the vice president of Yakutsk. He gave us an official welcome and was very effusive about what our swim meant to Russia. We had headsets translating what he was saying thank goodness! It was an honour and a very novel experience to sit around a table having tea with the vice president.

After that, we went to a religious ceremony in a small building that I think was some kind of place of worship. We arrived to find a log as the centrepiece of the room. I was looking at Paolo as if to say, 'What in God's name is going on here?' A man was babbling away in Russian, but even if I'd been able to understand, I'm sure he wouldn't have been making sense! As his rant continued, something told me he was going to burn the log. And sure enough, he did. He burned the thing in this tiny room, apparently to get rid of all the bad spirits for our swim. I started scouting out my exit points thinking, I don't know about this! I'd gone from sharing tea with the vice president one minute to choking on smoke at some religious ritual the next! It takes all sorts, I suppose.

In the afternoon we went to a function with a bunch of Russian sports writers. We had to walk up onto this stage two by two, like animals onto Noah's Ark. I felt like a display item! Not everyone likes ceremonies and media presentations, and I get that, but I guess when it comes down to it, you have to be grateful to find yourself in that situation at all.

Our 'opening ceremony' that night was small but lovely. As we stood listening to the voice of an angelic Russian singer, rain started to fall gently. It was a beautiful moment. But I think my favourite part of the day was the flag swim across the Irkutsk River. The idea is to swim breaststroke with one arm and hold up your nation's flag in the other. Unfortunately I'd never heard of a flag swim before. If I had, I certainly wouldn't have brought the pitiful excuse for a flag that I did. I tucked the 'pole' inside my goggles as we swam across the Irkutsk River, but it was virtually invisible! The water was about 17 degrees, beautifully warm. Enjoy it while it lasts, I thought. This was about as warm as it was going to get for a while.

When we got to the other side of the river, the vice president was standing there applauding with almost everyone in town! They were just loving it. Like the people of Medellín, they were so proud to be playing host, to be sharing their little corner of the world with us. And it was infectious! I swelled with pride myself, thinking, this is why I swim. To make people happy. You do a lot of individual swims aiming to meet your own personal goals. But being part of something bigger brings something entirely different. To have the vice president shaking our hands, to have a whole community clapping and cheering for us, and to be able to celebrate it together… It was one of the great days of my swimming career. And we weren't even at Bering Strait yet!

The next day, we flew in a majestic Russian military plane complete with tables and legroom to Kamchatka, where we would board the boat. Upon arrival we attended yet another ceremony, a few of the guys did yet another flag swim, and yet another girl sang to us to wish us luck. We finished the day with a dinner to officially open the swim, which I loved.

After dinner we went to the grocery store for some last-minute shopping. In hindsight, it was the worst-planned shopping trip of all time. We were all so preoccupied with cravings that we completely failed to consider the actual necessities. We were well stocked with chips, nuts, and chocolate, but toilet paper or soap? Forget about it. Of course, we wouldn't realise the error of our ways until it was much too late.

Only a couple of hours later, all sixty-five swimmers and about another sixty staff boarded the Russian military ship that we would call home for the next twelve days. Nothing I can say could describe the size and scope of this ship. A hundred metres long and about seven storeys high, it was totally kitted out with a spa and sauna, a medical area, a meeting area, a kitchen, a dining area… and that was just the beginning. A whole floor was dedicated to men's bedrooms, and another to the women's. There was a shower wing, and a toilet wing. It was a mammoth ship. But then it was a mammoth undertaking.

I was stoked to find out that I would be rooming with Craig Lenning, an American swimmer. He took me under his wing, realising that navigating a gigantic ship wasn't going to be that easy for a blind guy. It seemed like whenever I needed a hand, there he was waiting to help. He's so confident and upbeat, and always knew the right thing to say in the toughest times. But we also enjoyed giving each other a bit of a hard time! Every time I put my water bottle down I'd kick it over, and without fail he'd be there saying, 'He's kicked his water bottle over again. Here we go!' Some people would probably have hated it, but to me it just showed me that he didn't think of me any differently to everyone else. He didn't feel the need to tread on eggshells just because I'm blind.

Once we were on the boat, it would take four days to travel out to Provideniya, where the swim would start. We got into a bit of a routine over those four days. At 7.30 am we'd have a breakfast of sludgy porridge, and way-too-strong tea or coffee. At midday we'd have lunch: some kind of unidentifiable meat dish with gluggy rice, watered-down soup and stale bread. At 5.30 pm we'd have dinner, which was invariably dry, bony fish. Again and again, we endured the same disgusting menu. Finally, at 7.30 pm we'd have tea or coffee with sweet biscuits, or – Annica would shudder to hear me say this – reindeer. Ironically, the reindeer was the only food for the entire day that didn't make me want to retch. But it was a bit of a bonding experience I think, this shared suffering!

Paolo quickly worked out how to say 'I don't want fish' in Russian, and every night at dinner that's what he'd recite to the kitchen staff. It worked – they just gave him rice and potatoes. Hardly a wholesome meal, but a whole lot better than getting bones stuck in your teeth. Even the pescetarian adopted Paolo's 'I don't want fish' system (in fact, the fish was so bad that when we got to America he ordered a beef burger!). Every day someone else would approach Paolo to ask for the 'magic words'. It was very funny.

At the end of each day we'd gather in the gym, for a lengthy meeting, delivered exclusively in Russian. Yes, they translated it, but with fifteen non-Russian nationalities in the room it was bloody hard work. On our first day, we had a lunchtime meeting where they went through the entire history of the swim. God, I thought. I already know the bloody history. I spent most of July going through it! At times I could feel myself starting to drift off to sleep. This would set the tone for the rest of the meetings on the ship. Within only a few days we were conditioned to cringe the minute we heard the word 'meeting'. I tend to think the meetings were even more boring for me than everyone else. Not only did I have to sit through a lecture in Russian, I couldn't even look around for distraction!

Most of us just sat through the meetings motionless and blank while arguments went on around us. But there were two people who took it upon themselves to look out for the swimmers. Two people who put in the effort not only to stay awake through these blasted meetings but to ask all the right questions: Ryan Stramrood, from South Africa, and Nuala Moore, from Ireland. I don't know how they maintained such focus, but they never missed a beat. Ryan was the pragmatist. He was the one you'd go to with problems. He always knew what to do. Nuala, on the other hand, was the eternal optimist. Even when things were going poorly, you could always rely on her to stay upbeat, to cheer everyone on, and to maintain faith that ultimately, things would work out. Even towards the end of the swim, when most of us could barely walk, she was trying to drum up a group to dance with her in the gym! The two of them became our unspoken representatives. We were very lucky to have them.

One of the things I enjoyed most was that we were out there completely on our own, cut off from the rest of the world. It was quite an amazing feeling, to think that you were out there in the middle of the Bering Strait, on a Russian military ship, miles and miles from civilisation. We didn't have computers; our phones didn't work; there were no video games. The only mode of entertainment available to us was good old-fashioned reading or talking. We had no choice but to make friends – not that it was a chore! All day we'd be back and forth from each other's rooms, whether it was telling our life stories or just talking crap and having a laugh. Ryan would often sing and play guitar. I reckon we heard Simon and Garfunkel's 'The Boxer' almost every night. We really got to know each other in a way we never would have if we'd still been in the world of telecommunications. It was fantastic.

But it was hard being away from Jenny. In twelve days, I spoke to my wife once. We'd all put in for a sky phone so we'd each have a chance to take a few minutes to call home about halfway through the swim. When I got on to Jenny she was out at function for Annica at Sydney Middle Harbour Yacht Club. It wasn't the ideal scenario! There was quite a din in the background and all I managed to say was 'oh yes, it's going well' before the phone cut out. But just to hear her voice lifted my spirits enormously. It was hard being away from my family for the two weeks, of course, but I knew they'd been genuine in their support of the swim, and Jenny was happy to know that I was having a good time.

What I really loved about this group of sixty-five swimmers is that we shared a passion and a background in swimming, but that was where the similarities ended. We'd all got there through such different paths; we all had our own individual levels of ability, strengths and weaknesses. Craig had swum six of the Oceans Seven. Anne Marie had attempted the Scotland to Ireland swim – the hardest swim in the world – four times, and finally succeeded. That takes real guts. Paolo had completed the Manhattan Island Marathon in swimming *and* the New York Marathon in running. Mariia from Finland had done the 'ice mile' – a mile in sub-5-degree water. Incredible people, incredible swims. But now, in the Bering Strait, it wasn't about how good a swimmer you were. It was about how you worked in a team, and how you hacked the cold. And that's how we ended up with everyone from Jackie, who had done the longest crossing of the English Channel ever, to Mariia, who rarely swam more than a kilometre at a time. That was the beauty of this swim. It didn't matter who you were, if you had the motivation, you could be a part of it.

Back in 1988, the year of the first Friendship Flight, could you imagine a blind person being asked to go and swim with a group of able-bodied people? Not a chance. So it was a great thrill to come on this adventure as an equal. But also to be treated with care and respect when my vision loss did pose an issue. The Russians in particular always seemed to be ready to help. But Craig was the standout. He seemed to spend every spare minute helping me around the ship. He kept our room impeccable, he put ropes on doors so I could tell which room was which by feel, he was always there to guide me to the dining room at meal times. And any time I had any concerns or worries, he was first on the scene to have a chat and help me through them.

This swim will go down not only as one of the greatest swimming feats of all time, but as the greatest social swim. It was about including people of diverse backgrounds, abilities, political persuasions, and languages, and combining them to create something bigger than all of us.

Those four days, before the pressure was on, were just magical. But by the same token, excitement was mounting for the actual swim. The aim was to do a continuous swim the entire way, kicking off with an American in Russia and finishing up with a Russian in America. It was the perfect way to commemorate the Friendship Flight.

I'd been told that a small, covered boat would be taking six of us out at a time, and that we'd all wait on that boat until everyone finished their turn. The reality was nothing like that. We had two little open inflatable boats in which three swimmers at a time would get jammed in with a driver, a cameraman, and an observer. The first person would do a 10-minute block then high-five the next person, who would jump in to start their 10 minutes. Rinse and repeat. While this was going on, the second inflatable boat would load up with another three swimmers, and be out there ready to replace the first before the half-hour of swimming was up. If I'd known what it was going to be like beforehand it probably wouldn't have made much difference, but it was still a bit of a shock! Melissa O'Reilly, an American, was the first cab off the rank. When she came back in someone asked her how it had gone. 'Yeah, it was cold all right! I did okay, but the hardest thing was getting back up onto that inflatable boat. I feel like I've had my ribs torn apart.' To get up on the back of the inflatable boat, you had to get past the motor and up over this bar, then then try to sit down and get your gear back on. It doesn't sound all that hard, but when you've been in sub-5-degree water for 10 minutes, your muscle function is far from optimal! Poor old Melissa, the right side of her rib cage was killing her for the next 24 hours, and when she got in for her second leg the next day she did the left side too. The poor girl was turning black and blue! Everyone ended up with their fair share of bumps, bruises, and scrapes, but we all got out relatively unharmed. I'm utterly shocked that no one did a serious injury. But that's how good the Russians were at getting us on and off the boats.

They decided not to send me out in the first couple of slots, because the conditions were tough and getting on and off that inflatable boat from the main pontoon was precarious at the best of times. It was disappointing, but a good decision. As much as I wanted to get out there, when Craig came back to our room later on that first day and gave me a running report, I was glad the organisers had stuck to their guns and not let me out there. He said, 'Mate, it's 5-metre swells out there. I've just seen Jack almost get impaled against the side of the ship. Nuala and Anne Marie almost missed the boat on their jump off the pontoon. There's no way in hell you could have done it.'

Despite the difficulties with the pontoon, the atmosphere was buzzing. The first group of sixty-four – me excluded – went through without incident, and the second round began. But when my turn came around it was the middle of the night, and again they didn't want to send me out. It was 3.2 degrees in the water at that point, so I wasn't too devastated! But when the third round came and I still wasn't allowed out, I was itching for my chance to get out there. I spent a lot of time in the dining room hearing back from all the guys about how everything was going. They came back with some amazing stories and I loved sitting there chatting about the swim, but the more I heard about it the more I just wanted to experience it for myself.

On the fourth round I finally got out there, and it was just an amazing feeling. This was really happening! I was with Paolo and his English roommate Jack Bright, and Craig came out as well to give me a hand. The conditions were beautiful and calm, and it was still difficult. Thank goodness I hadn't challenged the decision not to go out in rough conditions or at night! It took 7 minutes to get out to our starting point, and when we got there the last person from the group before us was just starting their swim. Ten minutes later, he high-fived Paolo, and Paolo jumped in. Jack would go second, and Craig and I would go third. Third position was good because you had a chance to sit there and work out how it was all going to work, but bad because you were getting cold before you even hit the water. But then, if you got in first, you were stuck waiting 20 minutes afterwards, which would have been even colder! You were stuffed either way, basically!

The wind was fierce, and I was pouring all my energy into trying to stay warm. I put my hand into the water as we were waiting, just to see what I had to look forward to, and you know what? It wasn't that bad. After hearing sixty-four people complain about how cold the water was, I'd built it up so much in my head that I think I was anticipating below-freezing temperatures! It was 5 degrees, and I'm not going to pretend it wasn't extremely cold, but I expected it to be far worse. At least one part of the swim might be a bit easier than expected! That gave me a bit of confidence.

Paolo got back, high-fived Jack, and the next leg began. Then, another 10 minutes later, it was my turn. At the last possible second, I tore my jacket off, stood up, and jumped in. We tried to use the loudhailer, but the guy operating it was struggling because he had never used one before and besides, it was barely audible, so having Craig by my side made a world of difference. By the end of my 10 minutes I couldn't feel a single one of my digits, but I didn't care. I don't know whether my body is good at cold, or whether it was all those morning swims in my parents' pool finally paying off, but I'd done my 10 minutes, and I was really happy with the way I'd swum.

Now for the high-five! This was probably the trickiest part of the relay, at least from my point of view. Or, more specifically, getting close enough to the boat to do the high-five. Craig was frantically yelling, 'Quick! Go! To your left. More to your left. There he is! Put your hand up!' I don't know how much of it was Craig's expert instruction and how much was just blind luck, but I felt my hand collide with the Czech's, and he took off. Craig and I swam back to our boat, and suddenly I was feeling the nerves again. Here came the hardest part of all: getting back on the boat. I couldn't see and my hands and feet seemed to have lost all function, yet somehow I had to get myself up and over this bar.

But Craig helped me through, and I sat down and went, 'I've swum in the Bering Strait. How damn good is that? For the rest of my life, I can say I've swum in the Bering Strait.' I'll never forget that feeling. It was bizarre beyond belief that I'd found myself in this situation. Fifteen years ago, when I was swimming the English Channel, if you'd said to me that I would eventually find myself high-fiving a Czech just shy of the International Date Line in the Bering Sea without a wetsuit, I would have laughed out loud. What a ridiculous prospect. Yet here I was, living that reality.

It will go down in my life as one of the great moments. I remember Craig saying, 'We won't be able to shut this bloke up ever again. All he's ever going to say is, 'I swam in the Bering Strait!'

Damn right! It's funny, when I finished the English Channel in 13 hours and 50 minutes, of course I was absolutely delighted. But today, I'd swum for 10 minutes in the Bering Sea and I was even more in awe of what I'd done. Strange the way life works out.

On the boat ride back we all sat in frozen silence, just huddling under blankets and trying to conserve what warmth we could while our feet sat submerged in an ever-deepening pool of ice water. The 7 minutes back to the main boat seemed to drag on forever. Finally we got back up on the pontoon – another struggle – and planted our feet on solid ground. Well, solid boat. You beauty! We had our medical, had a sauna, and took a shower. As my blood started to flow again, I was able to relax a bit and really let it sink in. I was part of a history-making swim in the Bering Strait. What an experience. It really was one of the greatest thrills of my life.

The next day we got a beef kebab at lunch. Acceptable food! This could only mean one thing. We must be in American waters! Indeed, we had crossed the International Date Line. We were officially on US territory. And it was time for my next relay leg.

Everything went along smoothly as it had the first time, only everything was that little bit easier having already done it once before. The other big difference this time was the temperature. I never thought I'd consider 7 degrees warm, but everything in life is relative! It definitely made things easier, and I had a great swim. We set off back towards the main boat, but after about a minute we stopped. Jack, who speaks four languages, had started arguing with the observer and the driver in Russian. I'm pretty sure there were a few swear words thrown in there, but that's about as much as I could glean. Meanwhile, we were just sitting there, not moving.

'Hey, Jack!' I said, 'Fill me in here!' Jack turned to me and said coarsely, 'Well, James, it's nothing for you to worry about, mate, because we're lost in the fog, and you can't see that.' It was an absolute classic comment, but I knew better than to treat it as a joke. I could tell from his tone that we were in a serious bind. I'd have felt sorry for myself, but I was too busy feeling sorry for Paolo. The poor bloke had swum first and he'd been out here wet and freezing cold for 20 minutes now.

We just sat there motionless for 25 minutes. We couldn't find the ship, and speeding off in an unknown direction certainly wasn't going to help matters. We were in real trouble. Yet here I was battling a serious case of the giggles. It wasn't that I didn't appreciate the seriousness of the situation, it's just that there was something kind of funny about being unable to find a ship 100 metres long! I managed to hold the laughter in, thank goodness. Finally we managed to make our way back using the GPS. Poor old Paolo, 45 minutes on that boat. He must have been frostbitten. I laugh about it now, but it could have gone the wrong way.

I didn't think about it until we got back in because we were too busy trying to sort ourselves out, but the boat after us was stuck out there in the same conditions. I found out on the way back from the sauna that the Czech I'd high-fived had been the last to swim before they decided to call it off for the day. I wasn't surprised. You can't fight Mother Nature. Our dream of a continuous swim was shattered. We had no choice but to turn it into a staged relay. But maybe it was a blessing in disguise. I'd only done two swims, but the rest of the swimmers had done four or five by now, and the fatigue was starting to show.

Next morning when I woke up, Craig said, 'James! We're not on the American side of the Date Line anymore. I can see the Diomede Islands over there on our right. We've gone backwards!' He ran out to investigate, and came straight back and said, 'We've got a meeting in 10 minutes, mate. Up you get.'

Irina looked strained. 'We have a problem, guys. We haven't got a permit to get into America. It ran out overnight, and we had to go back into Russian waters. We're working on it, but we're not going to be able to swim for today.' Things were getting interesting, in the worst possible way. At least Claudia would sleep soundly knowing she'd absolutely made the right decision not to come along!

They managed to get the permit granted for the next day, but after spending over 24 hours twiddling our thumbs we had to get a move on. We made our way back to the GPS coordinates where we'd finished last time, got back in the water, and swam right through the night. But the conditions were getting hairy and again, a decision had to be made not to send me out. It was a hard blow after I'd had such a good time on the two previous rounds. I thought about challenging the decision, but Craig convinced me otherwise. 'James,' he said, 'We're struggling ourselves, and we can see. The waves are getting to 6 metres. Getting on and off that pontoon is diabolical. Nobody's questioning your ability. We know how bloody well you can swim. We know you're doing all right in the cold. You're great at what you do, no doubt about it. But we're talking about safety here. There's no way we're sending someone out there who can't see. It's just not on.'

By the end of the next day we were within 30 kilometres of Alaska. We were almost home, or so it seemed. But we didn't know what lay hidden under the water's surface. It wasn't marked on any nautical charts. No one knew, and there's nothing we could have done to prepare for it. It was the North Alaskan current. A current so fierce that a team of absolutely brilliant swimmers couldn't manage to swim more than a few hundred metres a day. Paolo would joke, 'Oh, the seventh of November? Yes, we'll be here. The eighth? Definitely.' It was decided that we'd send out the twenty-seven best swimmers to try to get through this current, then let everyone else go after them. Obviously I wasn't chosen, and for once that was absolutely fine with me!

The rest of us fell back into the routine of the first few days on the boat, just sitting back, relaxing, and having a good old yarn. When the three South Africans came back in from their swim, I said, 'So how far did you get?'

'90 metres.'

'Seriously? In 30 minutes?' I didn't mean to rub it in, I just couldn't believe it!

'Yes, James.'

I said to Ryan, 'How far did you get?'

'130 metres.'

The other two looked at me and said, 'Let's have it, then.'

'Wait a second... so in 20 minutes, you two went 40 metres backwards.'

'Yes, James.'

It was at that moment that the gravity of the situation really sunk in. If three of our best swimmers were swimming at 180 metres per hour, we really would be here until November. For all his joking, Paolo might actually be right. People were getting pretty nervous, but most of the time we managed to see the funny side. Craig said, 'I hope it wasn't me that jinxed us when I said we'd be home shortly. Is it too late to take that back?' Sometimes the humour was the only thing keeping us calm.

Then another problem presented itself, almost as dire as the first. We were running out of toilet paper and soap. Yeah. We had problems all right. We were getting low on food as well. We were still 30 kilometres from Alaska, and at the rate we were going, we were going to be here for weeks. My flight was leaving from Seattle in seven days!

This went on for a whole day and a half. The twenty-seven chosen ones were buggered. Gone was the luxury of an 11-hour break between legs. Now they were getting little more than 4 hours, and they were getting absolutely smashed out there. The water temperature had increased to 8–10 degrees, which was something I suppose, but it was still incredibly tough going. They were sleep deprived and physically spent from giving their all on our collective behalf, and coming in and seeing the rest of us sitting around fresh as a daisy added insult to injury.

These guys ended up doing eight, nine, ten swims each, until finally someone broke. Anne Marie was the first to just put her foot down and say no, and a few others quickly followed suit. Those remaining were left with even narrower windows between swims, but thankfully it wasn't too much longer before we made it through the current. It was time for those of us that had been kicking back for the past day and a half to get ourselves back into gear. We were now within sight of Cape Prince of Wales, so we probably wouldn't all get a final shot, but it didn't matter. We had started as a team, and we would finish as a team.

I was pretty far down the list of swimmers, so I was pretty sure I wouldn't be getting back in the water. I'd just come back to my room after having something to eat, when Craig popped his head around the corner and said, 'Come on then!'

'What are you talking about?'

'They've given you the penultimate swim, mate.'

I was speechless for a moment. What an honour. But there was no time to sit around reflecting. 'Let's get out there!' I said.

By now it was almost 12 degrees – heaven! Craig came out and swam with me until we got to about 150 metres from shore, then I high-fived the Russian. But he didn't start his swim just yet. The beauty of the swim now being a staged relay was that we could take a break whenever we wanted – all we had to do was mark the GPS coordinates and resume from there later on. So we all headed back to the ship together for one last meal before we brought this thing home.

For me, swimming the penultimate leg of the first-ever staged relay swim across the Bering Strait was an absolute privilege. An honour, that people thought highly enough of me to choose me out of a group of sixty-five phenomenal swimmers. I'll never know why I was chosen, but the privilege certainly wasn't wasted on me. I couldn't have been prouder to get out there and represent Australia for the second-last leg. It was just brilliant, and I'll never forget it.

We decided that to really end this thing in style, someone from each country would do a flag swim. Again I would live to regret my choice of flag. Everyone had put up their flags up on the outside of the boat early on, and my little skimpy one ripped in half within hours! But right when I thought I was going to have to go flagless, a bunch of women from the staff came in and asked for my flag. It was in tatters, but I still had it with me, and I handed it over. An hour or so later, they came back and presented me with the most marvellous creation I've ever seen. They had stitched the Union Jack, the southern cross and the seven-pointed star onto a big blue towel, and attached it to a wooden pole. It was perfect. I was almost brought to tears by what they'd done for me, and that flag is still in my house to this day. I have many souvenirs from that swim, not least of all my medal, but there is nothing I cherish as much as that flag.

As soon as the final swimmer, Oleg Dokuchaev, hit the shore, we all poured out of the inflatable boats, and one of us from each country swam our flag into America. It was my first time doing a flag swim with an actual flagpole, and it wasn't easy trying to hold the thing, but it was one of the most enjoyable struggles I've ever experienced! We got to the end and stood in the shallows together splashing around, giggling like children and whooping and waving our flags like maniacs while startled beachgoers fumbled for their cameras.

Flag swimmers on completion of Bering Strait Swim.

The inflatables ferried us all back to the boat and we all hopped into the sauna. The mood was one of pure elation. I guess it's not often that so many people get to share – really share – in such a momentous achievement. We'd completed the first-ever staged relay swim across the Bering Strait. We'd faced that terrible Alaskan current together, and we'd come through it together. I can't tell you how delighted we were to have finished.

It was a magnificent moment for me, but I realised that for those who had been through the failed attempts in 2011 and 2012, it must have felt even sweeter. I'd been building up to this for two months, but they'd been building up to it for over two years. Some people are just lucky and some aren't, and I think I've been very lucky throughout my entire swimming career. I was invited at the eleventh hour, I had the means to get there and a family that backed me, I got to be there for the first time the swim actually came to fruition, and I got the penultimate swim. If that's not lucky I don't know what is.

The English Channel, the Oceans Seven, the Scotland to Ireland, they're all great swims, and I have the greatest admiration for anyone that completes them. But they tell you nothing about what kind of person someone is. A swim like this, a team effort in every sense of the word, shows a whole different kind of greatness. To come together with people from all over the world for a single purpose, to get along, to support each other, to overcome adversity… That is the real achievement. It was an incredible feat of organisation, too – to pull together sixty-five swimmers from sixteen different countries, to cater for them for twelve days, to get all the boats and equipment together, to find a dedicated staff to look after everything… just incredible.

Looking back on the past two months, I could hardly believe it. On 18 June 2013, I had nothing planned for the year except for one little charity swim, and by 11 August 2013, I'd swum in the Bering Strait. Not only that, I'd swum in it four times, and I'd done it with nothing more than a cossie, cap and goggles.

That night we had a ceremony where everyone went up to the front of the room in turn to receive a certificate and a medal. When it was my turn to get up everyone went nuts cheering for me. It was the only time for the entire two weeks that I had been treated any differently. But I loved it. It meant an enormous amount to me that everyone in the room, with all their different worldviews and values, recognised how special this was for me. A blind man had come halfway across the world to stick it to his disability and prove that just because he couldn't see didn't mean he couldn't get out there and put in the same effort, handle the same conditions, and make the same contribution as everyone else. It embodied the spirit of the swim, and the volume of the applause very much reflected that. Occasionally life turns up moments that you just know, no matter how long you live, you'll never forget. This was one of those moments.

I still have the medal and certificate in my bedroom, and I treasure them for the memories they elicit, but that's all. At the end of the day, they're just things. The memories, the lifelong friendships, and the immense sense of accomplishment – they're the real rewards. I consider myself a team player in every facet of life, and that's why this swim meant more to me than any individual swim. Knowing that I had been liked and respected by everyone on the team showed that I lived up to that self-perception.

Our celebrations had to be cut short to deal with the logistics of getting all our crap together. Overnight we would travel the 10 hours from Cape Prince of Wales, where we had finished, to Nome, where those of us staying in America would alight. There was wet clothing strewn across every surface as we all trudged around zombie-like tackling the mammoth task of recovering twelve days' worth of possessions. The adrenaline had worn off, and our battered bodies were just giving up!

By morning we had reached Nome. Well, sort of. The ship was so big we could only get to within 2 or 3 kilometres of Nome Wharf, so the poor old inflatable boat drivers put in one last effort to transport us and our masses of luggage back to land. It took about four or five laps back and forth, and I'm sure they must have been wondering when it was ever going to stop. A few Russians took the opportunity for a holiday, but most of them stayed on board and continued back to Russia. It was now 12 August, and I had two days to get back to Seattle.

We were met by a single immigration officer. He stamped our passports production-line style, said, 'Thanks for coming', and continued on his way. I looked around thinking, where is everyone? Don't they realise we've just done one of the greatest swims of all time? We just made history. This may never happen ever again! And all they could muster for our arrival was an immigration officer.

Someone went off to tackle the unenviable task of finding accommodation for twenty-five people in a small city, and a few hours later I found myself in a single room – a rare luxury! I would have been quite happy to just sit down and enjoy the solitude, but someone suggested we all go out for a meal and I went along. My eyes nearly popped out of my head when one of the South Africans ordered soup. I said, 'You've just had twelve days of bloody soup! What are you doing?!' One thing for sure, I wasn't wasting *my* first proper meal in days on soup. I had known what I was going to order for over a week: the biggest, meatiest pizza I could get my hands on! Through every bowl of sludgy porridge, every dry piece of meat, and every bony fish, this is all I'd been thinking about. When it arrived at the table someone looked at me and started laughing going, 'Surely you're not going to eat all that?' I said, 'You'd better believe it.' I barely stopped for air.

Craig was sitting there on his laptop, and I had him email Jenny to say we'd arrived safely. Jenny wrote back almost immediately saying, 'Thank you. And congratulations! Good to hear you're all well.' It was a very simple interaction, and delivered via a third party at that, but it was the first contact I'd had with my wife in a week. It was a huge weight off my shoulders – and Jenny's, I'm sure! – that my family knew I was okay.

The next day the mayor of Nome flew in to say a few words in recognition of our achievement. Her PA had this terrible barking voice, and the mayor herself delivered her speech in the most laboured monotone I've ever heard. I thought, you know what? You're really not endearing yourself to me at the moment. You're making out as though this is some massive effort, when you should be honoured to be involved with one of the great sporting feats of all time. If you only knew the logistics, the politics, the effort that went into this. She looked as though she was here purely out of duty, and it was an insult to the importance of our achievement.

It's funny, because when we left Russia, we had three opening ceremonies, a personal meeting with the vice president, people singing to us, people lining up along the Yakutsk River to shake our hands... And here we were in America and the only reception we got was an immigration officer and a stony-faced mayor. I've said it before – I'm a huge fan of the Americans, but on this occasion they'd gravely disappointed me. Craig and Melissa deserved better from their fellow countrymen. We all deserved better. This feat merited recognition and celebration, and we got neither.

That night we went down to the wharf to see off the Russians and bring them supplies: toilet paper, soap and so forth. Just as they were about to depart, one of the Russian blokes came up to me and Paolo, put his arm round my shoulder and said, 'Respect.' I hadn't forgotten what that meant! Out came the vodka! Every time Paolo heard the word 'Respect', he'd surreptitiously decant his cup into mine. After about four shots I said, 'That's about enough respect for one night, thank you!' The vodka didn't go down particularly well, but it was the perfect parting memory of the Russians.

The next morning we gathered at Nome Airport and flew to Anchorage. Looking out for me right until the very end, Paolo and Craig helped me get to my gate. It was finally time for us all to go our separate ways. Time to say goodbye. I knew it was coming, but now that the moment was here I was surprised at the waves of emotion. Tears welled in my eyes as I shook their hands and thanked them for everything they'd done for me. We'd had the time of our lives together, but all good things must come to an end.

At Seattle Airport, I was shocked to see Claudia Rose and her partner getting off the same flight. It turned out they had been in Alaska preparing for a swim. We had a lovely dinner at the airport and I told them the incredible story of the past two weeks. When I thanked her for getting me involved with the swim, I almost choked up again. Without her, none of it would have been possible.

When I got into my hotel room I gave Jenny a call. There was one thing I'd been hanging out to say to her. 'Thank you so much', I said. 'Thank you for encouraging me to do this. Without your support, I would have missed out on one of the greatest experiences of my life. I'm the happiest man on earth right now, and it's all thanks to you.' Hearing her voice and her laugh was just wonderful. I never wanted to hang up.

Finally, on the morning of 16 August 2013, I arrived back at Sydney airport. I looked and felt completely out of it. I'd crossed the International Date Line six times in two weeks. I had no idea what time it was. I wasn't even sure what day it was! As I arrived at customs to declare my wooden flagpole and hand-stitched Australian flag, a bloke said to me, 'And what do you call that?'

It seemed pretty obvious. 'A flag!'

'Where on earth did you find that?'

'I didn't. The ladies on the Russian military ship made it for me while we were swimming the Bering Strait.'

He stood there sizing me up for a minute, trying to work out if I was having him on. I don't know whether he decided a story that crazy had to be true or whether it was just a problem he didn't want to be dealing with, but he said, 'Mate, here's your flag. Go home.'

I thought later about what it would have been like to have brought together all these people of all these nationalities in 1988, the year of the first Friendship Flight between Russia and America. Finland, Estonia, Latvia, Ukraine, USA and China all hated Russia's guts. Ireland was still battling with England over Northern Ireland. England and Argentina had been at war six years earlier. Nelson Mandela was still in jail, and South Africa was under apartheid. Today, twenty-five years later, South Africa had escaped apartheid; Nelson Mandela was still alive (though he would die three months later); Finland, Latvia, Estonia and Ukraine had separated from the Soviet Union; there was no Berlin Wall; there was no Cold War; relations were good between Argentina and England, Ireland and England.

I thought to myself, what a quarter-century it's been. We've come so far and done so many amazing things. And our swim epitomised that. Sixteen countries. Sixty-five swimmers. One massive achievement. Politics, religion, culture, disability, all put aside to swim together as friends. Twenty-five years ago they couldn't have even imagined it, and twenty-five years from now maybe it will seem just as incredible. It may never happen again. But in my lifetime, it happened. And I got to be a part of it. It proved what I have always believed: that sport can break down any barrier.

## Chapter 19
## Freedom Swim

While I was out in Bering Strait, there was talk about the Robben Island to Blouberg swim – 8 kilometres from Robben Island Prison, where Nelson Mandela was incarcerated from 1963 to 1990, to Blouberg, in 13-degree water. I knew exactly what it was, because I'd actually planned to attempt it way back in the early 2000s. But I'd heard too many stories about sharks, and I never quite worked up the courage to do it! Out there in Bering Strait, though, I felt a sense of invincibility that erased any fear I might have felt. The second I heard that Ram Barkai, one of the South Africans, was organising a 'Freedom Swim' at Robben Island, I knew I was in.

The swim would take place on Freedom Day, the anniversary of the first democratic election in South Africa in 1994. Believing as I do that Nelson Mandela is the greatest human being that ever lived, there was no way I could pass this up. I never thought I'd get the chance to do something like this, but with Ram's help, I had that chance. Since then, the swim has not only become an annual event, but has sparked an entire 'Freedom Series' celebrating significant days in South Africa's history and raising funds for worthy causes.

I was very fortunate that Alasdair, the photographer on the Bering Strait swim, said I could stay with him at his parents' house. If he hadn't volunteered I guess I would have hired a flat, or stayed in a hotel, but I wouldn't have enjoyed the experience half as much. I'm always happiest when I have people around, and none of my mates were coming with me. So to be able to go home to a room in an actual house, have a proper hot shower, and sit down for a home-cooked meal with some lovely people, I can tell you, that makes all the difference. It means you're getting a good night's sleep. It means someone is caring for you, providing for you, giving their heart to you. And when you can't see, it doesn't hurt to have someone to help you get around as well.

Alasdair's parents, Margaret and Ivan, were magnificent. Any time I wasn't training, they were there showing me a good time. The day after I arrived, they took me around Cape Town, finishing with a tour of the 146-hectare Klein Constantia winery, where Margaret boasted about my swim and I was given a beautiful bottle of wine in a lovely glass box. We're saving it for a special day. One afternoon, Ivan and I took a walk around a park where there were horses. I'm not a great walker, but for a whole hour and a half I really enjoyed walking, chatting, and being around the horses, dogs, and cyclists coming back and forth. Margaret had me make a speech at a lunch for the National Sea Rescue Institute. They totally embraced me, and I really enjoyed speaking with all the sea rescue volunteers. I'm always in awe of people who save others' lives.

A couple of days after arriving I decided it was probably time to see what I was in for here. It was a beautiful sunny day, and when we got to Three Anchor Bay the water looked lovely. But I wasn't fooled! I'd heard how cold the water was going to be in South Africa – 12, 13 degrees even coming out of summer. Yes, I'd survived 5 degrees in Bering Strait, but that was over six months ago. I'd trained, but I hadn't trained in cold water. I'd gone through a whole summer season of 23 degrees-plus since then. This was going to be a test. I braced myself and jumped in. And you know, I didn't feel too bad. I spent about half an hour in the water, and I not only survived, I felt good. If this was how it was going to be on the day, I'd be fine.

A couple of days before the swim, we had a briefing where Ram gave us a rundown of how it would all work. He emphasised that this would be no walk in the park. It was going to be damn cold, and good luck if you hadn't acclimatised yourself beforehand! I could hear the pride in his voice as he spoke about getting the swim running again after three years of downtime. And he should be proud. The swim was to raise money for a disadvantaged school, and they'd arranged for the school kids to present us with our medals. Fundraising for a good cause is always rewarding, but when you get to actually physically interact with the people you're helping, it's really special.

After the presentation, we would head straight to the medical room to be examined and collect our warm gear, which they'd collected and labelled for us beforehand. What a fantastic way to do a swim. You get to meet the school kids and receive your award, but then you get a chance to properly collect your thoughts and wind down in the medical room without a million people competing for your attention. Save for Willy Schultz's briefing in Alaska in 2007, I'd never been so impressed. I walked away from the briefing with complete confidence.

The day before the swim we were up before the sun to get out and do some pre-swim filming. Alasdair wanted to photograph and film as much as he could of my swim, and was keen to get some shots of me on the beach and in the surf. Needless to say, when we arrived at the beach we were the only ones there. What was I thinking being out there in the coldest part of the day, with the winds ripping through me? But as that question played on my mind, a bird descended from the skies and settled into a hover about three feet from my head. Granny was in town! Whenever she turned up I knew she was 100% behind me in whatever it was I was doing, and seeing her flitting back and forth in front of me hammered it home that I was here for a reason. There was real meaning and significance behind this swim.

The day of the Robben Island swim arrived, and Alasdair and I were up early to go down to the wharf and meet the other swimmers. When we got there, Ryan, who I knew from the Bering Strait, walked over and said, 'It's going to be 11 degrees. This'll be tough.' I don't know whether he was just trying to prepare me for the worst or whether he knew it to be fact. Either way, it got me worked up! Here's a bloke who's done this forty-nine times, and he's saying he thinks it's going to be tough. What does that mean for me?! I was also facing the challenge of swimming with two kayakers who had never used the whistle system before. And I knew there was a possibility we might encounter sharks. It was going to be an interesting day, that's for sure.

It was still a bit foggy, so the swim was delayed by half an hour. I couldn't have been happier. I had half an hour to properly take in the situation. As I stood and gazed at Robben Island Prison, chills ran down my spine. I said, 'Thank you, Nelson. Thank you for everything you've done to make this world a better place. Today I will do my family proud, and I will do you and your family proud.' It was the closest I have ever felt to a man that inspires me more than I can say.

The moment was interrupted by the announcement of the final briefing. I nodded towards the prison one last time, and headed back to the group of swimmers. Ram said, 'The penguin colony is mating at the front of the island, so we can't swim from there. We'll go off the side of the wharf, and you'll swim around to meet your kayakers.' I knew that everything had to go to plan for this to go well, so when I heard that the very first step of the plan had been changed, I was none too happy. But Ram said he'd swim with me to my kayakers, so that was some solace.

I got in the water and was pleased to find that Ryan's claim that it was 11 degrees was false. It was 13 degrees, and it actually felt pretty good. Not much swirl, not much wind, lots of sun. Someone up there was looking after us. Making sure this swim was going to work. As I took off with Ram I was still within sight of the prison, and I imagined what it must have been like to have been imprisoned for all that time. I imagined what it must have been like to finally get away after twenty-six years. At least, I tried to imagine. But of course, we were swimming away of our own accord. Nobody but Nelson Mandela himself could ever really know how it felt to finally regain his freedom.

Ram and I swam around the front of the island, and he helped me find my two kayakers. They settled beautifully into the whistle system and did a great job with the feeds. It helped that the conditions were very calm of course, but still, I was impressed to see how quickly they picked it up. The first couple of hours went really well. For me, anyway! One of my kayakers fell in, which slowed things down for a minute, but it was worth it for the laughs!

I felt completely comfortable in the water. The current was with me and the wind wasn't a factor. I was finding it really easy to focus on the whistles, and I wasn't feeling a hint of fatigue. At one point the rescue team asked if I was cold. I was being completely honest when I said no. The temperature never even crossed my mind. If anything I felt warm!

It's really hard to gauge distances when you're trying to swim towards land. At the 2-hour mark my kayakers told me I only had about 2 kilometres to go, yet half an hour later, it felt like I hadn't gone anywhere. That's another reason it's so important to trust your team. They're in a much better position to judge the best approach than you are. It's also one of the reasons I'd been nervous about swimming with two kayakers I didn't know, but they did such a good job I didn't question a word they said. Finally we were in the home stretch, and they told me to start veering to the left. On the way in we'd be facing a current to the right, so I needed to be in a position to let it bring me to shore.

Ram had promised to swim in with me once I got within 300 metres of the shore, and sure enough, there he was waiting for me. When I heard his voice I couldn't believe I was at the end already. I'd swum really well all day, the feeds and whistles had proceeded uneventfully, I hadn't felt cold or tired, and the current had been with me the whole time. I tried to remember another swim that had gone as well, and I couldn't. We swam into shore, and I emerged from the water with a broad grin plastered across my face. I turned back to Robben Island and took this last chance to remember why I was here. The sacrifices Nelson Mandela had made for us even to be *able* to be here today.

Now all that was left was to enjoy my victory. I didn't win, of course, but it was certainly a personal victory to do such a good job in honour of my hero. A kid from the disadvantaged school put a medal around my neck, a beanie on my head, and a towel around my neck. It meant more to me than any other presentation that these kids had come along to thank us in their own way. I was delighted to be able to actually shake the hands of the people I was directly helping with my swim.

Someone helped me to the medical room to have my body temperature taken. 'Your core temperature is down 2 degrees, mate', the doctor said. 'After 3 hours and 4 minutes, that's a pretty bloody good effort. Here's some hot chocolate. Stay here by the heater for 20 minutes and warm up, just relax and take your time.' Only when my body temperature came back to baseline would I be able to meet up with my family and friends. Not that it was a burden – I was glad I'd have the chance to again just reflect on the day. But somehow a reporter got in, and denied me that chance. The doctor took it as a good sign though. He said, 'That interview's got you going. I can tell your body's responding.' He took my core temperature again and said, 'You're up to normal. You're free to go.' I grabbed my gear and went straight outside, where Margaret, Ivan and Alasdair were waiting.

At the presentation lunch Ram gave a speech acknowledging the winners of the different categories, then introduced a man called Eddie Daniels. Eddie was a former anti-apartheid activist who had been a prisoner with Nelson Mandela for fifteen years. He spoke about his experiences and the amazing contribution Nelson Mandela had made to humanity, and he gave a heartfelt thank you. Thank you to South Africa for supporting the cause, to the swimmers, the organisers, the winners. But at the end of his speech, he thanked one person specifically. He thanked a blind man who wouldn't quit.

He said, 'I can't believe a blind bloke swam all that way.' He couldn't praise me enough for my commitment and my contribution. Never have I felt so proud, yet so humbled at the same time. At the end of the presentation, he came over, and I said, 'Can I embrace you?' And so an Australian blind man with a passion for history and charity embraced a South African ex-prisoner who had spent fifteen years in jail with Nelson Mandela for fighting for his beliefs. It was an absolutely outstanding moment. A moment I will never forget.

That night Alasdair was out with mates, so I sat down for dinner with just Margaret and Ivan. A beautiful dinner to cap off a beautiful, beautiful, day. I'd completed an historic swim, I'd been given a medal by disadvantaged children, and I'd been embraced by a man who had fought for equality with Nelson Mandela. I slept easy that night.

The next morning when I woke up, the change in weather was dramatic. Horizontal sleet, raging wind, and fog so thick you couldn't see more than a couple of feet in front of you. We were planning to have a swim with Ram and all his mates, but obviously we had to call it off. We thought we might climb Table Mountain, but they weren't even allowing the cable cars to go up in that fog. So we gave up on adventure and just spent the afternoon in a café.

Finally, it was time to go home and see the wonderful wife and daughter without whom I would never have even set out on this incredible journey. I would never have done the Bering Strait relay. I would never have met Ram, Alasdair, Ryan, and their mates Andrew and Toks. I would never have been invited to do the Freedom Swim. And I would never have been able to pay such beautiful homage to the man I admire more than anyone else in the world. To think that less than a year ago the whole chain of events hadn't even begun. And now that year, that magnificent year, takes pride of place as one of the best years of my life.

# Epilogue

After Robben Island, I knew without a doubt that I would never again compete in an international open-water event. People often ask me if I'm sad to have had to let it go. I'm not. I had more opportunities in my twenty-year career than most people get in a lifetime. How could I be anything but happy? It's been a bit of an adjustment losing that constant contact with my team, but I am still very close with Narelle, Brooke, Matt and Sticks. I may not see them as often as I once did, but every time we come together it's as if no time has passed.

Besides, when one door closes another opens. Swimming always came at the cost of time with my family, and getting to spend more time with Jenny and Annica has filled me with more joy than any swim could offer. We've finally had the chance to travel as a family. In 2015 we toured Tasmania, and in 2016 we caravanned around Queensland and the Northern Territory for three and a half months. Jenny's a meticulous planner, and we knew how the trip would run to the day before we even stepped out the door! Sometimes I still can't believe I managed to find my soul mate online. I honestly don't know what I'd do without her.

And Annica! I won't pretend I'm not biased, but she is the most delightful kid I've ever known. She's stubborn, and cheeky, and mischievous, and I wouldn't have it any other way. She has a zest for life like nothing I've ever seen. With Jenny as a role model, she has been completely behind me in all my swims and I could barely contain myself when she decided she wanted to follow in my footsteps. She has done her first ocean swim, and after a bit of a poor start, she pulled herself together and completed the whole 800 metres. I couldn't have been prouder if she'd won the thing.

I think of my mother often. Until the day she died, Mum always called me her little boy. She would say it every time I walked into their house. I miss that more than anything. She started losing her memory around 2008, and it was very difficult to watch that fierce intelligence dwindle away. But I never once heard her complain. Even as her memory failed her, she found ways around it. She entered every event, big or small, in her diary and studied her own life every day. She worked so hard at it sometimes you'd almost forget she even had a problem. Finally, on 11 February 2015, she passed away. It was one of the saddest days of my life, but I'm glad she left us while she was still smiling. Dad took a while to get over her death, but I think he's in a good place with it now. Our relationship is as strong as ever, and he adores being a grandparent.

I continue to be involved with my big charities, and it gives me great pleasure to be able to invest my love of swimming in a whole new way. I am hoping to do a massive fundraising swim for The Fred Hollows Foundation as of October 2017 involving swimming pools all around Australia. The Rainbow Club is still going strong, and the Malabar swim is getting bigger and better every year. In my own little way, I'm helping make life a little bit easier for blind and disabled children, and I can't tell you how good that feels.

You know, I've never been one to blow my own trumpet, and telling my story has been a huge personal challenge. But my hope is that with the publication of this book, my journey can inspire others to reach for their own goals. Hardship or disability shouldn't be an obstacle – it should be a motivator. I should know.

www.ingramcontent.com/pod-product-compliance
Lightning Source LLC
Chambersburg PA
CBHW071221080526
44587CB00013BA/1451